The Pragmatics of Style

The Pragmatics of Style

edited by
Leo Hickey

R
Routledge
London and New York

First published in 1989
by Routledge
11 New Fetter Lane, London EC4P 4EE
29 West 35th Street, New York, NY 10001

© Selection and Editorial Matter: Leo Hickey 1990

Typeset in Linotron 100 10/11pt Times
by Scarborough Typesetting Services
Printed in Great Britain
by T. J. Press (Padstow), Cornwall

British Library Cataloguing in Publication Data

The pragmatics of style.
  1. Language. Style
  I. Hickey, Leo
  808

  ISBN 0-415-02617-2

Library of Congress Cataloguing in Publication Data

The Pragmatics of style/edited by Leo Hickey
      p.   cm.
  Bibliography: p
  Includes index.
  ISBN 0-415-02617-2
  1. Language and languages – Style. 2. Pragmatics. 3. Style.
Literary. I. Hickey, Leo.
P301.P65   1989
306.4′4 – dc20
                      89–6204
                      CIP

Contents

Contents

Notes on contributors

Diane Blakemore is a lecturer in linguistics at the University of Southampton. Most of her publications have dealt with pragmatics including her book *Semantic Constraints on Relevance* (1987).

Raymond Chapman is Professor of English Studies at the University of London and Head of the Department of Language Studies at the London School of Economics. He is author of several books, including *Language and Literature* (1984).

Nils Erik Enkvist is Professor of Stylistics and Text Research at Åbo Akademi, the Swedish-language university of Finland. His civil and academic honours as well as his works on style, text and discourse, are numerous, and include *Coherence and Composition* (1985).

Leo Hickey is Professor of Spanish at the University of Salford. His publications deal with stylistics, linguistics and modern Spanish literature, including *Curso de pragmaestilística* (1987).

Flora Klein-Andreu is a professor in the Department of Hispanic Languages and Literature at the State University of New York at Stony Brook. Her published work has centred on syntax and discourse, including a volume which she edited on *Discourse Perspectives on Syntax* (1983).

Gun Leppiniemi took her MA in English at Åbo Akademi in 1983 and is research assistant in that institution.

Claes Schaar, until 1986 Professor of English and American Literature at the University of Lund, has published several books on literary subjects including *The Full Voic'd Quire Below: Vertical Context Systems in 'Paradise Lost'* (1982).

Margret Selting is Wissenschaftliche Mitarbeiterin at the University of Oldenburg. Her publications and interests centre on speech styles and conversational analysis; they include *Verständigungs-probleme: Eine empirische Analyse am Beispiel der Bürger-Verwaltungs-Kommunikation* (1987).

Carmen Silva-Corvalán is an associate Professor in the Department of Spanish and Portuguese at the University of Southern California. She is co-editor of *Studies in Romance Linguistics* (1986).

Jenny A. Thomas is a lecturer in the Department of Linguistics and Modern English Language at the University of Lancaster. She has published several papers on pragmatics and has two books forthcoming, *Speaker Meaning* and *The Dynamics of Discourse*.

George W. Turner is a reader in English at the University of Adelaide. He has published several books and numerous articles on language and linguistics, including the Penguin book *Stylistics* (1973).

Introduction

Leo Hickey

In the general area of style study or stylistics there is no shortage of ideas, definitions or published works. As long ago as 1971 Tzvetan Todorov could justifiably write: 'The bibliographies of stylistics contain thousands of titles, there is no lack of observed facts; however, the polysemy of concepts, the imprecision of methods, the uncertainty about the very goal of this research hardly make for a prosperous discipline.'[1] It is hoped, in the present volume, to contribute to the prosperity of the discipline mainly by clarifying and exemplifying how pragmatic considerations may be relevant to any study of style, in the conviction that pragmastylistics is more interesting and useful than stylistics on its own.

The starting point must be a brief survey of the definitions of style and stylistics. The very form of the latter term suggests a scientific and orderly, rather than an intuitive or impressionistic, investigation of style. Charles Bally, the father of modern stylistics, remarked that 'stylistic observation', that is, the study of the nature of what he called *faits d'expression*, must be distinguished from the observation of facts of style, that is, the use which any particular person may make of such expressive facts.[2] Thus we detect two separate levels of study: one, a general, methodical and scientific discipline; the other, an application of its methods or postulates to the analysis of the 'style' of a specific utterance, text, speaker, writer, movement or period. Although Bally would call the former 'stylistics' and the latter 'the study of style', it is clear that, in order to approach either, we must first attempt to understand style. At the outset it must be confessed that, perhaps somewhat arbitrarily, we limit our investigation to verbal style and do not refer to any of the non-verbal arts, such as painting, sculpture or music, much less to other activities like fashion, hair design, upholstery or playing golf, all of which undoubtedly display style and styles. However, it is important to stress that we have in mind the styles of every type of verbal text: written or oral, literary or non-literary, scientific or general, technical or lay.

The best known definition of style is Buffon's 'Le style c'est l'homme même', by which he meant that, whereas ideas are never original, the form of their expression belongs to the individual and in this sense style is the 'order and the movement' which one imposes on one's thoughts. R. A. Sayce varies this, declaring that style is 'the work itself' while Rémy de Gourmont claims that 'style is the thought itself'.[3] In a work on the philosophy of style, Gilles-Gaston Granger defines style as the individual aspect of any work, and more particularly as the 'modalité d'intégration de l'individuel dans un processus concret qui est travail'.[4] Just as there is a philosophy of style, so also there is a psychology of style and Henri Morier begins his work on this subject by explaining that style is 'une disposition de l'existence, une manière d'être',[5] thus seeming to locate style within the person, independently of its physical or material manifestations. Later he distinguishes objective stylistics, which studies general linguistic facts, from subjective stylistics, which deals with psychological facts in reference to choice of linguistic expression.[6]

Perhaps more practical is Pierre Guiraud's suggestion that style is 'une manière d'exprimer la pensée par l'intermédiaire du langage',[7] although it brings to light two problems which run right through the subject. The first is that, ironically, some authorities would hold that thought, 'la pensée', is precisely what style does not express: it conveys emotions, feelings or attitudes, but not conceptual thought.[8] The second is that the indefinite article in Guiraud's definition implies that there is more than one way or expressing a single thought while leaving the thought itself unchanged, and this may not be universally accepted either. According to this last approach, style is what distinguishes one utterance from another when both denote the same, or approximately the same, thought: it is the aspect of an expression or text which contrasts with another when both communicate 'the same' content. We shall see that, however problematical, this concept is virtually essential for the existence of stylistics.

It accepts that there are different 'ways' of doing 'something' (in our case, of writing or speaking), and *what* is done is different from *how* it is done. To put it the other way round, it supposes that one can express the same message, 'say the same thing', using different formulations, and these differences are said to be differences of style. However, as we have indicated, this may not be unanimously admitted. For instance, members of the Bloomfieldian school would probably reject it on the grounds that two utterances which do not coincide in form cannot coincide in semantic content. Referring to Bloomfield's hypothesis that 'formally different utterances always differ in meaning', Graham Hough insists that the matter-manner distinction is dead and that 'style is an aspect of meaning', although he accepts that according to generative grammar the differences between synonymous sentences may be called stylistic.[9] If it is denied that two sentences or utterances may be synonymous then style must become a matter of meaning if it is to exist at all.

Richard Ohmann reflects more general assumptions when he suggests that the common-sense notion of style is that it 'applies to human action that is partly invariant and partly variable. A style is a *way* of doing *it*',[10] where the constant part is *it*, what is done or said, and could probably have been done or said in another way, while the variable part is the *way* in which it is done or said in a particular case. He goes on:

> To put the question more concretely, the idea of style implies that words on a page might have been different, or differently arranged, without a corresponding difference in substance. Another writer would have said *it* another *way*. For the idea of style to apply, in short, writing must involve choices of verbal formulation.[11]

This idea is developed by Olga Akhmanova, when she writes: 'The concept of style presupposes the existence of objects which are essentially identical but which differ in some secondary, subservient feature or features.'[12] The trouble with terms like 'secondary' or 'subservient' is that they might seem to imply some quantitative or qualitative subordination. What this means in practice is that 'Linguistic style is that part of language which is used to impart to the message certain expressive-evaluative-emotional features . . .' and expressive-evaluative-emotional overtones are superimposed on the main semiotic content.[13] The style, by this account, is 'additional' to the semiotic element or message, which can be regarded as the important element. Whether this message is 'content' in the sense of something linguistic, that is, inherent in the language used, or something pre-linguistic in the sense of thought in existence prior to the utterance, although an interesting point, does not directly affect the concept of style, which is considered to be somehow posterior to either of these. Needless to say, this last possibility might not find favour with some theorists, for instance of the structuralist or poststructuralist schools.

Along similar lines, Michael Riffaterre, though dealing with literary style, gives a definition which would seem applicable to any written or spoken utterance: '*Style* is understood as an emphasis (expressive, affective or aesthetic) added to the information conveyed by the linguistic structure, without alteration or meaning. Which is to say that language expresses and that style stresses.'[14] Perhaps his use of the word 'added' is problematical in that it may suggest that the information conveyed by the linguistic structure, or even the linguistic structure itself, is chronologically anterior to the style, whereas it is more useful to conceive of the style simply as one aspect of the linguistic structure.

If it is admitted that one and the same 'message' may be expressed in more than one way, it follows that the writer or speaker has to choose between alternatives available to him, that is to say that at least one alternative must have been rejected – consciously or not – and this factor provides the basis of several mainstream definitions of style: style is the choice actually made from a number of linguistic options. As Jean Marouzeau put it: 'Si l'on s'applique à les distinguer, il semble que l'on puisse définir la langue comme la somme des moyens d'expression dont nous disposons pour mettre en forme l'énoncé, le style comme l'aspect et la qualité qui résultent du choix entre ces moyens d'expression.'[15] He goes on to remind us that there are, of course, limits to the choices available, limits set by grammatical rules or by the intention to convey a particular sense, among other constraints. We might add that further restrictions derive from the situation, that is from pragmatic factors, which are particularly relevant to our present study.

Thus we could suggest that style is the result of choice of linguistic features, made from among a range of available possibilities offered by a given language, which is not a direct, immediate or exclusive function of what the speaker or writer, consciously or voluntarily, wishes to express. Some authorities believe that a number of other conditions must also be fulfilled if a particular choice is to be called stylistic: for instance, it has been postulated that a single choice does not constitute style, but that it must be repeated, it must be systematic or characteristic of the text or class of texts being studied.[16]

Let us now return to the question of the correlation between linguistic choice and nonlinguistic objective phenomena, such as the situation, or particular aspects of the situation, in which the speech event takes place. It is commonly understood that linguistic features are selected according to such pragmatic factors as the speaker's or hearer's perception of the relationship between the 'message' and the situation, in its widest sense, of which the language-use tends to form only a part. Here such elements as the physical setting, the speaker's role, purpose or objective, the medium used (basically written or spoken), the personal and social relationships between the interlocutors, the degree of formality, etc. are relevant, and all of these elements receive at least some treatment in the present volume, representing points at which pragmatics influences style. Indeed Nils Erik Enkvist defines style as 'contextually restricted linguistic variation',[17] although it is possible that this might go beyond what would normally be considered style, to include the whole linguistic activity: the topic discussed, what is said about it, who speaks first, etc.

The definitions we have been treating up to now approach style as emanating from the author or speaker, as something in the genesis of the text and seen from that perspective. Once a text has been written or spoken, however, it becomes an object in its own right, with some standing in the empirical world, and another approach to a definition is based on the premiss that the style of a text derives from the differences between it and some other text, usually called the 'norm', from which it can be regarded as 'deviating' by reason of these differences. According to this view, 'the essence of variation, and thus of style, is difference, and differences cannot be analysed and described without comparison.'[18] Style is thus a deviation from a norm, the norm being any text, real or imaginary, which may serve as an ideal or standard for comparison, while the deviation is the actual text to be studied.

It is now many years since Paul Delbouille formulated what may be understood as 'norm' in this connection as (i) common usage of language, (ii) neutral expression devoid of any affective value or (iii) a kind of average of individual usages.[19] Whether this notion of style as deviation from a norm is substantive (i.e. style *is* the differences) or merely methodological (i.e. the style of a text can be *studied* by comparing it with another text), it has a long and respectable history. Bally wrote: 'Un principe important de notre méthode, c'est l'établissement, par abstraction, de certains modes d'expression idéaux et normaux; ils n'existent nulle part à l'état pur dans le langage, mais ils n'en deviennent pas moins des réalités tangibles.'[20] At least for Bally it was, apparently, part of a method.

Riffaterre develops this approach in a somewhat idiosyncratic but important manner. According to him, a stylistic device is any linguistic element which stands out from its own context in such a way as to attract the reader's attention and provoke a reaction. He has in mind the breakdown in predictability which can be caused by some element or elements deviating from the pattern set up previously in the text itself, or the context as he calls it.[21] In other words, the context itself serves as a norm in which stylistic devices (other authors speak of 'style markers')[22] occur and these stylistic devices, by definition, contrast with the rest of the text. It is therefore the opposition between context and contrasting features that constitutes the stylistic device. Riffaterre is thinking of literary writing and of how a reader can be surprised by unexpected elements, but the great virtue of his theory – elaborated in many works over the years – is that it allows each text to have its style and style markers in itself, without the need to compare it with anything extraneous to itself. There would seem to be no reason why this notion should not apply to the style of any text, literary or not.

An underlying problem in all these attempts at definition is to establish a method to determine which elements, features or forms in the linguistic system are stylistic and which are not, because they all assume that there are also 'common-core' or neutral parts of every text which seem to play no part in determining its style. In this regard it might be possible to set up a vertical axis and a horizontal axis, on the former of which might be situated a continuum of quality, ranging from formal to informal, or from rhetorical through poetic, colloquial, popular to vulgar, etc., and on the latter all possible occupational uses of language: legal, journalistic, medical, etc. One could then identify, for instance, formal legal style, and point to features – linguistic features – in a given text which would be its exponents. In a scheme not unlike this, it has also been suggested that an axis of sociolects might be added to show 'pragmatic space', thus manifesting, for example, language-use in the workshop, the design office, salesroom, lecture theatre, court-room, etc.[23] Sometimes such variations have been referred to as languages, sub-languages or registers, but the fact is that they seem to have much in common with styles, especially since the Prague School has established that functions of language constitute a consideration relevant to the question of style. For instance, in an interesting work on language variety,[24] there is a study of control tower language, and this is referred to as 'an excellent example of a specialised sub-language'. It might not be unreasonable to regard such language-uses as styles, but then the criterion of style would no longer be choice (at least exclusively or in these cases), since in such situations the speaker exercises little personal choice in the linguistic forms used.

As we have already hinted, one of the concepts that occupies a central place in many definitions of style is that of connotation, with its related notions of expressive or emotive features. This concept derives from the idea that every semantic unit – word, phrase, sentence, etc. – has a primary, literal, basic or referential meaning (its *denotation*) and may have other indirect or more figurative meanings (its *connotation*). Hence style is sometimes seen as the connotative level of language-use, as distinct from the denotative level. For instance, Akhmanova writes that 'linguostylistics concerns itself with the nature (peculiarities) of the expressive-evaluative-emotional features of linguistic units'[25] and there is no reason not to extend 'linguistic units' to include texts of any length or type.

While linguistics investigates and describes or explains the various linguistic levels of the surface and deep structures of utterances – phonetic, phonological, morphological, syntactic, lexical, semantic, etc. – stylistics, by this account, studies how each utterance differs from others in transmitting, conveying or expressing different connotations as well as, or over and above, the 'basic' idea or message which pure communication would contain.

It need hardly be repeated that style and stylistics refer to all types of utterance or text and everything we have suggested up to this point applies with equal validity to the study of style in every possible type of language-use, from the most formal to the most colloquial and from the most literary to the most prosaic. Nevertheless it must be said that some authorities have tended to make a distinction in practice between 'literary stylistics' and 'linguostylistics' or 'linguistic stylistics'. The difference relates mainly to the type of text studied and the actual purpose of a particular investigation, in that the object of the former type is usually related to criticism, appreciation or interpretation of 'literary' works, while the purpose of the latter type is usually more general, referring to linguistic analysis of any kind of text or language study.

How, then, does a pragmatic component contribute to stylistics or to the study of style? The routes along which pragmatics has developed have been rather distant from those of stylistics, mainly since 1938 when Charles Morris defined language in the semiotic sense as the use of signs governed by syntactic, semantic and pragmatic rules, and since 1959 when Rudolf Carnap took up this distinction and clarified that pragmatics refers to the relationships between signs and their users. It is now well understood that in using language, people do not merely talk or write but they perform actions also, that language is employed in situations which typically include both a linguistic and a nonlinguistic context, that part of the global context consists of the knowledge, beliefs and assumptions of the people involved and that at least one participant is trying by means of language to change the inner state or system of another or others.

This last element is fundamental, in that speakers and writers intend to bring about some (more or less specific) modifications in the knowledge, attitudes, beliefs or behaviour of others. Pragmatics focuses on the conditions which permit or impede the fulfilment of this purpose: it is interested in what language-users mean, what they do and how they do it in real situations, what they speak or write to be heard or read by one or more people, whom they intend to affect in one way or another.

Pragmastylistics, therefore, or stylistics with a pragmatic component, can be described as a study of language-in-use which pays special attention to the choices made from among the various grammatically correct ways of expressing one and the same thing, which is semantically or truth-conditionally equivalent. It also describes how such choices relate to the overall situation in which the language is used, including what the interlocutors already know or do not know, and what the speaker or writer wishes to achieve through his language-use. Pragmastylistics will always attempt to show how the different possible ways of saying 'the same' thing (style) depend on the factors which compose the situation (pragmatic factors). In other words, the linguistic surface will be seen as determined by some kind of 'fit' or relationship between stylistic choice and the nonlinguistic situation. That is to say, utterances with the same or virtually the same meaning (in the sense of correspondence to truth conditions, semiotic content or semantic value) may differ in their linguistic form and situational appropriateness, and these differences may have pragmatic explanations.

The domain of pragmastylistics, then, includes the study of all the conditions, linguistic and extralinguistic, which allow the rules and potential of a language to combine with the concrete factors of a situation in order to produce a text intended to bring about certain internal changes in the receiver. It distinguishes the abstract, theoretical or semantic meaning of the utterance or text from its usage or effectiveness in a concrete situation and what the enunciator means or intends to achieve by using it. It follows that pragmastylistic studies may focus on any expanse of language-in-use, ranging from the phrase or clause to a complete discourse, conversation or text. In practice, spoken uses of language are given a high priority by students of any kind of pragmatics, a tendency that is heavily reflected in Section II of this volume, which concentrates on pragmastylistic aspects of conversation. Of course written forms are also studied, whether they be general or literary, and written language is treated in Sections I and III.

No single study could attempt to cover more than a few aspects of the varied relationships between style and pragmatics. In the present volume, the first two chapters deal with general pragmastylistic questions and the third with a specific example taken from written language; the following four concentrate on conversational styles and the final three on literary texts.

George W. Turner's treatment of speech acts goes to the heart of pragmatics in pointing out that, while sharing, shaping and showing (or informing) pervade all language-use and take many forms, 'the most basic pragmatic element of language and the most pervasive' is sharing and he examines the kinds of language used to achieve this. The thorny problem of how a hearer chooses, from a range of possible assumptions, those which are relevant in order to interpret a particular utterance is tackled by Diane Blakemore. This involves a framework for explaining the relations between linguistic form and pragmatic interpretation and how the style of a communication varies as the speaker aids the hearer to identify the thought behind an utterance and the implicit interchanges with the explicit. Leo Hickey, using Spanish data, investigates linguistic elements which not only express but announce the topic to be treated in certain types of utterance, where the topic is morphosyntactically disjoined from the rest of the utterance, which is usually grammatically complete in itself. These forms of topicalization, conditioned by pragmatic factors, appear to have definite implications for the level of style, usually making it informal.

Also using a Spanish corpus, Flora Klein-Andreu defines somewhat similar phenomena, which she calls X-forms. These appear when a speaker mentions a referent that is closely related semantically to the reference of a nearby utterance, but without any morphosyntactic indication of the nature of the relationship. Asking why these X-forms occur, she concludes that they always express a referent that is important to the speaker. Carmen Silva-Corvalán explores certain linguistic means which a speaker may choose in order to express degrees of assertiveness or certainty, as against 'hypotheticality'. Style as choice thus relates to the pragmatic factor of the speaker's meaning.

Rather than viewing style as a juxtaposition of preconceived linguistic forms and particular extralinguistic or contextual features, Margret Selting, referring to German data, discusses how style can shift and switch as a conversation moves between extremes of personal antagonism and co-operation. Dealing with conversational interactions in clearly defined hierarchical situations, Jenny Thomas examines the main devices by which a dominant speaker may seek to control the discourse, in the sense of laying down the purposes and boundaries of the interaction, keeping the subordinate speaker within the lines established, marking new stages or signalling the end and forcing the subordinate to give particular 'on-record' responses to specific questions or remarks.

'The value of dialect in the novel', writes Raymond Chapman, 'is probably less synaesthetic than pragmatic'. He suggests that orthographic signalling of sub-standard speech in fiction fulfils the function, not so much of imitating characters' speech, but rather of signalling the pragmatic factor of the relationships between them. He finds that Thomas Hardy's 'concern for the pragmatic response to dialect', or indeed to standard speech, allows him to imply strangeness or isolation, social difference, emotional pressure, ease of intimacy or dominance of the explicit message over any interest in the way a character speaks.

In a discussion of what he calls vertical context systems, in the sense of 'infracontexts' or contexts which, though not explicit in a text, affect the meanings of words or brief phrases, Claes Schaar applies the concept to five types of 'inscription' or word-group. These can be fully and satisfactorily interpreted only by looking at the infralevels or packages of meaning derived from overtones and previous uses.

Nils Erik Enkvist and Gun Leppiniemi have teaching in mind as one objective of a number of experiments in protocolled reading, which they describe. These consisted of administering a short poem in a number of successive fragments to groups of students, asking them to note their anticipations of what they were about to read and their disappointments as they continued reading. 'The entire process of anticipation, confirmation and disappointment is an essential aspect of text comprehension', they conclude.

As the interdisciplinary subject with which this volume is concerned develops, no doubt new insights will emerge into the rich potential for the enhancement of style studies by the rapidly expanding field of pragmatics. This volume is not intended in any way to delimit, or even to predict, the forms which such insights may take; rather, it is intended to welcome any approach to stylistics – in every sense and definition of the term – which incorporates a consideration of the users of language, the relationship between them, the situation in which they communicate and what they do by means of their language-use. Although the prefix 'pragma' is adjectival and the root 'stylistics' is nominal in the term 'pragmastylistics', the subject allows the focus to fall on either end of the interdisciplinary scale, the pragmatic or the stylistic, or anywhere inbetween. To questions like 'What choice of linguistic form is exhibited in this text or utterance?' 'What is the effect of the form of this text?' the student of pragmastylistics will add 'What does this text or utterance do and how does it do it?' or 'What do the people involved in this language-use do and how do they do it?'

If stylistics studies the form of linguistic utterances, while pragmatics is interested in the formal analysis of the dependence of a text in respect of its situation or context or in 'that part of linguistic knowledge and behaviour which pertains to speaker-sentence-context relations',[26] it seems certain that only a stylistics which includes a pragmatic component can claim to be complete.

Notes

1 Tzvetan Todorov, 'The Place of Style in the Structure of the Text', in *Literary Style: A Symposium*, edited by Seymour Chatman (London and New York: Oxford University Press), 1971, p. 29.

2 Charles Bally, *Traité de stylistique française* (Heidelberg: Carl Winter's Universitätsbuchhandlung), 1909, vol. 1, pp. 25–6.

3 See Pierre Guiraud et Pierre Kuentz, *La Stylistique; lectures* (Paris: Klincksieck), 1970, Introduction, pp. 3–14.

4 Gilles-Gaston Granger, *Essai d'une philosophie du style* (Paris: Armand Colin), 1968, p. 8.

5 Henri Morier, *La Psychologie des styles* (Geneva: Georg éditeurs), 1959, p. 7.

6 ibid., p. 20.

7 Pierre Guiraud, *La Stylistique* (Paris: Presses Universitaires de France), 1954, p. 7.

8 See, for example, Stephen Ullmann, *Language and Style* (Oxford: Basil Blackwell), 1964 and *Meaning and Style: Collected Papers* (Oxford: Basil Blackwell), 1973, *passim*.

9 Graham Hough, *Style and Stylistics* (London: Routledge & Kegan Paul), 1969, pp. 4–8.

10 Richard Ohmann, 'Generative Grammars and the Concept of Literary Style' in *Word* 20, 3, December 1964, 426.

11 ibid., p. 427.

12 Olga Okhmanova, *Linguostylistics: Theory and Method* (The Hague: Mouton), 1976, p. 3.

13 ibid., p. 15.

14 Michael Riffaterre, 'Criteria for Style Analysis' in *Word* 15, 1, April 1959, 155.

15 Jean Marouzeau, *Précis de stylistique française* (Paris: Masson), 1946, 10th edn, p. 10.

16 See Werner Winter, 'Styles as Dialects' in *Statistics and Style*, edited by Lubomír Doležel and Richard W. Bailey (New York: American Elsevier Publishing Co.), 1969, p. 3. Rolf Sandell offers a preliminary definition of style as a 'characteristic way of making nonsemantic linguistic choices' in Rolf Sandell, *Linguistic Style and Persuasion* (London and New York: Academic Press), 1977, p. 6.

17 Nils Erik Enkvist, *Linguistic Stylistics* (The Hague: Mouton), 1973, p. 51.

18 ibid., p. 21.

19 Paul Delbouille, 'A propos de la définition du fait de style' in *Cahiers d'Analyse Textuelle* 2, 1960, 94.

20 Charles Bally, *Traité de stylistique française*, pp. 28–9.

21 Michael Riffaterre, 'Stylistic Context' in *Word* 16, 1, April 1960, 207–18.

22 For a useful treatment of style markers see Nils Erik Enkvist, 'On Defining Style', in Nils Erik Enkvist, John Spencer and Michael Gregory, *Linguistics and Style* (London: Oxford University Press), 1964, pp. 34–8.

23 J. C. Sager, D. Dungworth and P. F. McDonald, *English Special Languages* (Wiesbaden: Brandsetter), 1980, pp. 6–7.

24 W. H. Sumby, 'Control Tower Language' in *A Reader on Language Variety*, edited by C. S. Butler and R. R. K. Hartmann (Exeter: University of Exeter), 1976, pp. 56ff.

25 Olga Akhmanova, *Linguostylistics: Theory and Method*, p. 15.

26 Asa Kasher, 'Mood Implicatures: A logical way of doing generative pragmatics' in *Theoretical Linguistics* 1, 1974, 7.

Section I

Style in Communication and Comprehension

In one of its most basic senses, pragmatics is concerned with language in use, attaching special significance to those aspects of meaning not explained by semantics. In practice, this frequently involves distinguishing what speakers or writers mean from what their utterances mean. Pragmaticists also spend much of their energy trying to discover how hearers or readers understand what language-users are doing as well as what they are saying, usually in cases where there appears to be some discrepancy between the linguistic level and the actual import of the communication. At least since the publication of J. L. Austin's *How To Do Things With Words* in 1962, it has been understood that, in using language, people not only say things but also do things. In elucidating what is done and what is meant, the context (linguistic and extralinguistic, whether built into the utterance in some explicit way or not) often plays a vital part, as do inferences, implications, the balance between the explicit and the implicit level of the message, the appropriate conditions for performing particular actions and many other pragmatic factors. The style is the result of the choices made relating to the linguistic methods used to do or to mean whatever is done or meant.

In this Section, three aspects of language-use are studied in particular, namely the basic action of sharing, the problem of interpreting and the effectiveness of announcing what is to be talked about.

The number of actions that can be performed by the use of words is probably not infinite, although some of these actions may be more pervasive than others. George W. Turner suggests that three of the most fundamental are sharing, shaping and telling, but he shows that, if telling (in the sense of informing) is perhaps the least efficient, 'sharing is the most basic use of language, animal or human; it approaches pure communication without information'.

13

Diane Blakemore is concerned with how a hearer or reader actually interprets an utterance, since there seem to be many ways of saying the same thing and two utterances may convey one and the same meaning. Sentences do not express propositions, she explains, they only provide a linguistic blueprint for constructing them, and a receiver has to turn to inference and general communicative principles in order to work out what is meant. What is said is not, of course, the same as what is implied, which in turn is not the same as what is meant. Since a hearer may have to use various types of relevant contextual information, he may recover any proposition from a whole range of possible ones: how, then, does he decide which contextual information is relevant to interpreting a particular utterance? How does he know whether what he understands coincides, with or even resembles, the speaker's intention or not?

Utterances which are identical in semiotic content may differ in pragmatic organization and, consequently, in style. Leo Hickey discusses style both as the surface or linguistic features of a text and as the subjective reactions stimulated in the reader or hearer. Whatever structure a speaker decides to impose on his text, and especially whatever means he uses in order to distinguish between what he wants the hearer to understand and what he assumes is already known, will affect the style. As an example of how pragmatic factors determine style, he studies the degrees of formality manifested in the construction he calls the dangling topic, a structure chosen, not just to express the topic to be talked about in an utterance, but expressly to identify and announce it. Using a Spanish corpus, he suggests that this construction contributes to effective communication but produces informal style. The interrelation of pragmatics and style is therefore a very close one.

Chapter one

Sharing, shaping, showing: the deep uses of language

George W. Turner

Our cat has a habit of putting his paw over his eyes while sleeping. My wife and I find this pose rather fetching and either of us might say 'Look at him now' or 'The light's too bright' or (to the cat, but usually only if the other is present) 'Is the light too bright for you?' The cat, however, never comes to me if my wife is asleep to say 'Look at her. Isn't she nice?' Animals appear not to have developed the sophisticated patterns of sharing found in human society, though warning cries represent a very basic form of communication already found in animals, and it would be interesting to examine other animal behaviour to find what patterns of sharing they exhibit. Sharing is the most basic use of language, animal or human; it approaches pure communication without information.

Institutionalized or stereotyped sharing becomes ritual or liturgy. Patrick White[1] includes rustic conversation in this category. Ritual may take the form of dance-drama and the earliest forms of narrative and lyrical literature.

Virginia Woolf describes a language that is almost pure sharing, a husband and wife conversation 'which no third person could have understood'.[2] She points out, more acutely than linguists have done, that

> When two people have been married for years they seem to become unconscious of each other's bodily presence so that they move as if alone, speak aloud things which they do not expect to be answered, and in general experience all the comfort of solitude without its loneliness. The joint lives of Ridley and Helen had arrived at this stage of community, and it was often necessary for one or the other to recall with an effort whether a thing had been said or only thought, shared or dreamt in private.[3]

The antithesis of sharing is suggested here, what is 'only thought' or 'dreamt in private'. Such inner discourse is not wasted, since,

besides promoting sharing, language has acquired another function, that of shaping. As I write I have no immediate audience; what
I write is 'only thought', but I am shaping my thinking as I write and
revise and rewrite. J. S. Bruner describes this experience: 'Some
people write in order to find out what they think, I among them',[4] he
writes, and describes how with each succeeding paper his own views
changed and grew.

There is a complex pattern of shaping in literature in which a
writer shapes material and aims to shape the reader and is in turn
shaped by the experience of writing; the reader then interprets the
text, an activity involving further shaping. This activity on the
reader's part is an important element in a literary experience; the
reader is not passively shaped. That is why it is an objectionable
recent tendency in television programmes that canned laughter is
introduced at points in comedies meant to be funny. Not only our
thinking but even our laughing is being done for us in that sort of
television.

The shaping function of language has been emphasized by the
Russian psychologists Vygotsky and Luria[5] and must inevitably be a
part of a study of the acquisition and development of language by
children. In Sapir's words

> The product grows with the instrument, and thought may be no
> more conceivable . . . without speech than is mathematical
> reasoning practicable without the lever of an appropriate
> symbolism.[6]

Italo Calvino puts it in a literary way: 'It is only through the
confining act of writing that the immensity of the non-written
becomes legible.'[7]

Not only thinking but conduct may be regulated by a reflexive
shaping in the form of a vow, or, if uttered and in favour of a hearer,
a promise or, institutionalized, an oath.

Sharing is the most basic pragmatic element of language, and the
most pervasive. Even the solitary student shaping a thought, or the
speaker who mutters alone, has temporarily become both writer
and judge, both speaker and hearer, and the two elements share
language as other communication does. Sharing must therefore be
reciprocal and have a plural subject, or imply or lead to a phrase
beginning with 'with', but shaping may be either reflexive, as one
shapes one's own thought through language, or transitive as one
uses language to shape another's thought or conduct.

The shaping of another's thought, the informative or regulatory
use of language, showing (telling that) or commanding (telling to),
has received most attention from linguists and many write as though

showing or 'telling that' were the only important use of language. In fact 'telling' is the least efficient use of language and the most liable to misunderstandings. Even sociolinguists usually work with an ideal, an ideal combination of a speaker and a hearer without lapses of attention, preconceptions and preoccupations that distort meaning, misinterpretation of directives or bees in bonnets. We assume that people not only do share but want to share. It is a useful assumption which we will retain for the time being, but many uses of language rely on misunderstandings of linguistic situations which can be manipulated by charlatans, confidence men, propagandists and other hidden persuaders. It would be dangerous to leave out a linguistics of error, inadvertent or promoted, in a total theory of pragmatics.

The shaping of others may be regarded as a factitive version of sharing. Each of its manifestations, 'telling that' and 'telling to', informing and commanding, itself has a reciprocal or factitive version, the two being served by one verb 'ask' in English. One asks for information or one asks to be permitted to do something. There is a merging of 'telling that' and 'telling to' in 'telling how' or instruction. The instructor tells that it is done this way, or tells the learner to do it this way. Teaching is an institutionalized or iterative form of instructing. It has a passive, one of the meanings of 'learn' ('to be taught' in perfective sense) but a more important kind of learning, which an enlightened teaching will try to promote, is the reflexive form of shaping, to make discoveries by thought, especially by writing.

These categories may have subdivisions. With an increased element of sharing, a command might be a request. With a perfective element, informing might be convincing and requesting might be prevailing upon or (in one of its senses) persuading. Persuading may in another sense be an inceptive command (urging) or an iterative one (insisting). Asking may be reflexive, wondering, or, more perfectively, speculating. In a strict sense commanding is a perfective version of demanding, with a suggestion of institutional backing.

Is negating to be regarded as a speech act? We are so schooled in a view that double negatives are equivalent to positives that we are predisposed to think of negatives in terms of meaning. The attractive 'kernel sentences' of early transformational grammar fell victim to a feeling that a negative sentence differed too strongly in meaning from its positive counterpart to be derived from it by an optional transformation. Yet when Miss Miggs says of Mrs Varden (in Chapter 19 of *Barnaby Rudge*) 'I never see such a blessed one as she is for the forgiveness of her spirit, I never, never, never did. No more did Master neither; no nor no one – never!', we begin to feel that she is doing something (negating) more than saying something with her battery of negatives.

The uses of language are various, perhaps infinite, and ordinary language provides numerous terms for speech acts. For example, stating, informing, 'telling that', is usually thought of as neutral with regard to the aggrandizement of the speaker, but in the special case of boasting this element is prominent, and when speakers, instead of boosting themselves, seek to diminish the environment and the opportunities it offers them, we call their statements 'complaining', if they are intransitive general ones, or 'blaming', with its iterative 'nagging', if transitive, or directed against a specific object or person. Some speakers enhance themselves by denigrating others. Conversely a speaker may enhance another by praising or commending. Apologizing may be regarded as a reflexive form of blaming.

Sharing, shaping, and telling do not occur as separate activities but are elements in varying proportions in all language. If I tell my wife there is a magpie on the lawn, my purpose is sharing, even if she cannot see it from where she is sitting, because we both like having birds around, but there is also an element of information in my remark. If I am by the window and she is not and I tell her that someone is coming up the drive, my purpose will be primarily informative, though there is a trace of sharing. At least we have to be 'on speaking terms'. A scientist, telling us that the Australian magpie of genus *Gymnorhina* was once thought to be of three regionally dispersed species but that since they have been found to interbreed they are now classified as one species, is being informative, but expects a reader to share an interest in such factual details. When on the other hand, a poet, Judith Wright, writes

Along the road the magpies walk
With hands in pockets left and right

she is not so much telling us as sharing, inviting us to recall how Australian magpies walk (rather than hop) and have markings suggesting hands in pockets, but there is information too, about a detail of a magpie's habits. Perhaps the scientist and the poet can be said to agree in persuading us to take an interest in magpies, a step towards a feeling of oneness with living creatures. So the teller and the sharer shape us in the direction of a higher sharing.

Though literature, as opposed to science, aims at sharing rather than telling, nourishing 'the creative faculty to imagine that which we know'[8] rather than seeking an accumulation of novel facts, there are two senses in which poets are makers or shapers. Not only do they shape readers by sharing with them, but, unlike scientists or historians, creative writers are able to shape their material. For them situational constraints become a matter of choice. When Arnold Bennett in *The Old Wives' Tale* chooses a dead elephant rather than a dead horse to provide excitement to the people of the Five Towns, he is constrained not by history but by the symbolic needs of his story. This plasticity of narrative seems to be less evident in oral literature in which traditional tales and traditional expressions acquire fixed forms. Children often demand a similarly invariant telling of a favourite story.

One's view of language is shaped by the most readily available examples of it. For most people such sources will be speech, but scholars, especially while at work studying language, are in the abnormal situation, each one alone among books, of having available, and in the centre of their vision, written language, which has the advantage of permanence. It stands still while you look at it. One result of this preoccupation is that the language usually studied is monologue. Exchange, conversation, is the normal mode of language, another way in which sharing is basic; writing is abnormal, though less abnormal than our usual accounts of it suggest.

A writer, alone among familiar books, is, as we have suggested, two people, questioner and answerer. Writing is a debate, one in which victory is assured, certainly, since all writers, like poets and novelists, have control over their material and can marshal arguments without the unexpected twists of real conversation. They can decide what is given to a shadowy opponent in a subordinate clause and what answers it in a main clause. A writer begins 'although . . .' and there is drama as an opposing argument is allowed to build up; then, with all the force of a main clause, the opposition is crushed.[9]

The writer is not only a shaper of language, but is also shaped by it. The language will tend to run in traditional grooves, in clichés at its worst, and so the writer, to be creative, must struggle against society, or those parts of society that are not fresh and growing, as society, acting through its language, exerts pressures in prescribed directions. To that extent sharing has to be resisted, a too facile sharing of unexamined metaphors and figures from which the community is better saved.

How much we are predisposed by the language we are born into to think in stereotyped ways has become a special study within linguistics, a study of linguistic relativity or, popularly, the Sapir-Whorf hypothesis. Bréal,[10] for instance, thinks European languages predispose us to animistic thinking. Perhaps so: I have noticed children saying 'my trike can't go' where our adult idiom favours a more animistic 'won't go'. How much this actually shapes our thinking is what the debate is about.

The uses of language are sometimes marked by special grammatical forms, asking by interrogative, commanding by imperative, for example. The most basic, sharing, shaping, telling, are too pervasive to require clearly marked individual grammatical indicators though some general tendencies can be noted. The indicative mood is especially associated with telling but not confined to it; an imperative more clearly marks the special use 'telling to' (command, request, etc.). Forms especially associated with sharing are questions, especially tag questions, which acknowledge and emphasize the presence of a hearer, the use of second-person pronouns or verb forms, and imperatives (especially of advice or 'telling how'). Many languages retain separate singular and plural second-person grammatical forms allowing a derived use as instruments promoting relations either of solidarity, the more sharing alternative, or of power. In modern English decisions to use first names or surnames and titles have a similar function. Shaping is reflected in all the forms of inner speech (tendency to isolated predicates, subjects hardly needing explicit stating to the thinker) and all the forms of writing (where absence of an immediate shared environment makes the specification of subjects especially necessary).

Even where uses of language are marked by a special grammatical form, it is well known that an actual use may not coincide with the grammatical form. A question form may disguise a command, a statement may seek information. Subtle nuances lurk behind the indicatives of prose. Consider the following sequence from a student newspaper:

> In 1984 the combined total military expenditures of all countries was \$A1,208,000 million. That works out at about \$2.3 million each minute. If we started spending money at the same rate on providing clean, safe, water supplies for all people in the world, it has been estimated we'd have achieved that goal after only five days.

This is, to use a dated terminology, scientific, not emotive, prose. It appears to be 'telling that' but it is obvious that these facts told in this way introduce an element of 'telling to' in its purpose. It asserts a different scale of priorities from those currently acted on. Its exact purpose is perhaps not to establish those priorities, since it is hard to imagine that the argument will actually bring the desired change, so much as to create a mood of anger which will gradually urge various decisions along a desired line of development.

A similar but perhaps more convincing approach shows the need for changed priorities within a concept of defence itself, when Professor Quirk, addressing a conference on research problems and the teaching of English, concludes:

> Our work is being demanded of us in the interests, we are told, of international relations; yet virtually all of it could be financed with the money spent by the Ministry of Defence in a single hour.[11]

Because the purposes of language are normally mixed, there is likely to be argument about the mix. Is literature pure sharing (art for art's sake) or is there always an element of shaping (all art is ultimately didactic)? Is, for that matter, science all telling or does it promote a rationalist outlook which may appear as opposed to religion, and, taking the form of the social sciences, have far-reaching repercussions on modern life and politics?

On the religious side, what are we to think of Tolstoy's view that Christian art should deal in universals, what is shared already?[12]

What of literary criticism? People like to discuss plays or films they have seen in each other's company and it is pleasant to read a book at the same time as a friend and be able to discuss it together. This is sharing and it is the basis perhaps of literary criticism. It is a sort of 'metasharing', sharing the experience of sharing with an author. Of course the element of sharing is seldom pure. Perhaps I've encountered one example of literary criticism which was pure sharing when a student, asked to present to a small class an analysis of a rather complex literary work, began 'Well, it's sort of got a sort of – you know?' (with upward intonation). It seems that communication was complete since the half dozen students in the group all said enthusiastically 'Yeah!'. Usually literary criticism is more shaped – but might talk of 'a certain elusive *je ne sais quoi*', I suppose.

Not only literature and science, of course, show the mixed motives of language. An apparently innocent statement may be a complaint or blaming, perhaps only fully perceived by its victim. It is not enough to analyze conversation in terms of commands, requests, explanations, labels, and so on, but very difficult to assess the more complex motives which activate individual or class forms of language. There are unintended effects of language (to bore, offend, embarrass, irritate) and these very effects may in particular cases be deliberately aimed at. Teasing might be deliberate embarrassment, but then teasing can also be affectionate. In order to assess the exact force of a particular utterance we might need to know the whole history of speaker and hearer, and not only know it but understand it.

A further complication is the need to take context into account in assessing meanings or motives. In isolation the following passage is ambiguous.

> Five thousand diners were finishing five thousand dinners, their eyes undisturbed by the presence of advertisements on the walls.

It would be a better sentence with 'the presence of' omitted, but in its context[13] it is clear there are no advertisements. In Adelaide some time ago a political party was offended by a local newspaper called *The News*. Bumper stickers appeared bearing the legend 'No News is Good News', which, while perhaps retaining the potential ambiguity of its structure, was quite unambiguous in its purpose to those who knew the circumstances.

The basic linguistic situation consists not only of a speaker and hearer in a social situation but also of language itself. Language may be shaped in a process of naming, in which case the name given by a properly constituted authority is generally adopted, or in neologizing, in which case general approval is much less certain.

Writers of fiction enjoy special privileges of naming. Not only may they create names for their characters but these names may be appropriate, part of the shaping of the character. Obvious 'talking names' in the unexpectedly similar *Pilgrim's Progress* and *The Way of the World* gave way to less obvious but still appropriate names in Dickens or Trollope. One is most aware of the subtle influence of these names when another member of a family necessarily but inappropriately shares a name. Mercy Pecksniff is not a comic character.

The ease with which names can be shaped contrasts with the recalcitrance of things. Failure to apprehend this clearly leads to a belief in magic and spells, including the manipulating of things and people through their names. Because of this (even in societies that have outgrown magic) people are frequently found to be reluctant to mention their own names. You do not bluntly ask a person's name but say 'What was the name please?'

One's name is part of one's sense of identity, which in other ways too depends on language more than we usually realize. The foreigner in a strange land feels lost and begins to feel stupid until he learns to share a new language. Even a different surrounding dialect or accent (regional or class) leaves one feeling isolated and, in its original sense, excommunicated.[14] Languages provide devices (greetings, etc.) to maintain the presence of a shared language (the phatic use) and the spirit of sharing (politeness formulas).

It is possible for telling or referring to relate not to an external situation but to language itself. This is the metalinguistic use of language, mentioning an expression rather than using it to refer to something outside it. One theory of irony[15] is based on this distinction; an utterance used in a situation which seems not to fit it may be being mentioned rather than used and the listener is led to seek a reason for the discrepancy and so to sense irony. Another approach to irony sees it in terms of a double audience, a naïve one taking a statement seriously while a more sophisticated one enjoys the ironical intention.[16] This view provides a motivation for the indirectness of an ironical utterance.

Yet another aspect of irony is brought out by Northrop Frye,[17] who stresses the self-deprecatory use of irony to render oneself invulnerable to criticism by forestalling it. It is perhaps a variety of apologizing or self-blame, but marked by an intention the reverse of humility since, as Frye goes on to point out, in literature it becomes most commonly a technique for saying as little and meaning as much as possible. Like other forms of irony it works by avoiding a direct statement and must be interpreted in total context.

A particular kind of 'mention' is parody, usually with some distortion of what is mentioned or with a heightening to the point of absurdity of some features of a style. Among freshly painted graffiti on a wall in 1978 was 'Mussolini out of Libya now', presumably a parody (like 'Land Rights for Gay Whales!')[18] hinting at a degree of impotence or failure to relate to practical issues in slogans. Perhaps unfairly: the slogan as a speech act is probably as effective as advertising in influencing attitudes (shaping) and, especially if giving notice of rallies, has an added function in co-ordinating action (promoting sharing), but perhaps the writers of one kind of graffiti, racialist slogans, are more aptly compared with animals that mark out territory by urinating on walls.

Both shaping and sharing enter into both science and literature. Scientists shape their theories in order to add to a stock of shared knowledge; poets share their experience to shape their readers' values. Neither science nor literature has traditionally been shared by a whole society. Scholars have shared their findings with each other, rather than the public, in a special language (Latin) or the vocabulary, and to some extent the syntax, of a special language grafted on to a vernacular grammatical stock (modern scientific technicality). Scientists are initiated into such devices as footnotes, acknowledgements, bibliographies and citation indexes which allow the sharing of knowledge; writers, less corporate in outlook, nevertheless come back from time to time to a sense of tradition and by allusions and favoured styles build up something akin to the scientists' pool of knowledge and paradigms of approach. But ultimately science has to do with controlling (shaping) and the arts, particularly dancing and music, with sharing.

More immediately influential than writers and scientists, though perhaps less permanent in their effects, are the politicians. Rhetoric is their science of shaping, once to inform and persuade, increasingly, as the platform is superseded by the television screen, to control and not to convey information but to conceal or distort it.[19] The suppression of information is aided by censorship, official secrets acts, and the promotion of taboos against explicit discussion, in the most widely shared styles of the language, of such matters as sexual habits and hygiene. Even trade names represent an intrusion of privatization into the communal language.

Against this gloomy view, there are moves to make legal statutes more accessible to the public and journalists are not always the puppets of the politicians. Nevertheless politics remains an area where shaping and telling tend to be opposed.

The fundamental elements of language are a speaker (first person), a hearer (second person) and the world outside them in which their language operates (third person). Thus it is a universal constraint on grammars that persons can only be three in number. Rare languages with a fourth person merely divide the third person into two items in order of mention, as we do ourselves with 'the former' and 'the latter'. Language is a code to link the three elements of the linguistic situation and its deep uses emphasize one or the other element.

If emphasis is on the third person, on the world outside the linguistic group, shaping in its transitive sense, telling (that) is dominant. If second and third person of the linguistic situation are both relevant to the utterance, instructions (telling or showing how), commands (telling to), prohibitions (telling not to), warnings and threats (commands or prohibitions incorporating an element of 'telling that') are indicated. Institutionalized, these are the basis of law. With an element of sharing (linking all three persons) we have asking (in the sense of requesting information or, with emphasis more strongly on first and second person, the sense of asking permission). Telling is the basis of science; asking of philosophy.

If emphasis is on the second person of the triad, in practice the relation of first and second person, the function of language is sharing. Phatic uses of language are perhaps the best documented instances of sharing, though they are often linked with the shadowy extra element in the linguistic situation, language itself, and compared with testing that the channels of communication are open, as one does when whistling into a microphone before opening a meeting. It seems better to see them as a testing and maintenance of the social situation, not the language itself. If a friend seems not to want to speak to me I worry about our relationship, not the decline of English. Phatic uses might aid or damage friendships if we include among these teasing, bullying, and sneering as well as the more amiable uses of language such as greeting, congratulating, or wishing someone well.

A phatic element may enter into other uses of language. A teacher can enjoy a tutorial as a social occasion without departing from its instructional purpose. A writer might cultivate lucidity in the interests of a reader, or achieve a rhythm that seems to invite a reader to share a dance, or, on the other hand, he may wall himself in with rhythmically awkward jargon.

At an informal level, slang carries a strong sense of sharing or belonging to a group, but equally a strong sense of exclusion, since the group is defined by the exclusion of outsiders. Slang is especially attractive to the young who seem to need the comforts of its conformity as they shape a growing individuality first by being shaped by this provisional social product. Do national languages in developing countries have a similar role?

If emphasis is on the first person alone, we have wondering, speculating, and (in its first phase) writing.

If we add modifications such as reflexive, inceptive, factitive, perfective, to our basic sharing, shaping, and showing, we can characterize some of the speech acts that have been described by philosophers and linguists interested in pragmatics. A perfective telling (showing) is convincing; asking is in one sense factitive (or causative or induced) telling, in another sense factitive permitting, perfective if successful, or conative if not. Permitting itself is an induced command. Prayer may be seen as reflexive shaping, family prayer with an element of sharing. Special terms may merely reflect special technical areas of language; in law a command may take the form of a statute or of a will or of a sentence according to circumstances; a statement made by the foreman of a jury is a verdict.

According to J. L. Austin there are over a thousand verbs in English describing speech acts.[20] In view of this we hardly need to be warned by P. F. Strawson that '. . . we can scarcely expect a general account of linguistic communication to yield more than schematic outlines, which may almost be lost to view when every qualification is added which fidelity to the facts requires.'[21]

Eventually perhaps the right elements will be located to set up a matrix of distinctive features or a set of Venn circles to account for the various uses of language. At present the study has the mark of an early stage where little is certain but much is potential. I happily

25

leave the elaboration of detail, with the necessary restriction of potentiality, to others.

Notes

1   P. White, *The Twyborn Affair* (Ringwood, Australia: Penguin), 1981, p. 250.
2   V. Woolf, *The Voyage Out* (Harmondsworth, Penguin), 1970, p. 194.
3   ibid., p. 193.
4   J. S. Bruner, *Child's Talk* (Oxford: Oxford University Press), 1983, p. 9.
5   'Words play a central part not only in the development of thought but in the historical growth of consciousness as a whole' – L. S. Vygotsky, *Thought and Language*, edited and translated by Eugenia Hanfmann and Gertrude Vakar (Cambridge Mass.: MIT Press and Wiley), 1962, p. 153. Cf. A. R. Luria 'The Directive Function of Speech in Development and Dissolution', *Word* 15, 3, 1959, 341–52.
6   E. Sapir, *Language: An Introduction to the Science of Speech* (New York: Harcourt Brace & World Inc.: Harvest Book), n.d., p. 15.
7   I. Calvino, *If on a Winter's Night a Traveller*, translated from the Italian by William Weaver (London: Picador), 1982, p. 144.
8   P. B. Shelley, *A Defence of Poetry* in *Shelley's Literary and Philosophical Criticism*, ed. John Shawcross (Oxford: Oxford University Press), 1909, p. 151.
9   I notice I am slipping into the conventional metaphor of argument as conflict, when, as George Lakoff and Mark Johnson point out in *Metaphors We Live By* (Chicago: Chicago University Press), 1980, p. 5, it might equally well in an ideal language be represented by a dance. Indeed the shadowy conflict of writing, where opposite views may not be so much stated as merely countered in their absence, perhaps resembles a dance more than a battle.
10 M. Bréal, *Semantics: Studies in the Science of Meaning* translated by Mrs Henry Cust (New York: Dover), 1964, p. 3.
11 R. Quirk, *Essays on the English Language Medieval and Modern* (London: Longman), 1968, p. 93.
12 L. N. Tolstoy, *What is Art and Essays on Art*, translated by Aylmer Maude (Oxford: Oxford University Press), 1929, p. 241.
13 A. Bennett, *City of Pleasure* (New York: Doran), 1907, p. 30.
14 G. W. Turner, 'Language and Belonging', *New Zealand Speech Therapists' Journal* 25, 1, May 1970, 5–13.
15 D. Wilson and D. Sperber, 'Irony and the Use–Mention Distinction' in P. Cole, ed., *Radical Pragmatics* (London: Academic Press), 1981, pp. 295–318.
16 G. W. Turner, *Stylistics* (Harmondsworth: Penguin), 1973, p. 217.
17 N. Frye, *The Anatomy of Criticism* (New York: Atheneum), 1967, p. 40.
18 The genesis of this often quoted Australian parody is discussed in S. Murray Smith, *The Dictionary of Australian Quotations*

(Richmond, Australia: Heinemann), 1984, p. 227. Aboriginal rights to ownership of traditional land is an issue supported by the Left.

19   cf. Paul E. Corcoran, *Political Language and Rhetoric* (St. Lucia, Queensland: University of Queensland Press), 1979, p. xv.

20   J. R. Searle ed., *The Philosophy of Language* (Oxford: Oxford University Press), 1971, p. 39.

21   ibid., p. 38.

Chapter two

Linguistic form and pragmatic interpretation: the explicit and the implicit[1]

Diane Blakemore

I The message: what hearers understand

As every writer knows, the problem in achieving successful communication is not always a matter of deciding what to say: it is often a problem of deciding how to say it. There is always, it seems, more than one way of saying the same thing. In fact, as I shall show in this chapter, this is a problem for every communicator, and while the writer may devote more time and effort to its resolution than a speaker in everyday discourse, and while the solution she adopts in a particular instance may not be the one adopted by a speaker, their decision is, in the end, constrained by the same cognitive pragmatic principle.

Clearly, the fact that some communicators do spend time and effort on this problem suggests that they believe that their decision does matter, will have some effect. But what is this effect if it is not, as I have seemed to suggest, an effect on the actual content of the message? At this point it may be objected that there is no decision that a communicator makes regarding the form of her utterance (written or spoken) that does not affect the message she conveys, and hence that no two linguistic forms could ever be used to convey the same message. Equally, it may be claimed that these effects are purely aesthetic and hence that their study belongs more to the domain of a theory of aesthetics than a cognitive theory of pragmatics. Thus for example, according to the first view, the message conveyed by the metaphorical utterance in (1) could not have been communicated by any other utterance, whereas according to the second view, this utterance is simply a more decorative or ornamental way of communicating the message in (2):

(1) He was burning with anger.
(2) He was extremely angry.

Much has been written about these two views as they apply to the interpretation of figurative language.[2] Here I would like to discuss the question of the relationship between linguistic form and interpretation that is raised by a rather different set of choices available to the communicator. However, before we consider the variations in form that result from these choices, let us turn to the question that underlies the controversy outlined above: What is conveyed by an utterance? Or, in other words, when do two utterances convey the same message?

It is generally agreed that one of the things a hearer must do in order to understand an utterance is to identify the thought or proposition that it expresses. That is, she must be able to give a specification of the conditions under which what the speaker has said is true. Now, obviously, the truth conditions of an utterance are affected by the words it contains and their syntactic arrangement. However, this does not mean that the truth conditions of an utterance can be predicted simply on the basis of its lexical and syntactic properties. The truth value of (3) may vary according to who the pronoun *she* refers to, what *it* refers to, which box is being referred to, and whether *may* is intended in its permissive sense or its modal sense. In each case the interpretation supplied by the hearer depends on her assumptions about the world, or, in other words, the context. Similarly, it is only on the basis of her assumptions about the world that the hearer will be able to specify the domain of the quantifier in (4) and what it was too early for.

(3) She may put it in that box.
(4) Everyone turned up too early.

The suggestion, then, is that natural language sentences do not express propositions, but simply provide linguistic 'blueprints' for the construction of propositions. What we need is a theory which will explain how the hearer selects and uses the contextual information that enables her to develop the blueprint provided into a complete thought, and in particular, into the thought that the speaker intended to communicate. However, we also need a theory which will explain why the speaker chooses to use a particular linguistic clue for the communication of a given thought. Obviously, the speaker's choice is constrained by the grammar. A speaker could not, for example, expect to communicate the proposition that Mary knows that Susan admires herself by producing the utterance in (5). Nor could she expect the hearer to interpret the pronoun *she* in (6) as being bound by *every student*:

(5) Mary knows that Susan admires her.
(6) She thinks that every student will fail.

The point is that within these grammatical constraints the speaker still has a choice as to the form of utterance she may use for the communication of a given proposition. In particular, she must decide how specific her utterance must be, or, in other words, the degree to which she can expect the hearer to rely on contextual information. Thus, for example, in certain situations the speaker of (3) may have succeeded in communicating the same thought by producing the fragmentary utterance in (7):

(7)   In there.

On the other hand, assuming that *she* refers to Susan Jones, *it* to the book wanted by the addressee, and *that box* to the box on the speaker's desk, the speaker might have produced the utterance in (8) or the one in (9):

(8)   Susan might put the book in that box.
(9)   Susan Jones might put the book you wanted in the box on my desk.

I do not wish to suggest here that the sentences in, say, (3) and (9) are synonymous or have identical semantic representations. Nor do I wish to deny that there are any systematic connections between the semantic representation of a sentence and the thought communicated. The point is that because of the gap between the sentence meaning and utterance interpretation there is inevitably a variety of different sentences that may be used to communicate the same thought. Notice that even when the speaker is being more specific, as in (9), the sentence she uses could still express different propositions in different situations. That is, although she may need to supply less contextual information, the hearer still needs to supply some.

So far the discussion might seem to suggest that although the semantic representation of a sentence may fall short of being a complete representation of the proposition communicated, there is nevertheless a systematic connection between them. However, as is widely recognized, an utterance may communicate a number of thoughts whose content is not related to the semantic representation of the sentence used in any sort of systematic way. Consider, for example, the dialogue in (10):

(10)   A: Are you going to read this book?
       B: The author's a post-structuralist.

Whereas in one context the hearer may be expected to recover, in addition to information that the author of the book is a post-structuralist, the proposition in (11a), in another she might be expected to recover the one in (11b):[3]

(11) (a) The speaker will not read the book.
      (b) The speaker will read the book.

Clearly, the interpretation recovered by the hearer depends on which of the assumptions in (12) she holds:

(12) (a) The speaker never reads books by post-structuralists.
      (b) The speaker will read any book by a post-structuralist.

It is easy to imagine how a mismatch between the context envisaged by the speaker and the contextual assumption actually supplied by the hearer could lead to a misunderstanding. Misunderstandings do, of course, occur. However, given that communication does succeed, we need to explain the principles by which the hearer of an utterance like (10B) chooses the assumptions she brings to bear on its interpretation.

Equally, however, we need to be able to explain what leads a speaker to communicate a thought indirectly, as in (10B) instead of communicating it directly, as in (13).

(13) No I won't.

Notice that although there is no linguistically specified connection between (10B) and either of the propositions in (11), the hearer's choice of interpretation is constrained. That is, it is evident from B's utterance that she is expected to supply one or other of the assumptions in (12) and to derive one or other of the propositions in (11). In contrast, the hearer of the direct answer in (13) is not so constrained and is free to derive any implications she likes.

In this discussion I have attempted to distinguish between two sorts of information that may be communicated by an utterance. On the one hand, there is that information which I have referred to as the proposition expressed; that is, the proposition for which the sentence used provides the 'blueprint'. On the other, there is that information which the hearer infers from the proposition she takes to have been expressed on the basis of contextual information. To some readers this distinction might appear to correspond to Grice's (1967) distinction between 'what is said' and 'what is implicated', a distinction which for many followers of Grice is co-extensive with the distinction between the explicit and the implicit. However, there are two important respects in which the distinction I am making cannot be identified with Grice's distinction, and, consequently, it cannot be accommodated within a Gricean framework.

Grice's main concern in his 1967 William James Lectures was to find a non-semantic explanation for a range of phenomena that had posed serious problems for traditional theories of semantics, and, in particular, an explanation which could avoid postulating a large number of distinct but related senses for the so-called 'logical' vocabulary of natural language, for example, *and*, *or*, and *some*. Accordingly, he distinguished between 'what is said' – that is, those aspects of the total meaning of an utterance which are closely tied to the conventional meanings of the words uttered – and 'what is implicated' – that is, those aspects of meaning which are due to the interaction of linguistic meaning and general communicative principles (the maxims of truthfulness, informativeness, relevance, and manner). Thus, for example, one can maintain a purely truth-functional analysis of *and* in the face of examples like (14) and (15) by treating their temporal and causal connotations as 'implicatures' derived on the assumption that the speaker has conformed to the manner maxim which, amongst other things, requires speakers to be orderly.

(14)   He ran over to the window and jumped.
(15)   The road was icy and she slipped.

Similarly, in this framework the suggestion conveyed by (16) that not all of the students wrote essays is due not to the meaning of *some*, but to a general pragmatic principle requiring speakers to give sufficient information:[4]

(16)   Some of the students wrote essays.

The fundamental idea here is that in communicating, speakers aim to meet certain general standards, and that hearers interpret utterances with these standards in mind. As Grice himself realised, this idea has applications that extend beyond the analysis of the logical particles. There is a whole range of phenomena which could be treated as implicatures. In particular, Grice's approach makes it possible to explain how it is possible for a speaker to communicate a thought whose content is not related in any sort of systematic way to the semantic representation of the sentence used. Recall, for example, the dialogue in (10). The proposition that B's utterance expresses does not provide a direct answer to A's question and hence is not relevant as it stands. If B has obeyed Grice's maxim 'Be relevant', then it must be assumed that she intended to give A an answer. Moreover, if A has access to the assumption in (12a), then she can obtain the direct answer in (11a) from what B has actually said. In this way A may work out that B intended her to derive (11a) as an implicature.

This account leaves many problems unsolved. For example, although Grice recognized the importance of the context in working out implicatures, he did not explain what its role is or how it is selected to play this role.[5] Nevertheless in developing the notion of conversational implicature Grice drew attention to a fact of fundamental importance: there are aspects of utterance interpretation which cannot be explained in terms of decoding messages according to a set of linguistic rules, but which involve taking the meaning of the sentence uttered together with contextual information and inferring what the speaker meant on the basis of the assumption that the utterance conforms to very general principles of communication. While the importance of this idea has been recognized in so far as it allows us to explain phenomena such as the interpretation of utterances like (10B), it was not until comparatively recently that its full implications have been explored. In particular, it is only recently that it has been recognized that the role of inference and general communicative principles extends beyond the interpretation of implicatures to the determination of the propositional content of utterances, or, in other words, to the determination of what is said.[6]

As Grice himself pointed out, knowing what the speaker actually said in producing a particular utterance is a matter of, first, knowing what range of possible senses and possible referents could have been intended, and, second, knowing which sense and reference were intended on that occasion. We have already seen in the discussion of (3–4) that while the linguistic properties of an utterance may determine the first, they cannot determine the second. The following example (adapted from Wilson and Sperber (1981)), (17) has two possible senses, depending whether *admit* means 'let in' or 'confess to' and an indefinite range of possible referents for *them*:

(17)   I refused to admit them.

However, when it is produced in response to (18), the hearer can immediately eliminate all the possible interpretations except for the one in which *admit* means 'confess to' and *them* refers to the speaker's mistakes:

(18)   What did you do when you made a mistake?

Wilson and Sperber's point is that whatever the context of this utterance, it still has an indefinite range of linguistically possible interpretations, any one of which could have been intended by a speaker who was not observing the conversational maxims. However, as Grice claimed, hearers interpret utterances on the assumption that the maxims have been observed. Thus for example, the assumption that the relevance maxim is being observed will lead to the elimination of any interpretation for (17) in which *admit* means 'let in' and *them* refers to anything other than the speaker's mistakes. In other words, the sense and reference of an utterance is not fully determined by semantic rules, but is pragmatically determined by the context and the maxim of relevance.

As Wilson and Sperber point out, the pragmatically determined aspects of propositional content are not exhausted by disambiguation and the ascription of reference. Utterances are frequently elliptical or fragmentary – recall for example the utterance in (7) or such everyday utterances as 'Telephone' – and yet in every case the hearer is expected to recover a complete proposition. Further, there are cases in which the meaning of the words uttered determines a proposition which, although complete, is too under-specified to be taken as the one the speaker could have intended. Consider, for example, the utterance in (19) (taken from Carston (forthcoming)):

(19)   It will take us some time to get there.

In principle, the hearer of (19) could recover a complete proposition on the basis of its linguistic content together with reference assignment. However, she would not recover thereby anything she didn't know already: obviously the event of going to a location takes place over time. In this case, suggests Carston, the hearer's assumption that the utterance conforms to the maxim of informativeness will lead her to recover a much more completely specified proposition – for example, the one in (20):

(20)   It will take longer to get there than you think.

Carston goes on to show that this idea, that there are pragmatically determined elements of propositional content, has even wider applications. In particular, she shows that the evidence, first noticed by Cohen (1971), that argues against the classical implicature account of the causal and temporal connotations of conjoined utterances (see (14) and (15) above) is not evidence for a semantic account of these connotations, but rather for a pragmatic account at the level of what is said. Her account proceeds from the quite standard assumption that an utterance describing an event is interpreted as a proposition which contains a value for a time index determined on the basis of the context. The point is that given his background beliefs and general pragmatic principles, a hearer can go beyond the linguistic meaning of utterances like (14) and recover values for the time index in each conjunct so that if the value in the first conjunct is t, then the value in the second conjunct is $t+n$.[7] Thus as a first approximation, the proposition recovered from (14) may be represented as in (21):

(21)   He ran over to the window at t and he jumped at t+n.

In fact, the same pragmatic factors enable the hearer to recover a much more fully specified proposition than this. In particular, the hearer is able on the basis of the information in the first conjunct to identify the references of *he* in the second conjunct and the information that he jumped out of the window.[8] The proposition recovered is given in (22):

(22)   He$_i$ ran over to [the window], at t and he$_i$ jumped out of [the window], at t+n.

Within Grice's framework, the fact that the maxims play a role in the recovery of information from an utterance means that it is part of what is implicated rather than part of what is said. If we wanted to maintain this definition of an implicature, then we would have to say that the proposition in (20) together with the results of disambiguation and reference assignment should be classified as part of what is implicated and that the 'what is said' should be restricted to the range of possible meanings specified by the grammar. This is evidently inconsistent with Grice's original intention. Moreover, it undermines what pragmatists have generally regarded as the most intuitively appealing contribution made by his theory of implicature – namely, that it provides an account of how it is possible to convey more than just the propositional content of an utterance. Clearly, we do wish to maintain the distinction between the proposition that the speaker is taken to have expressed and the implications that follow from it. However, this is not a distinction between 'what is said' and 'what is implicated' – at least, not if 'what is said' is defined in terms of 'conventional' or linguistically specified meaning. Nor is it a distinction between the explicit and the implicit – at least, not if 'the explicit' refers to the linguistically explicit and the 'implicit' to that which is left unsaid. As we have seen, there are many elements of propositional content which are left unsaid.

It is clear that if explicit means 'linguistically explicit', then there can be no fully explicit thought. Even when the hearer is provided with a highly specific linguistic clue, as, say, in (9), she still has to rely on some contextual information.[9] As Sperber and Wilson (1986) put it, natural language sentences do not (and cannot) encode thoughts (1986: 192–3). On the other hand, it is clear that the propositional content of an utterance is always made explicit to some degree. That is, the linguistic properties of an utterance determine a semantic representation (or, as Sperber and Wilson call it, a logical form) which, given contextual information, can be developed and enriched into a complete thought. In contrast, the suggestion or implicature recovered from the proposition expressed (for example, the suggestion in (11a) recovered from (10B) is not a development of a semantic representation specified by the grammar, but is recovered on the basis of contextual information. That is, it seems that whereas the proposition expressed by an utterance may be explicit to some degree, the suggestions or implicatures recovered from it are always implicit.

This, essentially, is the distinction between explicit and implicit communication as it is drawn by Sperber and Wilson (1986). Their definition of explicitness is given in (23):

(23)   *Explicitness*
       An assumption communicated by an utterance U is
       explicit if and only if it is a development of a logical form
       encoded by U. (1986: 182)

As they point out, this is a comparative notion: there are degrees of explicitness. The more the hearer has to rely on contextual clues for the identification of the proposition expressed, the less explicit it is, and inversely. Thus, for example, the proposition expressed by (7) is less explicit than the one expressed by (3) which, in turn, is less explicit than the one expressed by the utterance of (9). Similarly, the complex proposition expressed by the utterance of (14) is less explicit than that expressed by the utterance of (24):

(24)   He ran over to the window and then he jumped.

However, all of these are explicit to some degree, or, to use a term introduced by Sperber and Wilson, they are all explicatures (1986: 192). Any assumption which is not a development of a grammatically specified representation is an implicature.

The claim that no thought can be completely represented by a natural language sentence (or, in other words, be fully explicit) might seem to imply that communication is impossible. How, in the absence of a linguistic or grammatical code, can a speaker guarantee that the hearer recover exactly the thought that she intended to communicate? Notice that this assumes, first, that successful communication involves exact duplication of thoughts, and, second, that successful communication can be guaranteed. Neither of these assumptions, argue Sperber and Wilson, can be maintained. On the one hand, communication may succeed provided that the proposition that the hearer receives bears a sufficient resemblance to the speaker's thought:

> We see verbal communication as involving a speaker producing
> an utterance as a public interpretation of one of her thoughts,
> and the hearer constructing a mental interpretation of this
> utterance, and hence of the original thought. . . . [W]e see no
> reason to postulate a convention, presumption, maxim or rule of
> literalness to the effect that this interpretation must be a literal
> reproduction. (1986: 230–1)[10]

The question that this approach raises is: how does the hearer know
how closely the proposition she recovers resembles the speaker's
thought? It also raises the question of what determines the hearer's
interpretation of an utterance as an interpretation of one thought
rather than another. For if, as we have seen, the linguistic
properties of the utterances do not fully determine the proposition
recovered and the hearer must construct it on the basis of contextual
information, then, logically speaking she may recover any of a
whole range of propositions. For in principle, a hearer may bring to
bear any of her accessible beliefs and assumptions upon the
interpretation of an utterance, which means that from a logical
point of view, her interpretation isn't constrained at all. While
successful communication may not be guaranteed, the fact that it
does occur suggests that the hearer's choice of contextual assumptions for the interpretation of an utterance is one that may be
exploited and manipulated by the speaker.

Neither of these questions arise in a Gricean programme, at least
at the level of propositional content (or 'what is said'). The fact that
Grice does not recognize the extent to which contextual information and inference rules may be involved in the identification of
'what is said' means that he has no notion of degrees of explicitness.
On his approach any contextually or pragmatically determined
aspect of meaning would have to be an implicature. At this point it
may be recalled that Grice distinguishes between two types of
implicature: 'non-conventional implicatures', propositions recovered from what is said entirely on the basis of contextual information together with the assumption that the maxims are being
observed; and 'conventional implicatures', suggestions which are
not part of the propositional content of the utterance but which
nonetheless are linguistically (or 'conventionally') specified. Probably the most discussed examples of the former type are the
conversational implicatures (illustrated above in (10B)). Unfor-
tunately, Grice had much less to say about the latter type and
confined his discussion to a few brief remarks about the role of
words such as *therefore* and *but*. Thus for example, according to
Grice's analysis, the use of *therefore* in (25) indicates that his being

brave is a consequence of his being an Englishman, but the speaker could not be held to have spoken falsely should the consequence in question fail to hold:

(25)   He is an Englishman; he is, therefore, brave.

The claim that there are elements of linguistic meaning which do not contribute to the propositional (or truth-conditional) content of utterances is difficult to reconcile with the programme, generally associated with Grice's theory of conversation, of maintaining a purely truth-conditional semantics. Equally, it is difficult to reconcile the claim that implicatures may be linguistically determined or explicit with the view, also generally associated with Grice, that implicatures are pragmatically determined and are hence part of implicit content.

Karttunen (1974) and Karttunen and Peters (1975) link Grice's notion of conventional implicature to the class of phenomena referred to in the presupposition literature as 'pragmatic presuppositions' (cf. Stalnaker 1974, 1975). While they recognize that the latter term has been used to cover a heterogeneous class of phenomena, and hence that it is unlikely that everything that has been called a pragmatic presupposition is in fact a case of conventional implicature, they suggest that Grice's claim about *therefore* applies equally well to sentences with words such as *manage, fail, again, even, yet,* and *too,* all of which have been said to carry pragmatic presuppositions. In fact, in this chapter I shall not be concerned with these words, but will be pursuing the line of inquiry suggested by Grice's example in (25). However, it is worth noting here Karttunen's suggestion about *too. Too,* he says is a 'rhetorical device' whose presence or absence does not have any bearing on what proposition the sentence containing it expresses, but rather relates the sentence 'to a particular kind of conversational context' (1974: 12). In other words, such expressions do not so much encode implicatures, as suggested by Grice, but rather impose constraints on the context in which the utterances containing them must be interpreted. If the appropriate context is not available, then the utterance (or, more particularly, the use of the expression in question) is inappropriate or infelicitous. As already noted, Karttunen owes much of this idea to Stalnaker's (1974) proposals about the relationship between pragmatic presupposition and 'common ground'. However, neither Karttunen nor Stalnaker provided a psychologically adequate account of the role and selection of the context in utterance interpretation, and, consequently, they were not able to explain why there should be linguistically specified constraints on the context.

In this section I have raised two problems for a Gricean account of the distinction between the explicit and the implicit. First, it takes no account of the role of pragmatic factors in the determination of the proposition expressed by an utterance and hence does not recognize that 'what is said' may be explicit only to a certain degree. Second, although Grice recognized the existence of non-truth-conditional linguistic meaning (for example, *therefore*), he did not provide a satisfactory account of the role such meaning plays in the determination of implicatures. As we have seen, both problems lead us to the same questions: (i) What is the context for the interpretation of an utterance; and (ii) What are the principles governing its selection and role in the interpretation of utterances? In the following section I turn to an account of pragmatic interpretation which provides a unified and psychologically grounded answer to these questions, and hence a framework for explaining the relationship between linguistic form and pragmatic interpretation.

II Recovering the message: constraints on relevance

Sperber and Wilson (1986) argue that an account of utterance interpretation must be based on a general cognitive theory of information processing. The basic idea underlying their theory is that in processing information people generally aim to bring about the greatest improvement to their overall representation of the world for the least cost in processing. That is, they try to balance costs and rewards. Obviously, not every addition of information counts as an improvement. A hearer's representation of the world will not necessarily be improved by the addition of information that it already contains. Nor will it be improved by the presentation of information that is unrelated to any of the information it already contains. The hearer's aim is to integrate new information with old, or in other words, to recover information that is relevant to her. Notice, too, that a hearer is not simply interested in gaining more information about the world: she is also interested in obtaining better evidence for her existing beliefs and assumptions. The point is, that in every case her search for relevance leads her to process new information in a context of existing assumptions.

In this theory computing the effect of a newly presented proposition crucially involves inference. That is, the role of contextual assumptions is to combine with the content of an utterance as premises in an argument. There is no space here to outline the nature of the inferential abilities that Sperber and Wilson believe to be involved in utterance interpretation. However, it is important to recognize that in this theory propositions are treated not just as logical objects but as psychological represen- tations, and that inferences are psychological computations per- formed over those representations. Their basic claim is that assumptions about the world come with varying degrees of strength and that logical computations assign strength to conclusions on the basis of the strength of the premises used in deriving them.

There are three ways in which an inference system plays a role in assessing the impact of a new item of information on an existing representation of the world. First, since an inference system can be used to test for inconsistencies in the propositions submitted to it, it can play a role in the hearer's decision to abandon an existing assumption in favour of the information that has been presented to her. Second, the fact that conclusions inherit their strength from the premises from which they are derived means that inference rules can be used to assess the extent to which an existing assumption is confirmed or justified by a new item of information. Finally, since the propositions which are taken as premises may be derived from the hearer's existing representation of the world, an inference system may play a role in the identification of what Sperber and Wilson call contextual implications. That is, it enables the hearer to add to her existing representation of the world by processing new information in a context of old information.

Intuitively, it is clear that the greater the impact a proposition has on the hearer's representation of the world the greater its relevance. For example, in normal circumstances the fact that the light goes on in my office when I flick the switch has fewer implications for me, and hence less relevance, than the fact that it does not go on. On the other hand, it has to be remembered that all information processing requires effort and time – that is, a cost – and that, other things being equal, the greater the cost of processing a new item of information, the less its relevance for the person processing it. In the case of verbally communicated information there are two types of cost involved. On the one hand, there are the costs entailed by the linguistic complexity of the utterance: the more complex the utterance the greater the processing effort required. On the other, there is the cost of accessing and using contextual assumptions. Although, typically, a hearer will have an enormous amount of encyclopaedic information available to her in memory, only a small subpart of this will be accessible to her at any given moment. Moreover not all information will be equally accessible to her at one time. For example, the most easily accessed information will include that which has been most recently processed – for instance, the information that played a role in the interpretation of the previous utterance together with the information derived from it. This initial context can be extended in various ways, for example, by adding information derived from utterances earlier in the discourse or from the physical environment. Indeed, the fact that the concepts present in the initial context being processed will themselves give the hearer access to propositions which contain concepts that give her access to propositions which contain concepts . . . and so on means that in principle the hearer could go on adding to the context indefinitely. But as the size of the context increases so does the cost of accessing and using the assumptions it contains, and a hearer who is searching for relevance will automatically process each new item of information in the context that yields a maximum contextual effect for the minimum cost in processing.

Obviously, it is in the interests of a hearer who is searching for relevance that the speaker should produce an utterance whose interpretation calls for less processing effort than any other utterance that she could have made. But equally, given that the speaker wishes to communicate with the hearer, it is in her interests to make her utterance as easily understood as possible. This means that the hearer is entitled to interpret every utterance on the assumption that the speaker has tried to give her adequate contextual effects for the minimum necessary processing, or, in other words, that the speaker has aimed at optimal relevance. Sperber and Wilson call the principle which gives rise to this assumption the *Principle of Relevance*.

On this view, the responsibility for success in communication is not shared, but taken solely by the speaker.[10] On the assumption that the speaker has aimed at optimal relevance, the hearer will simply go ahead and recover the optimally relevant interpretation. This means that a speaker who wants communication to succeed must have grounds for thinking, first, that the hearer has immediate access to a context which enables her to recover the right (that is, intended) proposition, and, second, that this context is one in which contextual effects may be obtained. Let us look at each of these points in turn.

As we have seen, the linguistic properties of an utterance are consistent with a whole range of propositions. However, the hearer assumes that only one of these is the one intended by the speaker. The question is, which one? The answer suggested above is: the one that is consistent with the Principle of Relevance, or, in other words, the one which yields adequate contextual effects for a minimum cost in processing. This might be taken to suggest that the identification of the propositional content of an utterance involves listing all the possible propositions and then ranking them according to their degree of relevance. However, this strategy is not consistent with the Principle of Relevance. As Sperber and Wilson point out, it would entail that all possible interpretations would require the same amount of effort, namely, the effort needed to construct and compare them (1986: 166). Consider their example given here in (26):

(26)   George has a big cat. (=Sperber and Wilson (65) p. 168)

Ordinarily, the first interpretation that will occur to the hearer is that George has a big domestic cat. While this may have some contextual effect for the hearer, it is quite feasible that any of the further alternative interpretations that George has a tiger/lion/jaguar have even more contextual effects, and hence that the hearer would find it more relevant to investigate other lines of interpretation. But recall that the Principle of Relevance entitles the hearer to assume that the speaker has produced the most relevant utterance she could for the communication of the information she wanted to convey. If the speaker had intended to communicate the proposition that George has a tiger, then she would have produced an utterance that would have saved the hearer the effort of accessing the first interpretation. For example, she would have produced either of the utterances in (27):

(27)   (a)   George has a tiger.
       (b)   George has a tiger or lion, I'm not sure which.

In other words, the only interpretation warranted by the Principle of Relevance is the first one found to be consistent with it.

This might be taken to suggest that a speaker who wishes communication to succeed – that is, who wishes the hearer to recover the right proposition – must produce an utterance whose form is such that it eliminates the hearer's reliance on contextual information, and hence the need to construct and evaluate hypotheses. But, as we have already noted, it is impossible for a thought to be fully explicit: the linguistic properties of an utterance always underdetermine the thought the hearer wishes to convey. Moreover, while such linguistic clues may reduce the hearer's reliance on contextual information, they add to the complexity of the utterance. If the effort that this increased complexity entails is not offset by an increase in contextual effects, then the relevance of the utterance will be decreased. Consider here the discourse sequences in (28) and (29) (both taken from Blass 1985):

(28)   He went to McDonalds. The quarter pounder sounded good and he ordered it.
(29)   The river had been dry for a long time. Everyone attended the funeral.

Whereas the mention of McDonalds in the first sentence gives a Western hearer access to contextual information that can be brought to bear on the interpretation of the next, in (29) there is nothing in the first sentence that helps the hearer with the interpretation of the second. In contrast, for a speaker of Sissala (a Niger-Congo (Gur) language), the sequence in (28) would seem incomprehensible and the one in (29) perfectly understandable.

A Western speaker who wished to communicate the information in (28) to a Sissala hearer would have to make the required contextual assumptions explicit – as in (30) – while a Sissala speaker who wished to communicate the information in (29) to a Western hearer would have to produce something like the sequence in (31):

(30)   He went to a place where food is cooked and sold. It is called McDonalds. There he saw ground meat which was formed into patties, fried, and put into cakes baked with flour. . . .

(31)   If a river has been dry for a long time, then a river spirit has died. If someone has died, then there is a funeral. The river had been dry for a long time. . . .

The point is, of course, that no speaker who wished to communicate with a Western speaker would have produced the sequence in (30). The extra complexity requires effort which is not offset by extra contextual effects, and the result is excessively ponderous and even patronizing in style. Indeed, a Western hearer presented with (30) might doubt that genuine communication was intended, and refuse to make the processing effort required.

While a speaker may have specific intentions regarding the proposition expressed by her utterance, it is not always the case that she will have specific intentions regarding the contextual effects that will be derived from it. On some occasions she may have only very general grounds for thinking that the hearer will derive some contextual effect. For example, if a stranger asks you the time, you will assume that your answer is relevant to her even though you may have no idea of the conclusions she will draw from it. In other cases the speaker may have an idea of the range of contextual effects her utterance will have, but not have any specific expectations about the conclusions the hearer will draw. For example, it will be rather difficult to pin down the exact contextual effect produced by the utterance of (32) made in a shop where piped music is being played:

(32)   I can't stand this type of music.

However, as we saw in the discussion of (10B), there are cases in which the speaker makes it manifest to the hearer that specific contextual assumptions are to be supplied and, hence, that a specific effect is to be derived. Let us take a different example, and suppose that Tom offers Ann an apple which has a small sticker saying 'Cape'. Although Tom does not know that this means that the apple was exported from South Africa, and Ann knows that he doesn't know this, Ann may still expect Tom to interpret her response in (33) as conveying the information in (34):

(33)   I never eat South African fruit.
(34)   Ann does not want to eat the apple.

Obviously, Ann would not have made this response unless she had grounds for thinking that Tom could supply the contextual assumption in (35):

(35)   The apple comes from South Africa.

However, in spite of the fact that there is nothing in the linguistic structure of her utterance which indicates that this is the interpretation she intended, it is evident that Ann is not really taking a risk here. Indeed, it is difficult to see how Tom could have interpreted her utterance in any other way.

By asking Ann whether she would like the apple, Tom is suggesting that he has immediately accessible a context in which either the information that she does want it or the information that she doesn't is relevant. This means that Ann would have satisfied the Principle of Relevance by answering him directly. But she didn't. This means that if Tom wishes to maintain his assumption that Ann was aiming at optimal relevance, then he will have to assume that she expects him to supply the premiss in (35) and derive the answer in (34). In other words, by answering him indirectly she has made a particular context immediately accessible to him, thus ensuring its selection under the Principle of Relevance.

But while this may explain why Tom interpreted Ann's utterance in the way he did, it does not, it seems, explain why she produced the utterance in the first place. If Ann was aiming at optimal relevance, then she should have been aiming to reduce the hearer's processing costs. Yet the indirect answer in (33) entails processing effort not entailed by the direct one. The fact that Ann has forced Tom to supply the assumption in (35) and derive (34) as a contextual implication may be explained if the processing effort these steps require is offset by the recovery of contextual implications that would not have been derivable from the direct answer. In other words, in producing the indirect answer, Ann is assuming that the extra information she is conveying is relevant in its own right. For example, it may be that Ann wants to alert Tom to the significance of the label so that he does not make the same offer again, or, assuming that Tom shares her opinions about buying South African produce, so that he will avoid buying food with these labels. Or perhaps she simply wants Tom to know that she is a person with principles. Notice that it may not be clear to Ann exactly what effects Tom will recover. The point is simply that she must believe that it is worthwhile for Tom to undertake the extra processing entailed by her indirect answer.

Whatever the relevance of the 'extra' information communicated by Ann's indirect answer, it is clear that Tom must supply the contextual assumption in (35) and derive the conclusion in (34). That is, there is a sense in which his choice of context and hence his interpretation is constrained even though Ann had not made her intentions explicit through the words she uttered. More generally, examples of this kind show how a speaker may exploit the hearer's aim of maximizing relevance in order to make her intentions about the implicit content of her utterance manifest.

However, as we began to see in the previous section, there are linguistic devices that the speaker may use in order to indicate what kind of contextual effects the hearer is expected to derive, or, in other words, to make her intentions regarding the implicit content of her utterance explicit. These devices do not contribute to the propositional content of the utterances that contain them: their sole function is to guide the interpretation process by specifying certain properties of context and contextual effects. As we have seen, the existence of such devices is difficult to explain given the programme, generally associated with Grice's theory of conversation, of maintaining a purely truth-conditional analysis of linguistic meaning. Moreover, even when the existence of non-truth-conditional elements of meaning is recognized, as in Karttunen's (1974) work, their contribution to the interpretation of the utterances that contain them is left unexplained in the absence of an account of the selection and role of the context. In Sperber and Wilson's relevance-based framework the existence of these devices, far from being a problem, is to be expected. On the one hand, given that the semantic representations of sentences do not encode propositions (that is, do not have truth conditions), there is no reason to expect every aspect of linguistic meaning to be directly analysable in truth-conditional terms. On the other, given the hearer's aim of maximizing relevance, and, in particular, of minimizing processing costs, the existence of structures and expressions which constrain the hearer's choice of context can be explained in both cognitive and communicative terms: their use ensures correct context selection at minimal processing cost.

To illustrate, consider the sequence in (36):

(36)   A: I wish I didn't have to work today.
       B: It's Friday.

Although A's utterance provides the hearer with an immediately accessible context for the interpretation of B's continuation, it is not clear exactly where the relevance of B's remark lies. For example, it could be relevant as an explanation of A's attitude, or as an attempt to dismiss her utterance as irrelevant, or as an objection to her remark. In real conversation, however, the connection between the two remarks would not be left unspecified, and B would have made her intentions clear either through intonation or through the use of such 'discourse connectives' as *after all, anyway, still*, and *nevertheless*. Thus (37–40) each suggests a slightly different interpretation:

(37)   A: I wish I didn't have to work today.
       B: You see, it's Friday.
(38)   A: I wish I didn't have to work today.
       B: Anyway, it's Friday.
(39)   A: I wish I didn't have to work today.
       B: Still, it's Friday.
(40)   A: I wish I didn't have to work today.
       B: Nevertheless, it's Friday.

(37B) suggests that the sentiment expressed by (37A) is to be expected given the fact it is Friday, (38B) suggests that A's wishes are irrelevant, (39B) suggests that the implications of A's having to work are cancelled by the fact that it's Friday, while (40B) suggests that A has to work in spite of her wishes. In other words, each of these expressions indicates how the relevance of B's remark lies in the way it modifies or affects the interpretation of the previous remark, and thus contributes to the overall coherence of the discourse.

Notice that in order to be able to establish the prescribed connection the hearer must supply further contextual assumptions. Thus, for example, the fact that it is Friday is only an explanation for A's wish not to work given some further information about Friday, for example, the information that A always feels negative about her work on Fridays. To underline this point further, consider Grice's original example, repeated here as (41) and the contrasting example in (42):

(41)   He's an Englishman; he is, therefore, brave.
(42)   He's an Englishman; he is, after all, brave.

Whereas in (41) the fact of his being brave is presented as proven by the fact of his being an Englishman, in (42) it is presented as proof of the assertion that he is an Englishman. That is, whereas *therefore* indicates that the proposition it introduces is a conclusion, *after all* indicates that the proposition it introduces is a premiss. However, in both cases the inferential connection is established only if the hearer supplies a further premiss, for example, the one in (43):

(43)   All Englishmen are brave.

In this way, the use of these words constrains the hearer's choice of context in that she must supply the contextual assumptions that allow her to establish the connection they express.[12]

Within the text analysis tradition (as, for example, in Van Dijk (1977)) the existence of expressions such as these is construed as evidence for the need for a grammar of discourse, that is, a set of rules for constructing and interpreting well formed (that is, coherent) text. However, while it is certainly the case that there are grammatically specified structures and expressions that contribute to the structure and organization of discourse, it is not necessarily the case that the coherence of discourse itself can be explained in terms of a set of ruler for producing and interpreting utterances.[13] As we have seen, utterances are interpreted against a context of background assumptions, and the actual context for the interpretation of an utterance is constrained by 'the organization of the individual's encyclopaedic memory, and the mental activity in which he is engaged' (Sperber and Wilson 1986: 138). Considered in this framework, such expressions must be construed as evidence for the existence of arbitrary links between linguistic form and pragmatic interpretation, or, more specifically, between linguistic form and implicit content.

In the previous section the notion of implicit content was introduced as that content which is not related in any systematic or grammatically specified way to the semantic representation of the sentence uttered, but which is derived from the proposition expressed entirely on the basis of contextual information. As we saw, it is not the inferential character of implicit content that distinguishes it from so-called 'explicit' content – the context and inferences are also involved in the identification of the proposition expressed by an utterance – but rather the fact that the semantic properties of the sentence uttered played no role in its recovery. But now we have seen that there are aspects of linguistic meaning which do play a role in the recovery of implicit content. Does this mean that implicit content can be explicit, or, less paradoxically, that there is no distinction to be drawn?

The problem is that we are conflating two different distinctions:

on the one hand, we have the distinction, drawn by Sperber and Wilson, between that content which is arrived at through the development and enrichment of the logical form encoded by the sentence uttered – that is, what I have called 'the proposition expressed' – and that content which is derived from the proposition expressed together with contextual information. On the other, we have the distinction between linguistically signalled aspects of interpretation and non-linguistically (or pragmatically) determined aspects of interpretation. The existence of expressions like *after all, anyway* and *therefore* does not undermine the first distinction. However, it does suggest that the semantic properties of sentences are not exhausted by those properties which encode what Sperber and Wilson have called 'logical form' or, in other words, by those properties which contribute to the determination of the proposition expressed. This leaves us with the question of what aspects of interpretation these expressions are used to signal.

Recall that according to the framework outlined here, utterance interpretation is not just a matter of identifying the proposition or thought expressed. The hearer is also expected to do something with that thought, to perform computations on it.[14] As we have seen, those computations involve combining that proposition with others supplied from the context for the deduction of further propositions (or, in other words, for the derivation of contextual effects). In the first section we were concerned with the way in which the style of a communication may vary according to the degree to which the speaker aids the hearer in the task of identifying the thought that is to be assessed for relevance: the greater the hearer's reliance on the context the less explicit the thought. In the second section we saw that the style of a communication may vary according to the extent to which the hearer is constrained in what she does with the thought expressed. On the one hand, she may be constrained by purely pragmatic factors (as in the interpretation of indirect answers). On the other, she may be constrained by the form of the utterance itself. The problem, then, is not so much that there is no distinction between explicit and implicit content, but rather that the distinction between the linguistically specified and the non-linguistically specified applies not just to representations or content but also to computations or processes.

Notes

1   This chapter owes a great deal to discussions with Robyn Carston, Ruth Kempson and, in particular, Deirdre Wilson. However, none of them are to be held responsible for the views it contains.

2　See, for example, Ortony (1979) and Sperber and Wilson (1986).

3　In spite of the problems just outlined, I shall, for the purposes of exposition, represent propositions with English sentences.

4　For a more detailed account of this type of phenomenon, see Gazdar (1979) and Levinson (1983).

5　For a more detailed criticism of these problems, see Sperber and Wilson (1986).

6　A notable exception here is Katz (1972) who points out that since the reference of referring expressions can depend on the assumption that the maxims are being obeyed, 'determining what is said depends on the principles for working out what is implicated' (1972: 449).

7　Carston's account is actually given within the relevance-theoretic framework of Sperber and Wilson (1986) which will be outlined briefly below. However, the point remains the same: the temporal and causal connotations of conjoined utterances must be analysed as pragmatically determined elements of propositional content.

8　In fact, this approach allows us to account for the whole range of suggestions recovered from conjoined utterances listed by Posner (1980).

9　This point is in direct conflict with Katz's (1981) Principle of Effability: 'Each proposition (thought) is expressible by some sentence in every natural language' (1981: 226). For Katz, this does not simply mean that every thought can be conveyed by the utterance of some sentence, but rather that for every possible thought there is in every natural language a sentence one of whose senses uniquely corresponds to that thought. But as we have seen, there are many thinkable thoughts for which there is no corresponding natural language sentence.

10　Notice that according to this approach, non-literal (or figurative) utterances are not departures from a norm (i.e. of literalness), a view which places Sperber and Wilson closer to the Romantic tradition (represented by Coleridge, and more recently Max Black) than to the classical Aristotelian tradition, and, of course the neo-classical Gricean tradition. However, their view is not identical to the Romantic view. For further discussion of the distinction between the Romantic and classical approaches to figurative language see Ortony (1979). For Sperber and Wilson's approach see Sperber and Wilson 1986 4.8.

11.　In this respect Sperber and Wilson's approach contrasts with the 'mutual knowledge' approach of, for example, Bach and Harnish (1979) who assume that the hearer's task in utterance interpretation is to identify the speaker's intentions, a task which necessarily involves a certain amount of speaker-hearer co-ordination, particularly with respect to the choice of context.

12.　I have considered here only a range of the expressions which can be analysed as linguistic constraints on the relevance of the propositions they introduce. Other such expressions include *so*, *moreover* and *however*. For a more detailed analysis of all these expressions within a 'relevance-theoretic' framework, see Blakemore (1986, 1988, 1989).

13. For a more detailed criticism of the coherence-based accounts of discourse, see Blakemore (1989) and Blass (1985).

14. In fact, people do not just construct and store propositions or thoughts. They entertain them in different ways or as the objects of different attitudes. This means that hearers must not just identify the proposition which is to be assessed for relevance but also establish whether it is relevant, for example, as a factual description of the world, as a promise, as a request for information, as a request for action. As many readers will have noted, the style of an utterance may vary according to the extent to which the speaker's attitude towards the proposition expressed is made explicit. However, consideration of this aspect of style must be reserved for a later paper.

References

K. Bach and R. Harnish, *Linguistic Communication and Speech Acts* (Cambridge, MA: MIT Press), 1979

D. L. Blakemore, *Semantic Constraints on Relevance* (Oxford: Blackwell), 1987

D. L. Blakemore, 'So as a Constraint on Relevance', in R. Kempson (ed.), *Mental Representations: the interface between language and reality* (Cambridge: Cambridge University Press), 1989

D. L. Blakemore, 'The Organisation of Discourse', in F. J. Newmeyer (ed.), *Linguistics: the Cambridge Survey* (Cambridge: Cambridge University Press), 1988

R. Blass, 'Cohesion, Coherence and Relevance'. (University College London, unpublished MS), 1985

R. Carston, 'Semantic and Pragmatic Analyses of *and*'. Paper read at the Spring Meeting of the Linguistics Association of Great Britain, 1984

R. Carston, 'Explicature, Implicature and Truth Theoretic Semantics', in R. Kempson (ed.), *Mental Representations: the interface between Language and Reality* (Cambridge: Cambridge University Press), 1989

L. J. Cohen, 'Some Remarks on Grice's Views about the Logical Particles of Natural Languages', in Y. Bar-Hillel (ed.), *Pragmatics of Natural Languages* (Dordrecht: Reidel), 1971

G. Gazdar, *Pragmatics: Implicature, Presupposition and Logical Form* (New York: Academic Press), 1979

H. P. Grice, 'Logic and Conversation'. William James Lectures, Harvard University. Unpublished MS, 1967

H. P. Grice 'Logic and Conversation', in P. Cole and J. Morgan (eds), *Syntax and Semantics*, Vol. 3, *Speech Acts* (New York: Academic Press) pp. 41–58, 1975

H. P. Grice, 'Further Notes on Logic and Conversation', in P. Cole (ed.),

Syntax and Semantics, Vol. 9, *Pragmatics* (New York: Academic Press) pp. 113–28, 1978

M. A. K. Halliday and R. Hassan, *Cohesion in English* (London: Longman), 1976

L. Karttunen, 'On Pragmatic and Semantic Aspects of Meaning', paper presented at the 11th Annual Philosophy Colloquium, 1974

L. Karttunen and S. Peters (1975) 'Conventional Implicature in Montague Grammar', Berkeley Linguistics Society 1, 1975

J. Katz, *Semantic Theory* (New York: Harper and Row), 1972

J. Katz, *Language and Other Abstract Objects* (Oxford: Blackwell), 1981

S. Levinson, *Pragmatics* (Cambridge: Cambridge University Press), 1983

A. Ortony, 'Metaphor: a Multidisciplinary Problem', in Ortony (ed.), *Metaphor and Thought* (Cambridge: Cambridge University Press), 1979

R. Posner, 'Semantics and Pragmatics of Sentence Connectives in Natural Language', in J. R. Searle, F. Kiefer and M. Bierwisch (eds), *Speech Act Theory and Pragmatics* (Dordrecht: Reidel), 1980

D. Sperber and D. Wilson, *Relevance: Communication and Cognition* (Oxford: Blackwell), 1986

R. Stalnaker, 'Pragmatic Presupposition', in M. Munitz and P. Unger (eds), *Semantics and Philosophy: Studies in Contemporary Philosophy* (New York: New York University Press) pp. 197–213, 1974

R. Stalnaker, 'Presuppositions', in D. Hockney, W. Harper, and B. Freed (eds), *Contemporary Research in Philosophical Logic and Linguistic Semantics* (Dordrecht: Reidel), 1975

T. Van Dijk, *Text and Context* (London: Longman), 1977

D. Wilson and D. Sperber, 'On Grice's Theory of Conversation', in P. Werth (ed.), *Conversation and Discourse* (London: Croom Helm) pp. 155–78, 1981

D. Wilson and D. Sperber, 'Inference and Implicature', in C. Travis (ed.), *Meaning and Interpretation* (Oxford: Blackwell), 1986

Chapter three

The style of topicalization, how formal is it?

Leo Hickey

Among its many functions, stylistics provides criteria to describe any linguistic utterance in terms ranging, for example, from formal to informal, noncasual to casual, written to spoken or literary to colloquial. The scales are open-ended but the qualities described have at least two characteristics in common, namely they represent or correlate with some objective linguistic features and they stimulate certain subjective reactions or cause certain impressions in hearers or readers. Stylistics attempts to identify and analyse such features and to explain such intuitive reactions. Style, then, has two closely related aspects: the language chosen by the speaker or writer (the enunciator) and the effect stimulated in the hearer or reader (the receiver).

With the development of pragmastylistics, we are in a position to examine the language of any utterance or text, not only from a linguistic point of view, but also taking pragmatic factors into account. This will involve, among other things, a consideration of what information the enunciator assumes the receiver already possesses and what he assumes to be new, and will go on to consider how this information-status is affected by the context and the choice of language. Pragmastylistics therefore analyses style using any linguistic means available and relevant (pragmastylistics is primarily stylistics) but, additionally, it asks how the style is affected by pragmatic factors. An important example of these is the manner in which the enunciator performs the pragmatic task of modifying the receiver's internal system or state of knowledge in the process of communication. Our main purpose here is precisely to see how style, as perceived on the formal-to-informal scale, is affected by one particular pragmatic factor, namely the identification and announcement of what is to be talked about within certain types of utterance, and to exemplify this from a Spanish corpus.

As we have just implied, language-in-use is always related to whatever relevant information the enunciator assumes to be possessed by the receiver or to be present to his mind, and utterances in any one discourse are connected to one another in such a way that utterance B is as it is, among other factors, because utterance A was as it was. Some part of each utterance expresses or refers to the item or items of the receiver's information which is to be modified, and some further information is expressed to modify it. It is now fairly well understood how these pragmatic factors influence structure and meaning.

We have already implied that style is also affected and in fact some of the most interesting examples show the relationships between stylistic effects and pragmatic objectives to be, in some cases at least, conflictual.[1] In an utterance like

All that publicity . . . of course, you have not encouraged it,[2]

the phrase 'All that publicity' clearly refers to something known to the receiver, and it is left dislocated to signal this status, to distinguish it from the 'new information' to follow, to reinforce its contextual dependence, to identify or announce (and not simply to express) what is to be talked about in the following phrase and for other pragmatic effects which positively help the communicative process. In a pilot survey which we devised and administered to a group of English graduates and teachers, this utterance was judged by a majority of our informants to be a) informal, b) ugly and c) more appropriate to spoken than to written usage. The reasons for their reactions are stylistic but the structure of the utterance is determined – apart from semantic considerations and grammatical rules – by pragmatic factors.

The terminology relating to this and analogous pragmatic divisions within utterances seems to be unsettled at present, partly because there is no total agreement on whether certain phenomena are the 'same' or 'different'. For example, it is not quite clear whether utterances like the following should be classified as showing the same pragmatic division or not, although it is certain that different pragmalinguistic explanations may be offered for each.[3]

My eldest son I am worried about.
My eldest son, I am worried about him.
With regard to my eldest son, I am worried about him.

We must leave the problem of terminology as it stands and state simply that we are interested in a series of structures which contain an element that not only expresses but actually identifies or announces what is to be talked about and which is syntactically (by left dislocation, right dislocation or the use of a relative connective or subordinator) and possibly otherwise (e.g. by comma, dash, suspension points, pause, intonation, etc.) disjoined from the rest of the utterance which generally, in turn, is grammatically (though not necessarily semantically) complete in itself. This may mean that the latter contains a pronominal copy, an almost exact repetition or a co-referential of the announcing element if the grammar requires or allows it, but there may be no such repetition.

Fully aware that the term may not meet with everyone's approval, we call the element which announces what is to be talked about a 'dangling topic', by loose analogy with Cinque's 'hanging topic',[4] which is somewhat different. We choose this term because, in the structures we study, there is almost invariably an element which remains dangling, disjoined or detached from a grammatically complete sentence.

If we wish to examine the style of any text, we are *ipso facto* interested in the means chosen to organize or articulate the information distribution, in van Dijk's term.[5] The concepts of given/new, old/new, theme/rheme, topic/comment, topic/focus, topic/tail, dislocation or detachment etc. are semantic-syntactic-pragmatic notions that refer to functions normally manifested within a single utterance, but the pragmatic conditioning of the structure comes mainly from outside the utterance. This is how the objective semantic material is carried into the receiver's mind and gets the communication moving forward, in some form of 'communicative dynamism'.

Here we wish to make a distinction between 'communicative dynamism', which according to the Prague School pushes the communication forward, and 'communicative effectiveness', which undoubtedly pushes it forward but also lays much store on the clarity of the message or takes steps to ensure that the receiver knows and understands what the enunciator is talking about. This may sometimes actually slow the communication down in the interests of security or agreement between enunciator and receiver.[6]

It is known[7] that languages differ in the degrees to which grammar determines word order and to which pragmatic considerations do so (normally in the form of topic/comment articulation). Spanish is a language in which grammar leaves word order relatively free, in the sense that it can be manipulated for stylistic and pragmatic purposes.[8] Diachronic evidence of word order used for purposes of topic/comment articulation in Spanish may be provided by a few examples from medieval texts,[9] in which the subject of an embedded clause is left dislocated out of its clause to signal it as what is to be talked about.

Sant Gregorio dizen que tanto hera dado a fazer limosnas
que . . .
> (*Libro de los exenplos por A.B.C.* 3358)

St Gregory they say that (he) was so given to doing alms
that . . .

Un ombre dizen que rrobo a un monje (Id 6014)
A man they say that (he) robbed a monk

Ell araña quando esta en su tela, viene la mosca
> (*El libro de los gatos* 1706)

The spider when (she) is in her web, the fly comes

E este ensueño dixo el marido que podría ser verdad
> (*Libro de los engaños* 940)

And this dream the husband said that (it) could be true

. . . quantos fazen romeryas . . . yo non digo que fazen mal . . .
> (*El Conde Lucanor* Exemplo LI)

All who make pilgrimages . . . I do not say that (they) do
wrong.

Utterances which are identical in semiotic content or in respect of
truth conditions may therefore differ in style or in surface structure
deriving from pragmatic organization. The differences between (a)
and (b) are not fundamentally semantic or based on truth conditions, but rather pragmatic and stylistic: pragmatic because they
articulate different theme/rheme or topic/comment organizations,
stylistic because they differ in surface manifestations (e.g. word
order and repetition or non-repetition of the direct object) and
would evoke different reactions in receivers.

(a) Eso también lo sabe   (b) También sabe eso
     That also (he) knows it   Also (he) knows that[10]

The structures we wish to examine are marked structures, which
typically retrieve a previous discourse topic or signal a changed
topic, about which something is then expressed. Contreras[11]
describes the dislocated element of some of our examples in terms
of Chomsky-adjunction, to explain its segregation from the complete sentence which either follows or (more rarely) precedes it and
which may or may not contain a pronominal or clitic copy of what
we have called the dangling topic. This is always identical with a
major constituent of the sentence, usually NP, VP or AP, in that
order of statistical importance. It is a structure used for pragmatic
purposes, namely to identify, introduce or announce (by position)
what is to be talked about, while the following complete sentence
then goes on to express (by lexis and syntax) how the receiver's

information concerning it is to be modified. Occasionally, the information to be changed is not directly of the topic itself, but of some other matter closely related to it.[12]

For the purpose of studying both aspects of style referred to earlier, namely surface features and reactions stimulated in receivers, and their relationship to these structures, we administered two test surveys to two groups of native Spanish-speakers. We adopted this experimental or empirical method because, although surface features are objective facts and largely indisputable, the impressions and reactions stimulated within receivers are subjective and therefore non-observable; only by obtaining a fairly broad consensus regarding such internal reactions could we confidently speak of the effects of the structures being studied. The first survey, administered to university graduates, consisted of fifty-two utterances (including four distractors and four examples of a different structure), all taken from published written material and representing some form of topic. We changed a small number of lexical items, including proper names, which we considered might have overconditioned the reactions. We asked the informants to situate each utterance on a scale of 1 to 5 referring to each of three gradations of quality: formal-informal or spontaneous (we used the adjectives *formal* and *espontáneo*), elegant-careless and written-spoken. The five points were: Very formal, Fairly formal, Neither formal nor informal, Fairly informal and Very informal, as follows:

Pasar, no pasó nada

Formal:	Muy	Bastante	No	Bastante	Muy	*Espontáneo*
Elegante:	Muy	Bastante	No	Bastante	Muy	*Descuidado*
Escrito:	Muy	Bastante	Ambos	Bastante	Muy	*Hablado*

A brief definition or explanation of each of these six terms was given in the preamble.

The second test, administered to university undergraduates, consisted of twenty-seven utterances (including two distractors) in which we transcribed the form to be tested randomly either before or after an alternative unmarked form. Here we asked only which of the two versions seemed more formal or whether they appeared to be equal in formality, as follows:

Eso también él lo sabe ( )
El sabe eso también ( ) =

In this paper, we shall refer almost exclusively to the formal-informal scale. In spite of the lexical changes made, one of the main difficulties which emerged was that informants seemed to react primarily to lexis and to poetic or lyrical concepts and images, often confusing these with formality, and we were reluctant to focus their attention directly on the phenomenon we were testing, namely word order as manifesting topic/comment articulation. We have therefore had to make some allowances for this kind of response, as we shall see.

We wish to deal with ten different but related types of surface structure, which we shall now outline in turn, in order to describe them, report on the reactions they evoked in informants and attempt to explain such reactions.

Type (1): The subject of an embedded clause is left dislocated and is not repeated in the surface structure of that clause. We have found no straightforward example of a left dislocated main clause subject (see 2g below) although this appears to be possible, e.g.

Juan, no cree que venga.
John, (he, i.e. John) doesn't believe that he/she (i.e. John or another person) will come.

where a comma or pause signals a gap or zero copy of the subject. Some of the examples tested will now be transcribed.

1a   Esta situación es urgente que termine.
      This situation (it) is urgent that (it) should end.

Esta situación is the subject of the embedded clause and alternative word orders would be:

Es urgente que esta situación termine.

or

Es urgente que termine esta situación.

The left dislocated subject leaves a zero copy in its place:

Esta situación es urgente que (ella) termine.

Such a pronoun would fulfil none of the conditions for the appearance of subject pronouns in Spanish and we have found no example in which it actually appears. On the surface level, the construction seems to involve merely a rearrangement of elements – marked word order, in effect. The example just quoted was perceived as informal by all informants in our surveys. Another example, 1b, was labelled as informal by most, but not quite all, informants, though some indicated that they regarded it as unacceptable.

1b   Este pintor, de 32 años de edad, es la segunda exposición
que presenta.
This painter, of 32 years of age, (it) is the second exhibition
that (he) has presented.

Example 1c received a more mixed reception, but here there are
factors (e.g. the end-weight rule) in operation which might have
influenced perception.

1c   La diferenciación entre un grupo y otro creen que es una de
las distinciones fundamentales para comprender el
problema.
The difference between one group and another they think
that (it) is one of the fundamental distinctions to
understand the problem.

Type (2): The direct object, whether noun or pronoun, is left
dislocated and repeated in the form of a pronominal copy. This, in
fact, is the most common manifestation of the types we are
discussing. The following example, 2a, was seen by virtually all
informants as informal or less formal than the unmarked alternative
with the subject in initial position.

2a   Esta posibilidad liberadora la brinda la experiencia de la
fiesta.
This liberating possibility the experience of the holiday
offers it.

The unmarked version presented to informants was:
La experiencia de la fiesta brinda esta posibilidad liberadora.

Examples 2b and 2c were seen as informal by most, but not quite
all, informants:

2b   Eso hay que beberlo en unos vasos especiales.
That we must drink it in some special glasses.
2c   Esto sólo lo decía el uno cuando el otro no podía oirle.
This the one said it only when the other could not hear him.

We used sentence 2d in contrast with 2e in an attempt to discover
whether it was specifically the addition of the pro-form which
conditioned the informal reaction, but in fact the former, with the
pronominal copy, was perceived as less informal than the latter,
suggesting that the left dislocation itself (also) carries informality.

2d   Este libro lo he leído.
This book I have read it.
2e   Este libro he leído.
This book I have read.

Although repetition or redundancy alone does not produce informal style (since in itself it is a normal linguistic phenomenon and neutral as far as style is concerned), we nevertheless regard this last point as still open to verification.

It is not clear why the expression of a (contrastive) subject pronoun should make any significant difference to the style, but the fact is that in our surveys it appeared to do so. Examples 2f and 2g were more consistently labelled as informal in relation to the two former sentences 2d and 2e, with the last example the most informal of the four. There are, however, variables in this last example (*esto del* is probably colloquial lexically) which are in themselves informal, and it would seem that both subject and object are left dislocated or the left dislocated object is not taken completely out of its clause.

2f   Eso también él lo sabe.
      That also *he* knows it.
2g   Yo esto del cierre no lo entiendo.
      I this business of the closure (I) do not understand it.

Type (3): The direct object is not a noun phrase, as in type (2), but a noun clause (introduced by the particle *Que*) which is left dislocated and is copied in the form of an anaphoric pronoun before the verb. The following was unanimously perceived as informal:

3a   Que el Rey es inteligente lo sé.
      That the King is intelligent I know it.

Type (4): The indirect object, whether noun or pronoun, is left dislocated and is copied in the form of a pronoun in the unmarked position, that is, before the verb.

4a   Al profesor le interesa saber los detalles.
      To the professor to him it is of interest to know the details.
4b   Al capitán le fue asignada una habitación cómoda.
      To the captain to him was assigned a comfortable room.
4c   A mí me dijeron que venía.
      To me they said to me that he was coming.

These examples evoked such mixed responses as to be inconclusive. We might speculate that the forms quoted are almost fully grammaticalized, that the unmarked alternatives are statistically infrequent and consequently seen as relatively unusual and that usage has determined stylistic reaction. It may also be that the first two examples were unfortunate in that 4a has a noun clause subject which would rarely be found in initial position (compare the

English: 'To know the details is of interest to the professor') and the second contains a passive with *ser*, a form which is sometimes regarded as stylistically less appropriate to some types of text than to others.

Type (5): This type represents only a slight variation on the last, in that no true indirect object seems to be involved, but rather an ethic dative. This use is extremely common in Spanish and is not genuinely comparable with any usage in English except in isolated instances, some of which are dialectical:

I bought me (myself) a new hat.
They stole his car on (for) him.

Example 5a was perceived as either very or quite informal by a slight majority of informants:

5a   Al chico le temblaba la barbilla.
     To the boy to him was trembling the jaw.

Type (6): In traditional Spanish grammar, the preposition known as the 'personal *a*' (derived from Latin *ad*) preceded a personal direct object. This use of the preposition has so proliferated that it might now be more accurate to suggest that any verb which may, or at least which usually does, govern a personal direct object, tends to be followed by this preposition before *any* direct object.[13]

Our examples of this feature show a left dislocated (personal) direct object with the preposition *a* and a pronominal copy following in the unmarked position. In the second survey we tested:

6a   Al miliciano le esperan los compañeros.[14]
     The militiaman his companions await him.

The sentence transcribed in the first survey was

6b   Al miliciano herido le velan los compañeros.
     The wounded militiaman his companions watch over him.

This evoked a very mixed reaction. We speculated that the image of the wounded militiaman being watched over by his companions, together with the choice of the lexical item *velan* (related to the English *vigil*) might in themselves be perceived as poetic and hence easily confused with formality. When the sentence was further edited in the second survey to the form first transcribed in 6a, the reaction was unanimously informal. A similar response was evoked by:

6c   A mí no me dejaron recojerlo.
     Me they did not allow me to collect him.

Example 6d evoked a more mixed reaction and this may be accounted for by the personification or personalization of *amor*:

6d   Al amor hay que ganarlo cada día, como se gana el pan.
       Love one must earn it each day, as one earns one's bread.

Type (7): Left dislocation of non-noun phrases, normally adjectives or infinitives, necessarily involves a copy or some form of repetition of the dislocated element: otherwise we would simply have either hyperbaton, inverted word order or no sentence at all.
Examples are:

7a   Pasar, no pasó nada.
       Happen, nothing happened.
7b   Estar, está. Todo lo demás carece de importancia.
       Be there, he is there. All the rest is unimportant.
7c   Verle le veía mal, porque él estaba muy lejos.
       See him, I saw him badly, because he was far away.
7d   Casado debía estar casado, de eso no había ninguna duda.
       Married, he must have been married, of that there was no doubt.
7e   Sólo como vegetales y sano lo estoy, pero tengo mucha hambre.
       I eat only vegetables and healthy so I am, but I am very hungry.

(In this last example alternatives would be: *Sano estoy*, and *Sano, estoy sano*.)

These examples were all perceived as informal.

Type (8): Right dislocation evoked similar responses to left dislocation. The subject is right dislocated in 8a, which was unanimously perceived as informal:

8a   Es una gran novela ésta de Gironella.
       (It) is a great novel this one by Gironella.

The indirect object is right dislocated in:

8b   Le dijeron que no al viento, a la niebla y al agua.
       To it they said 'no' to the wind, to the mist and to the water.

This was an unfortunate example because the personification of the wind, the mist and the water, together with the image of saying 'no' to them, are themselves poetic. Responses were mixed.
       In the examples which we noted of right dislocated noun clause direct object, the aspect marker *ya* was invariably found.

8c   Conozco a la señora; ya lo creo que la conozco.
     I know the lady; I should think so that I know her.

In the first survey, informants reacted unanimously to this as informal. However, the alternative offered in the second survey was

8d   La conozco. Ya lo creo.
     I know her. I should think so.

Responses to 8c and 8d were approximately equally divided possibly because, although unmarked, the second sentence of 8d is itself colloquial.

Type (9): This type involves the appearance of a topicalizer or topic-marker.

9a   Respecto a las comidas, los platos de Antonia eran
     deliciosos.
     With regard to the meals, Antonia's dishes were delicious.

This example seems to be similar to what Chafe calls Chinese style topic,[15] in that the expression of the topic is not repeated or copied, but sets a framework within which the main predication holds, manifesting a more general concept than what is actually spoken about in the following sentence.

This example was perceived as formal by a clear, but not overwhelming, majority of the informants. In an earlier and slightly different experiment,[16] we found an analogous response to topicalizers followed by pro-copies of the topic.

9b   Respecto a las enfermedades, pocas son las que sufre.
     With regard to illnesses, few are those which he suffers.
9c   En lo que respecta a Mordesa, tampoco le son precisas
     demasiadas deducciones.
     In respect of Mordesa, neither are too many deductions
     necessary for him (i.e. for César).

It would seem, therefore, that the topicalizer somehow 'formalizes' the left dislocated or dangling topic.

Type (10): The last type which we wish to discuss exhibits characteristics in many respects very different from those of the previous classes. However, we would claim that it has sufficient in common with them to be included here. The structure to which we refer is essentially as follows: a clause, followed by the non-case-marked relative connective or subordinator *que*, is followed in turn by a clause which contains a personal pronoun or possessive adjective marked for case and co-referential with a noun phrase in the clause preceding the relative.[17] Any case may be thus signalled, although subject pronouns are deleted. We would argue that the first clause functions as a kind of topicalizer, the noun phrase 'antecedent' functions as a topic about which anything can be enunciated in the following clause and the case-marked pronoun or possessive adjective takes the clause out of the ordinary category of relative clauses. Examples are:

10a.i   Aquel ladrón nunca vio objeto abandonado que no lo hiciese suyo.
        That thief never saw an abandoned object that he did not make it his own.

10a.ii Conviví en mi adolescencia con un grupo que lo componían García Lorca, Alberti y Neruda.
        I lived in my adolescence with a group that García Lorca, Alberti and Neruda composed it.

10a.iii Me parece bien escribir un prólogo, no sólo por mi afición a ese subgénero, que la confieso, sino porque en este caso es indispensable.
        I think it good to write a prologue, not only because of my affection for that subgenre, which I confess it, but because in this case it is indispensable.

10b.i   Se trata de problemas relacionados con las explosiones y que no debe ignorarse su existencia.
        I refer to problems related to the explosions and which one must not ignore their existence.

10b.ii Se trata de un compañero que al decidir un día hacer la guerra por su cuenta pasó inadvertida su desaparición.
        I refer to a companion that upon deciding one day to go to war on his own account his disappearance passed unnoticed.

10c.i   Son realidades que sólo puede uno acercarse a ellas con cautela.
        They are realities that one can go near to them only with caution.

10c.ii Hay escritores, afortunadamente, que les gustaría ser muy distintos.
        There are writers, fortunately, that it would be pleasing to them to be very different.

10d.i   Tiene una idea que no sé cuál es, pero es una idea muy buena.
        He has an idea that I do not know what it is, but it is a very good idea.

10d.ii Entonces sintió algo inmenso que todavía no sabía lo que era, pero que estaba ahí, rozándola, esperándola.

>   Then she felt something immense that she did not yet
>   know what it was, but which was there, touching her,
>   waiting for her.

10d.iii   Se trata de unos principios sencillos, básicos, que
           puede decirse que no tienen variación.
           I refer to simple, basic, principles that it can be said
           that they do not vary.

Let us comment briefly on each of the examples.

It will be noted that in examples 10a the direct object personal pronoun seems to 'disambiguate' redundantly, that is, to signal case when such a signal is not necessary from the grammatical or semantic point of view, since the non-case-marked *que* happens to be in the direct object form anyway, by coincidence, as it were. In these examples the pronoun could be deleted and leave a correct sentence from the grammatical and semantic points of view. Example 10a.i was generally, but not unanimously, seen as informal. Example 10a.ii was perceived as a little less informal, as was 10a.iii (10a.i has a subjunctive in the 'relative clause'), and this is interesting since these two examples show the direct object relative and the (redundantly disambiguating) personal pronoun actually side by side.

Examples 10b.i and ii were seen almost unanimously as informal. These involve a possessive adjective, *su*, indicating case after the relative. In some examples the preposition *de* appears whether the genitive is in fact relevant or not. Contrast the following two examples:

10b.iii   Así se producen accidentes de los que conocemos las
           dramáticas características que revisten.
           Thus accidents occur of (or about) which we know the
           dramatic characteristics that they exhibit.
10b.iv   Era una buena muchacha, una mujer de la que estoy
           seguro que me quería.
           She was a good girl, a woman of (or about) whom I am
           sure that she loved me.

It would seem, however, that despite the proximity of the genitive in 10b.iii, the use of *de* in both of these examples may be identical in function, having nothing to do with case, but being pragmatic (a relative topicalizer, perhaps) or semantic: 'accidents in respect of which the following can be said . . .', 'a girl in respect of whom I may say the following . . .' These examples show characteristics which are not uncommon in written and spoken discourse.

Examples 10c.i and ii were labelled as informal by virtually all informants. Here the pronoun may or may not take the preposition *a*.

Examples 10d involve a deleted subject pronoun in an embedded clause following the relative. 10d.i was unanimously seen as informal. 10d.ii evoked very mixed and curious responses, and indeed a majority described it either as very or fairly formal. However, if we compare it with 10d.i, we may speculate that the poetic semantics and choice of lexis may have influenced the reactions. 10d.iii was described in no consistent manner, varying from very formal to very informal.

Before we leave our examples of dangling topic, it may be relevant to confirm that the phenomenon which Flora Klein-Andreu calls X-forms,[18] and which seems to coincide to some extent with Cinque's hanging topic, does not appear to occur in written Spanish. X-forms express something closely related semantically to adjacent linguistic material, but without any morphosyntactic marking of the relationship. In other words, they are not case-marked and any case may follow in the ensuing sentences. Examples from Klein-Andreu's corpus of spoken Spanish are

Los cérvidos se les cae todos los años el cuerno.
The deer the horns fall from them every year.
Y yo me entró una tos que me ahogaba, del humo.
And I a cough got into me which was choking me from the smoke.

She suggests that such a structure is not used in the written language and we have found no counter-examples.

Much work has been done on the pragmatic aspects of the constructions which we have outlined, with the possible exception of (10). We take as well known and noncontroversial all the positive advantages of using left dislocation, right dislocation or topic structure, and we have treated the various forms as similar for our purposes. These structures are chosen by an enunciator because of their communicative dynamism, their thematic structuring capability, their value in functional sentence perspective, their marking of what is old information (or known) as distinct from what is new (or unknown), their ability to announce what is to be talked about, etc. These conditions may be summed up in the phrase 'effective communication' which is usually a desirable objective. The informality perceived in most examples seems to constitute at least part of the 'price to be paid' for this particular method of achieving it.

We now wish to offer a number of suggestions of a speculative nature to explain why these forms appear to be perceived generally as informal.[19]

First of all, they resemble or formally equal a repair strategy or premature subject, a pleonasm or even an anacoluthon.[20] Since style always involves choice, each of these constructions has, and must have, at least one formal alternative if it can be perceived as informal. Examples of type (1) look like ways of defrauding or cheating sentence plans, where the subject is left dislocated; the pronominal copy is deleted like most other subject pronouns, resulting in what may be perceived as unusually marked word order or some kind of subject-raising.

The second reason why they appear non-formal may be that (with the exception of examples like 10a.i) they consist of grammatically complete sentences with an extra element which remains dangling either before (left dislocation) or after (right dislocation) or in the middle (relative), and readers (as distinct from hearers, perhaps) are culturally and educationally conditioned to expect nothing but sentences in formal uses of written language. Examples under (2) show this most clearly. When the object is left dislocated leaving a pronominal copy, this copy completes the sentence grammar. Contrast 'El libro he leído' (meaning: The book I have read but, in contrast, the article, I haven't; the utterance as it stands is probably semantically incomplete) with 'El libro lo he leído' (where there is no contrast with any other object).

Third, it may also be that anything in the NP_1 position, i.e. the first noun or pronoun in the nominative case, *ipso facto* looks like a subject and, if it is not, the receiver must 'retrace' his reading and modify what he has understood. In some examples, for a moment there may appear to be lack of agreement between subject and verb, as in

El corazón del asunto no sé dónde está.
The heart of the matter (I) don't know where it is.

However, even when subject and verb coincide in person and number, they may not be related as subject to predicate:

Esta situación es urgente . . . que termine.
This situation (it) is urgent . . . that (it) should end.

In this case the reader has to read on in order to detect the non-agreement. An example like the following is grammatically and perhaps semantically ambiguous in that NP_1 may be subject or object:

El perro lo vio.
The dog saw it/him.
The dog (he/she) saw him (i.e. he/she saw the dog).

Such a structure may seem unplanned[21] in having the object NP in initial (subject) position and then an 'extra' object (*lo*). If an NP in NP$_1$ position turns out not to be subject, it will normally be read as contrastive or emphatic. That is to say, once an NP which is left dislocated is recognized as an example of left dislocation and not merely as a subject in the unmarked position, it may be read as being in focus, but normally such an element is not in focus because it tends to be topic, theme, old information or given. This point refers to the difference between contrastive word order:

El libro leí (el artículo no).

and left dislocation:

El libro lo leí.

So (for a moment in the reading) two incompatible signals seem to be given. Alternatively, two objects may signal two different points where the sentence may end (compare the 'loose sentence'), the first one signalling an end when in fact the sentence has not finished because the pronoun is cataphoric and its referent follows the sentence:

Ya lo creo . . . que la conozco.
I should think so . . . that I know her.

Fourth, the left dislocated constructions consist of an element which in speech would be articulated with level intonation, followed by full sentence intonation, so that what is announced (the topic) remains prosodically dangling. In the case of right dislocation, full sentence intonation is followed by another element. Here, we are complementing our second and third explanations, which referred to complete sentence grammar, by mentioning complete sentence intonation. Several examples under (1), (2), and (3) manifest this clearly.

Sometimes the syntax and semantics depend on other suprasegmental elements, such as pause or pitch, which are essentially spoken phenomena. When written, therefore, these structures require 'spoken intonation', as it were. Let us add two examples to illustrate this point:

Quienes le ven pasar, afirman que ha desaparecido de su gesto la sonrisa, así como que el rostro lo lleva comido por una adustez grave.

Those who see him pass affirm that the smile has disappeared
from his countenance and that the face (he) carries it/him eaten
by a grave sullenness. (Carlos Alfaro: *Crónica sobre César*)
. . . en el peor de los casos, tendría entre sus manos una persona
que podría pedirle un gran favor. (Juan Benet: *El aire de un
crimen*)
. . . in the worst of cases, (s)he would have in h(is/er) hands a
person that s(he) could ask h(im/er) a great favour.

The pronouns *lo* and *le* respectively in these examples are
grammatically ambiguous. *El rostro lo lleva* can be interpreted as
'The face carries him' or 'The face, he carries it'. In fact, in the
second example *le* does not refer to the subject of *tendría*; the
phrase *una persona que podría pedirle un gran favor* could, but here
does not, mean 'a person who could ask her a favour' but 'a person,
that she could ask him for a favour', that is, 'a person of whom she
could ask a favour'. The sentence in the original is

La Tacón [. . .] acreditaría con Medina [. . .] una deuda de
considerable cuantía y, en el peor de los casos [La Tacón]
tendría entre sus manos una persona que [La Tacón] podría
pedirle [a esa persona, a Medina] un gran favor.

This structure allows the enunciator to assign pitch prominence to
an element whose referent has low semantic weight in the sentence,
but which is important in the discourse.[22] This is similar to examples
(10).

Fifth, any device to announce what the enunciator wishes to talk
about may be useful in a conversation to catch the hearer's attention
or to ensure that the interlocutors agree on the topic of the
utterance. This is particularly appropriate for a noisy channel,[23] but
in writing or formal contexts it seems inappropriate because it may
be assumed that the hearer is attentive and knows what is being
talked about, except in certain cases, e.g. headlines or chapter
titles. In other words, the noise-to-signal ratio is high in conversation, and this structure is a way of identifying, or over-identifying,
the topic when the speaker thinks the hearer may have difficulty in
identifying the referent (examples 2–7). In other words, it is a
specifically oral device.

Topicalizers (type 9) seem to be stylistically neutral in this
function, as we have mentioned. Presumably structures with
topicalizers are more fully grammaticalized than the others, and
indeed they may be compared, on certain levels, with chapter titles
or headlines.

Finally, right dislocation often looks like an afterthought

expressed when the speaker belatedly thinks he has not been clear enough. The right dislocated element must be thematic, it would seem, so it appears as if the speaker thought at first that he would be understood as referring to a particular theme, but then he decides to express it after all, when it is grammatically redundant and stylistically too late, though still pragmatically useful. Right dislocation also hints at the spoken medium in that it is frequently used to introduce physical objects in the nonlinguistic context into a conversation.[24]

We are tempted to summarize our findings by suggesting that in practice effective communication frequently seems to have a 'higher priority' than formality of style, in the sense that it appears to prevail over this latter consideration in all sorts of text. Formality of style is perceived primarily as syntax, lexis and semantics, not as effective communication, and very often informal syntactic structures may best serve the cause of effective communication. Stylists have to settle in practice for some kind of compromise, more or less felicitous, between differing objectives. Pragmastylisticians can only comment on what stylists have managed to do.

Notes

1 Compare P. D. Teskey, *Theme and Rheme in Spanish and English* (Coleraine: New University of Ulster), 1976, p. 8 who suggests that 'the grammatical structure of a language forms a word-order principle in its own right, and this may run counter to the principle of FSP [functional sentence perspective], resulting in a tension which must be resolved'
2 Len Deighton, *SS-GB* (St Albans: Triad Panther), 1980, p. 181
3 See Carmen Silva Corvalán, 'Topicalización y pragmática en español', in *Revista Española de Lingüística* 14, 1, 1984, 1–3. It will be noticed that in this paper we do not deal with structures of the type 'My eldest son I am worried about'
4 Guglielmo Cinque, 'The Movement Nature of Left Dislocation', in *Linguistic Inquiry* 8, 2, 1977, 397–412
5 See Teun A. van Dijk, *Text and Context: Explorations in the Semantics and Pragmatics of Discourse* (London: Longman), 1977, p. 208
6 See Silva-Corvalán (1984) pp. 3–5
7 Charles N. Li and Sandra A. Thompson, 'Subject and Topic: A New Typology of Language', in Charles N. Li, (ed.) *Subject and Topic* (New York: Academic Press), 1976, pp. 457–518
8 We would contend that many phenomena which in the past were thought to be determined by stylistic considerations, e.g. emphasis,

might now be better regarded as determined by pragmatic factors, and word order is indeed one such phenomenon in many cases

9   We are indebted to our friend and colleague John England of the University of Sheffield for drawing our attention to these examples

10 Haldur Öim, 'Towards a Theory of Linguistic Pragmatics', in *Journal of Pragmatics* 1, 1977, 254–7, points out that a sentence is pragmatically ambiguous if it can communicate different messages or instructions for the hearer to modify certain information structures in his memory, while retaining one and the same form and describing one fact in the real world

11 Heles Contreras, *A Theory of Word Order with special reference to Spanish* (Amsterdam: North Holland), 1976, p. 83

12 See Wallace L. Chafe, 'Givenness, Contrastiveness, Definiteness, Subjects, Topics, and Point of View', in Li (1976), p. 50

13 The diachronic and descriptive aspects of this phenomenon are interesting but irrelevant here

14 The original version was a verse of poetry by Pere Gimferrer: Al miliciano herido le velan las ondinas de la nieve

15 Chafe (1976), pp. 50–1

16 Reported in Leo Hickey, *Curso de pragmaestilística* (Madrid: Coloquio), 1987, pp. 167–76

17 We do not wish to enter into a discussion concerning the exact status of this *que*: relative pronoun, relative adverb, conjunction or complementizer. Such a discussion would be irrelevant here

18 Flora Klein-Andreu, 'Why Speech Seems Ungrammatical', in *From Sign to Text: A Semiotic View of Communication*, edited by Yishai Tobin, (Amsterdam: Benjamins), forthcoming

19 Interestingly, Betsy Barnes, *Left Detachment in Spoken Standard French* (Amsterdam: Benjamins), 1985, p. 114 refers to left dislocation as 'a pragmatic phenomenon occurring in spontaneous speech'

20 See Chafe (1976), p. 51

21 See D. J. Allerton, 'The Notion of "Givenness" and its Relations to Presupposition and to Theme', in *Lingua*, 44, 1978, 158–61

22 See Carmen Silva-Corvalán, 'On the Interaction of Word Order and Intonation: Some OV Constructions in Spanish', in Flora Klein-Andreu, *Discourse Perspectives on Syntax* (New York: Academic Press), 1983, pp. 122–3

23 See Elinor Ochs Keenen and Bambi B. Schieffelin, 'Topic as a Discourse Notion: A Study of Topic in the Conversations of Children and Adults', in Li (1976), p. 350

24 Betsy Barnes (1985) p. 64.

Section II

Style in Speech and Situation

Essentially concerned with the study of all types of communication through language, pragmatists pay more attention in practice to spoken than to written forms. Indeed, conversational analysis has developed as a sub-discipline in its own right, with much cross-referencing between general pragmatic principles and models of interpersonal language-use in particular. As in all pragmatic studies, the objective is usually to provide an explanation of the devices or strategies used by interlocutors to organize, structure and develop their discoursal relationship so as to achieve the ends they have in mind. Whatever else they may be, styles in conversation are the result of choices made on the subject of such devices and they frequently manifest features not found in written texts. In a special way, therefore, speakers' choices are directly determined by what they are trying to do, and their style, in turn, is their way of doing it.

The chapters which comprise this section select four aspects of spoken language for detailed scrutiny. These are certain devices which show that particular referents are of special importance to a speaker, ways in which speakers express their attitudes to the truth or falsehood of what they say, means by which speech style is negotiated or interactively achieved by interlocutors and strategies used to negotiate power relationships in the course of an oral exchange.

Whereas the last chapter in Section I dealt with topicalization based on a written corpus (including dialogue in fiction), the phenomenon examined by Flora Klein-Andreu is found exclusively in spoken Spanish and indeed it might be regarded as a specifically oral version of topicalization. Her study is very much concerned with oral communication in practice and the feature discussed, the X-form, is essentially an informal style marker. The author suggests, however, that it is a way of expressing that the referent is important to the speaker for any number of reasons and not merely because the discourse is 'about' it, as would be central to most definitions of topic.

71

Carmen Silva-Corvalán discusses certain features which express speakers' attitudes to the possibility that the content of their propositions may or may not be true. Such features determine what she calls 'hypothetical discourse', and this may vary along a scale of assertiveness. The choice of language, resulting in style, is conditioned by pragmatic considerations, including the degree of the speakers' assertiveness, the effect they intend to produce and the formality of the situation. To the extent to which speakers select from the options open to them prompted by such factors, 'style necessarily becomes a question of pragmatics', the author concludes.

Also studying conversational speech styles, Margret Selting shows how the shifting and switching of such styles is not determined by extralinguistic or contextual factors, but by 'dynamic interactively-achieved ways of speaking by which participants signal and achieve the constitution of global and local dynamic conversational contexts interactively'. Using a German corpus, she shows how style in speech is the result of a developing partnership between the interlocutors as they go along, rather than something fixed *a priori* by their situation or anything else.

A very similar point is discussed by Jenny A. Thomas, who focuses in particular on devices used in conversation to affirm, negotiate or control power relations; she is interested in 'interpersonal pragmatics' with the objective of moving 'towards a more predictive and explanatory model of discourse organization'. Her examples are taken from 'unequal encounters', in the sense of conversations between superiors and subordinates, and her findings are similar to Margret Selting's, namely that style is not settled before the interaction commences but is established as the exchange proceeds.

Chapter four

Speech priorities

Flora Klein-Andreu

Introduction

I should like to take this occasion to continue examining structures that occur in conversational Spanish, but not, it seems, in the written language or in the more formal spoken registers, under the assumption that the characteristics of these oral forms are due to the speech situation itself. My discussion is based on speech recorded in Spain, and specifically on consideration of a particular kind of construction that I have studied in detail: the constructions I call 'X-forms' (Klein-Andreu, 1989)

1. The Spanish 'X-forms'

Consider the following examples:

(1) Y yo me entró una tos que me ahogaba.
(2) Tú te gustó 'Upstairs Downstairs'?
(3) El águila real, la pieza favorita es la liebre.

What these utterances have in common is that each begins by mentioning a referent that is closely related semantically to the reference of a neighbouring utterance, but without the expected morphosyntactic indication of the nature of the relationship. Thus, in (1) and (2) we find the free (or subject) pronouns *yo* 'I' and *tú* 'you (subj.)', where the actual role of the referents would call for the prepositional forms *a mí* and *a tí*, respectively, as in (1b) and (2b) below. Similarly, in (3) we find *el águila real* 'the royal eagle' preceding *la pieza favorita* 'the favourite prey', with no specification of the relationship between the two, where we would expect to find *la pieza favorita* in initial position, as 'head', modified by the prepositional *del águila real* 'of the royal eagle', as in (3b).

(1b) Y a mí me entró una tos que me ahogaba.
(2b) A tí te gustó 'Upstairs Downstairs'?
(3b) La pieza favorita del aguila real es la liebre.

Thus, examples (1), (2), and (3) are 'ungrammatical' in that they counter the expectations set up by grammatical prescription. Yet, though such constructions seem relatively common in ordinary speech, at all educational levels, prescriptive grammars do not actually mention them at all, even to condemn them. From this I conclude that they must not be common in writing or in the more formal or 'planned' registers of speech. For this reason, too, they have no traditional designation, so that I refer to them as 'X-forms'.

2. The problem and present approach

The questions to be asked, then, are *why* do such forms occur, and why do they occur precisely where they do – in ordinary conversation rather than in writing or in more formal oral registers. A common reaction is, of course, that such forms are simply errors, due to the time-pressure under which speech is produced. It seems to me, however, that this begs the question of just what is meant by an 'error' in the first place. Put differently, it is hard to imagine how we can ever hope to understand the characteristics of spoken language (or of any phenomenon, for that matter) if we start out by discarding examples of it from the outset, as 'erroneous'. I therefore take the position that one must instead start by investigating whether the phenomena in question exhibit any systematic characteristics at all, that might help to explain their occurrence and especially their occurrence in particular contexts rather than in others.

Of course, the kinds of systematic characteristics one looks for will depend on one's view of language. Thus, if one regards language as essentially an *instrument of communication* – the point of view that seems reasonable to me, though obviously not the only one possible – systematicity will be sought in *the relation between overt form(s)* and the *kinds of communications* with which they are associated, both at the local (syntactic/semantic) and at the larger (discourse-pragmatic) levels.

Accordingly, the next section summarizes some of the characteristics of the X-form's reference and discourse-function that I have found to be systematic, as discussed in earlier work (Klein-Andreu, 1989). We then go on to examine the relation between these findings and one of the concepts most often employed in work on discourse: the concept of *topicalization*. Based on examples of X-forms in their actual context, we consider whether and to what extent this concept is an analytically useful characterization of these forms. Finally, we attempt to determine just what functional characteristics seem to be shared by all X-forms, and how they relate to the kind of situation in which X-forms occur – namely, ordinary conversation.

3. X-forms' reference

Examination of X-forms' reference shows that their occurrence is not random, but rather seems to depend on the X-form's *referent* and *its relation to the discourse* in which it occurs. First, various statistical measures indicate that referents of X-forms typically are 'topic-worthy'. Thus, in comparison with an equal number of grammatical subjects of randomly chosen utterances without X-forms, produced by the same speakers, we find that the X-forms are more likely than the subjects to have *definite* and *animate* referents, and even to refer to the interlocutors themselves or members of their immediate family. Further, the most usual operational measure of a referent's *actual* topicality in a discourse – its frequency of mention in the immediate context – indicates that the referents of X-forms not only are topic-*worthy*, but actually are topic*al* or salient referents in the particular contexts in which they occur. Overall, the referents of X-forms are mentioned much more frequently in the immediate context than are the referents of the *grammatical subjects* with which they are most closely construed (that is, those perceived as being in 'the same utterance', such as *la presa favorita* in relation to *el águila real* (Klein-Andreu, 1989).

4. Are X-forms a kind of topicalization (and what is a 'topic', anyway)?

The finding that X-forms mention referents that are salient in the particular discourse in which they occur suggests that this manner of expression may be an example of 'topicalization' – presumably, the *presentation* of a referent *as salient*. Other characteristics of X-forms are also consonant with this view: as regards their reference, we often find repeated mention by X-form either of the same referent or of several referents being treated in the context as equivalent (for instance, as different examples of the same thing). As to their form, X-forms overwhelmingly are *initial* elements, in that they precede the remainder of the utterance with which they are most closely construed. This of course is a position of prominence (priority/foregrounding). But it also has the effect of presenting the X-form's referent *detached* from the associated utterance, by position, just as it is unrelated to it by morphological form.[1] It may be argued that morphosyntactic non-specificity and detachment also are consonant with referential salience, in that the actual role of salient referents (in particular, their relation to the remainder of the utterance) should be relatively easier to arrive at by simple inference. Finally, note that pronominal X-forms occur in the subject form – thus, the form normally associated with central referents.[2]

Yet, it seems to me that the explanatory value of such terms as 'topic' and 'topicalization' is limited by insufficiently precise definition and inconsistent use – as noted for example by Givón (1983: Introduction), Sanders and Wirth (1985), Tomlin (1985). Especially confusing is the non-obvious relation between various terms in this family, in particular 'topic' and 'topical' on the one hand and 'topicalization' on the other. It seems worthwhile to consider this matter in some detail. To begin with, as long as the main operational measure of topicality is frequency of mention, topicality will correspond to something like 'saliency in the discourse'. But this measure also establishes topicality (i.e. saliency) as a relative matter, so that various referents are more or less topical (salient). The extreme analytic consequence of this view is to treat all referents as 'topics' – in effect, the approach taken in Givón 1983.

But if everything that is mentioned at all must somehow be more or less salient (at least as compared to what is *not* mentioned), we are still left with the question of why, in particular utterances, the saliency of different referents is indicated in different ways. This in fact is the question addressed by Givón 1983. In general, the studies in Givón's volume support his contention that the encoding of different referents ('topics') is determined by their relative 'availability to the hearer', by which he means 'what may reasonably affect the *degree of difficulty* that speakers/hearers may experience in *identifying* a topic in discourse' (original italicization) (Givón 1983: 11). Specifically, he finds that, as expected, referents that are relatively *less* 'accessible or identifiable' are encoded by relatively more conspicuous and/or descriptive forms (e.g. by 'topicalizations' of various kinds, full noun phrases, or by stressed and unbound pronouns), whereas those that are more accessible (hence 'topical', in the sense of 'thematic') are mentioned with less conspicuous formal means (e.g. by anaphora, by unstressed or bound pronouns, or by grammatical agreement). This is a satisfying outcome in that it shows a straightforward and reasonable relationship between linguistic form and function. But at the same time it illustrates the confusing relation between 'topicalization', in the sense of conspicuous linguistic mention of *non*-'thematic' referents, and 'topic'/ 'topical' in the sense of 'theme'/'thematic' or more or less known or expectable referent.

In any event, the idea of foregrounding to facilitate access will not account for Spanish X-forms. Though X-forms are like other forms called topicalizations in that they amount to a conspicuous (and foregrounded) presentation, this cannot be attributed to their referents' 'inaccessibility' since they are mentioned so often in the context. Also, the fact that such a high proportion of X-forms refer to the speaker (43 per cent, as compared to 26 per cent of the grammatical subjects of other utterances) makes one wonder about 'difficulty of identification'.

As noted earlier, we would also want to understand why X-forms occur in certain contexts but not in others, and in this respect too they seem to differ from other forms described as topicalizations. It often is said that topicalization in general is more typical of spoken than of written language. Yet, of various forms that have been called topicalizations, to my knowledge only two are said to occur in colloquial speech only, like Spanish X-forms: so-called left-dislocation and right-dislocation in certain languages (Duranti and Ochs 1979: 379; Givón 1983: 19).

5. About 'aboutness'

It has been said that the essential characteristic of topics is 'aboutness': topics (presumably now in the sense of 'themes') are 'what the sentence or other discourse units are about' (Sanders and Wirth 1985: 12). If we ask whether the referents of Spanish X-forms are 'topics' in this sense, we find that the answer to this question differs in different cases. For instance, example (1.3) was taken from discourse that was indeed 'about' the royal eagle. But (1.1) occurs in a context that is not really about the speaker, but rather about a fire in a house where she was living. In recalling the events, however, she starts to recount her own experience of them. One might say, perhaps, that at this point the discourse comes to be 'about' the speaker, but I am not sure that such stretching of 'aboutness' gains us anything. We return to this point later. Before that it will be useful to examine some examples of X-forms in the actual contexts in which they occurred. Consider the following passage:

5.1   I: Bueno, entonces coges una cabeza de ajos. O según la
            cantidad de ajos que te guste, si te gustan los ajos
            fritos. Y sin quitarle la cáscara, lo partes por la mitad.
      A: Ah, sin la cáscara?
      I: Sin quitarle la cáscara, con la cáscara, o sea con la
            cáscara.

Y: Y ¿por qué esto?
I: Ah pues eso sí que no lo sé.
A: Ahora, desde luego la vitamina del ajo está en la
    cáscara, eh.
Y: ¿Ah sí?
I: Mira, *yo me gusta* luego coger el trocito de eso, así (se
    chupa los dedos)
A: A mí los ajos fritos me encantan.
I: Los ajos fritos me encantan. Bueno pues fríes los ajos,
    la cantidad de ajos que quieras, verdad (etc.) . . .
(100A: 15: 1/4)

In this passage, I – a middle-aged, upper-class woman from central Spain – is explaining the preparation of various Castillian recipes. As she explains how one must fry pieces of garlic to make garlic soup ('the amount of garlic you like, if you like fried garlic'), this leads her to manifest her own fondness for fried garlic by exclaiming that she likes to pick up pieces straight from the pan and eat them as is – as she licks her fingers. As she says this she refers to herself by X-form: *yo me gusta*, literally 'I (subj.) me (obj.) it-pleases (3p.)' (compare the following utterances which use prescriptive forms with *encantan* 'they-delight': the prepositional *a mí*, and the objective clitic *me* 'me' alone.). It hardly can be said, however, that the context is about the speaker – unless 'aboutness' is construed so broadly that it becomes virtually meaningless.

In my earlier work on X-forms I propose that mentions of the interlocutors, and especially self-mentions of the speaker, are so frequent in conversation because to a great extent we engage in conversation in the first place for *sociable* reasons – to establish or maintain contact, or to show solidarity – rather than because of a primary interest in the subject matter for its own sake (Klein-Andreu, 1989: see also Schiffrin 1984). Hence in conversation (in contrast to more 'formal' uses of the language, including most written uses), we often use a particular subject matter for purposes of self-affirmation, or to align ourselves 'with' our interlocutors. In the preceding example we see this happening immediately following I's exclamation: it prompts A to interject her own fondness for fried garlic (*A mí los ajos fritos me encantan*, literally 'to me fried garlic me-obj. they-delight-3p.'), which in turn is echoed by I (*los ajos fritos me encantan* 'fried garlic me-obj. they-delight-3p.'). Now if self-affirmation and/or expression of solidarity with interlocutors are indeed high priorities in conversation, then it is not surprising that self-mentions not only should be frequent but often presented as prominent too.

Consider now 6.2. Here the entire anecdote serves as an 'expression of solidarity', occurring in response to my saying that I dislike driving into big cities because I have trouble finding where I am going, to the point where on occasion I have had to engage a taxi to lead the way. This prompts P – a highly educated, middle-aged professional – to recount an amusing incident in which the same thing happened to him, in this case because he arrived in Cologne on Carnival Monday and all the passers-by were drunk:

6.2 P (a) ¿Sabes a mí eso donde me pasó? ¿Yo tener que coger un taxi para ir desde el aeropuerto?
(b) En Colonia hace cinco o seis años, llegué un lunes de Carnaval como a las 12 de la mañana. Y ¡me encontré con todo Colonia borracho! !Y que estaban borrachos hasta los guardias! Iba preguntando por el hotel, el hotel no sé cuantos, no me acuerdo ya, 'Chirichihof'. Iba con un amigo mío, y (dice) '¡Aquí están soplaos hasta los guardias!' Digo, 'Aqui hay una fórmula. Vamos a una parada de tasis, yo tomo un taxi y le digo el nombre del hotel, que creo que los tasistas no estarán bebidos.' Y así tuvimos que hacer.
(c) Porque *todo el mundo* que-que les preguntabas y se reía y te-te iba a abrazar por la ventanilla . . .
(d) *Algunos alemanes* que se lo cuento se ríen pero dicen que sí, que lo comprenden. Qu'és qu'el lunes de Carnaval en Colonia a las 12 de la mañana hasta los guardias están borrachos.
(108A: 1/3).

Here the referent of the first X-form – *todo el mundo que le preguntabas* 'everybody that you asked' clearly *is* what the anecdote is 'about': it would be impossible to recount these events without some kind of general reference to the passers-by and their usefulness as informants. But this cannot be said of the referent of the second X-form – *algunos alemanes que se lo cuento* 'some Germans that I tell it to'. Yet this referent is important to P's presentation of the events because he is using the Germans who hear the story, and the fact that 'they laugh and they say yes, that they understand', as *witnesses* to the central claim of the story: that 'on the Monday after Carnival in Cologne even the policemen are drunk'.

As I have noted elsewhere, invoking witnesses is a common strategy in conversation (Klein-Andreu, 1989, example II). Yet the above passage is unusual in one respect: As one might expect, in conversation the most commonly invoked 'witnesses' are those present – including the speaker – and their family and acquaintances. Consider 6.3:

6.3   JM: . . . Se está planteando el hecho de que a los
               maestros como él, que los van a jubilar, pues los van
               a tener que, digamos, hacer hasta un curso de
               adaptación.
        L: Ahí estoy de acuerdo, porque yo he visto que *mi
               padre*, si le hubieran hecho curso de adaptación, tal
               vez no hubiera perdido lo que perdió . . .
        Y: Es que es muy difícil jubilarse, sicológicamente.
        JM: Y más en una profesión como la de maestro.
        L: . . . Por ejemplo, *mi marido* será-sería terrible. . . .
               Por ejemplo, al marido aquí de M., le quitan de
               trabajar de golpe, y D. se muere, del susto.
        M: El tractor le tiene que coger diario, diario, aunque
               sea del corral aquí, de aquí al corral. (91B: 18: 1/3)

Here the problem of retirement has come up via mention of JM's
father, a semi-retired schoolteacher, and his outdated views on
education. It is briefly generalized by JM (himself a schoolteacher):
using the prescriptive prepositional form, he refers to the need to
offer a course in adaptation to retirement *a los maestros como él* 'to
schoolteachers like him'. But the issue is then seized by L – JM's
mother – who brings the problem home again. She refers first, by
X-form, to her father and to her husband (JM's father) – with the
latter reference preceded by *por ejemplo* 'for example'. Finally, she
refers to the husband of another of the persons present, L, the wife
of the local farmer D, in this instance in the prescriptive form with
the preposition *a* (*al marido aquí de M* 'to the husband of M here').
Of course, her mention of 'the husband of M' has the effect of
bringing M into the conversation, as witness to the truth of L's
contentions.

This example is especially typical of the progress of conversational exposition, which characteristically shuttles back and forth
between the general and the particular: on the one hand, personal
experience and opinions are dignified by generalization (as shown
in Lavandera 1985: 103); on the other, generalities are rendered
more vivid and credit-worthy by being referred – often explicitly
'for example' – to the particular experience of the interlocutors
themselves and/or other 'witnesses', preferably close to those
present.[3] Obviously, this kind of alternation has the effect of
exacerbating what I call 'competition for attention' between
referents, in this case between referents whose importance is
primarily *contingent* on the particular subject matter being
discussed, and others of *intrinsic* interest, for their relation to the
speech situation and the participants in it.[4] Thus, such competition

for attention would be a natural consequence of the speech situation itself. I have proposed that it is responsible in the first place for the greater prevalence in spoken language of what may be viewed as 'multi-centric' presentations: that is, constructions that present more than one referent as salient, in different ways (Klein-Andreu, 1989).[5] Obviously, X-forms are an example of this – as are also other constructions described as 'topicalizations' (as noted by Duranti and Ochs, 1979: 413).

The suggestion that X-forms are brought about by competition for attention between referents is supported by the nature of the 'local' contexts where X-forms most often are found: namely, in mentions of 'experiencers' and 'possessors'. In prescriptive Spanish usage, these referents would be relegated to secondary status in so-called 'experiencer' and 'possessor' constructions, centred about what is experienced and what is possessed, respectively. These are the contingently important referents: that is, they are topi*cal* in the sense that they are what the context is 'about'. Yet, as has been noted, the possessor and the experiencer are likely to be more intrinsically important or 'topic-*worthy*'; among other things, they are much more likely to be animate (see e.g. Givon 1979: 91).[6]

Note too that, especially in 'experiencer' constructions, the experiencer's referent should be intrinsically more salient than the subject's not only because the experiencer is more likely to be animate, but also because the subject's referent is more likely to be *in*animate, and in fact often is not an entity at all. Thus in these constructions the reference of both the subject and the experiencer typically conspire to insure that the experiencer's reference is likely to be the more intrinsically interesting of the two. It therefore should come as no surprise that expressions of experience are by far the most frequent contexts for X-forms – if X-forms are indeed multicentric presentations brought about by 'competition for attention' between referents.

To test whether *the subject's* referent affects how the experiencer is mentioned, as 'competition for attention' would predict, I did another count of all experiencer expressions – prescriptive (prepositional) and non-prescriptive (X-form) – produced by those speakers who had produced most X-forms. The results are in the direction that 'competition for attention' predicts: as Table 4.1 shows, non-entity subjects (e.g. *me gusta que cantes* 'I like you to sing', *me gusta cantar* 'I like to sing', *me gusta igual* 'I like it the same') improve the chances that the experiencer will be expressed by X-form, whereas nominal subjects (e.g. *me gusta la tortilla de patata/ eso/ lo que dices* 'I like potato omelette/ that/ what you say') favour its prescriptive expression, by prepositional phrase.

Table 4.1 Form of experiencer, as a function of the subject

Subject:	Experiencer:	
	X-form	Prescriptive form
Non-nominal: (N: 18)	10 (55%)	8 (45%)
Nominal: (N: 32)	10 (31%)	22 (69%)

What we seem to be confronted with here is particular reluctance to centre attention on the intrinsically *least* 'topic-worthy' (intrinsically salient) kinds of referents – those that are not entities at all – manifested at the local level in experiencer constructions, where an intrinsically more salient referent (an animate being) must also be mentioned.[7] What I propose, then, is that the apparent limitation of X-forms to conversational speech is due to competitive pressures of essentially the same kind, but operating at the *discourse* level, and in this case due to the relatively heightened saliency that the speech situation itself confers on the participants in it, the interlocutors, and especially on the speaker.

Finally, the nature of the larger context in which X-forms occur – ordinary, unprepared speech – also is consonant with the idea that they are multicentric presentations brought about by competition for attention, since such competition should be relatively harder to resolve under time-pressure (see e.g. Ochs 1979: 65f.).

6. '*Qui m'aime me suive*'

I think we must conclude, then, that the referents of X-forms are not necessarily presented as prominent because the discourse is 'about' them, in any meaningful sense of the term, nor to assist the hearer in identifying them. The only characteristic that all referents of X-forms seem to have in common is that they can be shown, in context, to be important *to the speaker*. This may be because the referent is an important element in the subject matter (for instance, *todo el mundo* in 6.2). In this case, of course, the discourse *is* about it, and this should be reflected in such quantitative measures as relative frequency of mention. But in other instances the referent is important only because of the way the speaker chooses to present the subject matter – e.g. by invoking witnesses (*algunos alemanes* in 6.2) – or simply because the speaker uses the subject matter as a vehicle for self-expression (*yo* in 6.1) or for expressing solidarity with the interlocutors. In the latter circumstances the referent may or may not be mentioned frequently – *algunos alemanes que se lo cuento* 'some Germans that I tell it to', for example, is mentioned only once in 6.2. Understandably, it is characteristic of conversation that referents are often invoked, and mentioned prominently, because to some extent they serve all these ends at once. So it is that referents of X-forms are mentioned frequently overall, though not necessarily in each individual case.

Accordingly, the referents of X-forms are by no means 'speaker/hearer neutral'; on the contrary, they seem to reflect the speaker's interests in the first place. Moreover, they take little account of the hearer, since they present referents prominently but do not indicate why.[8] This may be another reason why these forms occur in speech but not in writing or in the more formal or 'planned' spoken registers. On the one hand, the flexibility of multicentric present-ation is encouraged by the interests and dynamics of the conversa-tional situation – and by the 'time-pressure' it imposes: conversation implies the active participation of more than one person, with each participant interpreting ostensibly 'common' subject matter according to more or less personal priorities. But at the same time the speech situation itself makes it possible for each speaker to indulge his own priorities, even at the expense of morphosyntactic specificity, since the interlocutors can be expected to compensate for it by their co-presence and shared contextual knowledge (cf. Ochs 1979: 66; Tannen 1982: 2).[9] Of course, this flexibility presupposes that it is normal in actual use of language for 'receivers' (hearers/readers) to play an active part in its interpreta-tion, so that, in their turn as encoders (speakers/writers), they know when and to what extent they can rely on it.

Notes

This article is based on research that was funded, in part, by grants from the American Philosophical Society, the US-Spain Joint Committee for Educational and Cultural Affairs, and the State University of New York. I am grateful to Dwight Bolinger, Leo Hickey, Elias Rivers, and Suzanne Romaine for their useful and encouraging comments on my earlier work on X-forms, and especially to Erica García for providing the opportunity to discuss it with her in detail. I am of course most indebted to my informants, for their hospitality and their loquaciousness.
1   This is not the same as (affective) 'detachment' in the sense of Chafe 1982, but instead like what he calls (morphosyntactic) 'fragmentation'. Chafe considers fragmentation characteristic of spoken language, and its opposite, integration, typical of written language.
2   The Spanish pronominal paradigm is a favourable one for X-form presentation, since the forms used for subjects are also free forms, and

so can appear in foregrounded position. (For an analysis of the semantic import of subjecthood in Spanish see García 1975). This would not be true of English, for example, which could only foreground object forms, or reflexives. (I owe this realization to discussions with Erica García.)

3   I have referred to this strategy as 'particularization'. It may perhaps reflect what some researchers on reasoning call an 'empirical bias', by which 'personal knowledge and experience [are] used as . . . "proof" or verification of a conclusion reached through the use of problem information' (Scribner 1977: 491). They attribute this manner of reasoning especially to 'traditional societies'.

4   Compare the different bases for attention observed by psychologists: relevance to task at hand vs. personal value (Miller and Johnson Laird 1976: 132).

5   This may have been obscured by the fact that much work on discourse has used an experimental design, with controlled subject matter (e.g. Chafe 1980; Marslen-Wilson *et al.* 1982; Levy 1984). This has obvious advantages as to rigour and comparability of results, but is unlikely to elicit the kind of speaker-involvement characteristic of more natural conversation (as noted by Redeker 1984).

6   Presumably because of the 'conflict of interest' inherent in possessor and in experiencer expressions, not all languages assign prominence according to the same priorities (see e.g. Li and Thompson (1976) on Lahu and Mandarin; Comrie (1981: 217) on Maltese; Givón (1976: 59) on Israeli Hebrew. Compare also Old vs. Modern English usage with verbs such as *like*, and also the colloquial *I'm hurting* vs. *It's hurting me*.) Apparently, even in prescriptive Spanish usage experiencers are treated like subjects as regards their normal order with respect to the verb. Thus Bentivoglio 1985 finds that the unmarked order of subject and verb is VS with verbs of experience, in contrast to other verbs with which it is SV. With verbs of experience, then, the experiencer is mentioned first. (See also Bentivoglio and Sedano 1985, on the tendency to interpret animates as the subject of the Spanish 'impersonal' presentative *haber*.)

7   Understandably, the most common contexts for X-forms are expressions with *gustar* and the like; *parecer* 'seem' (giving such forms as *yo me parece* 'I me-obj. it-seems-3p.'); and *para mí* 'for me', i.e. 'in my opinion' (giving *yo para mí* 'I for me'). Note that in the latter expressions the subject is never an entity.

8   I suspect that where analysis of ordinary conversation is concerned, concentration on 'informativeness' or utility to the hearer may turn out to be misguided, and misguiding – not unlike 'truth value' in the study of morphosyntax.

9   Note that in some instances X-forms amount to 'simpler' (and less precise) presentations in yet another sense, also shared by grammatical subjects (and by accusatives): they are relativized by *que* 'that', arguably the vaguest relative in Spanish, without a preposition (e.g. the X-forms in 6.2, which prescriptively would be relativized by *a*

quien). Sometimes this permits still further simplification: For example
in the case of *mi padre* 'my father' in 6.3 has the effect of allowing *mi
padre* to be interpreted in two roles: as recipient of *hubieran hecho un
curso* '(if) they had given him a course' and as agent of *hubiera perdido*
'(he) would not have lost'. In this sense, too, X-forms favour agility of
expression at the expense of morphosyntactic precision.

References

P. Bentivoglio, 'Función y significado de la preposición del sujeto nominal
en el español hablado'. Paper read at 45th International Congress of
American Spanish, 1985

P. Bentivoglio and M. Sedano, 'Haber: ¿un verbo impersonal?' Paper
read at 45th Congress of American Spanish, 1985

W. Chafe 'Givenness, contrastiveness, definiteness, subjects, and topics,'
in *Subject and Topic*, edited by C. Li (New York: Academic Press),
1976

W. Chafe, *The Pear Stories: Cognitive, Cultural, and Linguistic Aspects of
Narrative Production* (Norwood, NJ: Ablex), 1980

W. Chafe, 'Integration and involvement in speaking, writing, and oral
literature', in *Spoken and Written Language: Exploring Orality and
Literacy*, edited by D. Tannen (Norwood, NJ: Ablex), 1982

B. Comrie, *Language Universals and Linguistic Typology* (Chicago:
University of Chicago Press), 1981

A. Duranti and E. Ochs, 'Left dislocation in Italian conversation,' in
Syntax and Semantics 12: *Discourse and Syntax*, edited by T. Givón
(New York: Academic Press), 1979

E. C. García, *The Role of Theory in Linguistic Analysis: The Spanish
Pronoun System* (Amsterdam: North Holland), 1975

T. Givón, 'Topic, pronoun, and grammatical agreement,' in *Subject and
Topic*, edited by C. Li (New York: Academic Press), 1976

T. Givón, *On Understanding Grammar* (New York: Academic Press),
1979a

T. Givón, *Topic Continuity in Discourse* (Amsterdam: Benjamins), 1983

E. O. Keenan and B. Schieffelin, 'Foregrounding referents: a
reconsideration of left dislocation in discourse,' in *Proceedings of
Annual Meeting of Berkeley Linguistics Society*, 1976

F. Klein-Andreu, 'Why speech seems ungrammatical', in *From Sign to
Text: A Semiotic View of Communication*, edited by Y. Tobin
(Amsterdam: Benjamins), 1989

B. Lavandera, 'Tensión entre lo personal y lo impersonal en la
organización del discurso,' in *Variación y significado*, edited by B.
Lavandera (Buenos Aires: Hachette), 1984

E. Levy, 'Communicating thematic structure in narrative discourse: the
use of referring terms and gestures,' University of Chicago
Dissertation, 1984

C. N. Li and S. A. Thompson, 'Subject and topic: a new typology of language,' in *Subject and Topic*, edited by C. Li (New York: Academic Press), 1976

G. A. Miller and P. N. Johnson-Laird, *Language and Perception* (Cambridge, Massachusetts: Harvard University Press), 1976

E. Ochs, 'Planned and unplanned discourse,' in *Syntax and Semantics* 12: *Discourse and Syntax*, edited by T. Givón (New York: Academic Press), 1979

G. Redeker, 'On differences between spoken and written language,' in *Discourse Processes* 7, 1984, 43–55

G. Sanders and J. R. Wirth, 'Discourse, pragmatics, and linguistic form', in *Beyond the Sentence: Discourse and Sentential Form*, edited by J. Wirth (Ann Arbor: Karoma), 1985

D. Schiffrin, 'Jewish argument as sociability,' in *Language and Society* 13, 3, 1984, 311–36

M. Sedano, 'Un análisis comparativo de las cláusulas seudohendidas y de las cláusulas con verbo ser focalizador en el habla de Caracas.' Paper read at 7th International Congress of ALFAL, 1984

S. Scribner, 'Modes of thinking and ways of speaking: culture and logic reconsidered,' in *Thinking: Readings in Cognitive Science*, edited by P. N. Johnson-Laird and P. C. Wason (Cambridge: Cambridge University Press), 1977

W. Strunk Jr and E. B. White, *The Elements of Style*, 3rd edition (New York: Macmillan), 1979

D. Tannen, 'The oral-literate continuum in discourse,' in *Spoken and Written Language: Exploring Orality and Literacy* (Norwood, NJ: Ablex), 1982

R. Tomlin, 'Interaction of subject, theme, and agent,' in *Beyond the Sentence: Discourse and Sentential Form*, edited by J. Wirth (Ann Arbor: Karoma), 1985

D. Zubin, 'Discourse function and morphology: the focus system in German,' in *Syntax and Semantics* 12: *Discourse and Syntax*, edited by T. Givón (New York: Academic Press), 1979

Chapter five

The pragmastylistics of hypothetical discourse

Carmen Silva-Corvalán

1. Introduction

This paper analyses the various manners in which speakers choose
to express their attitude towards the possibility that the contents of a
proposition or a number of propositions constituting a discourse
unit may be true in a present or future world, or could have been
true in a past world given certain conditions. The choice among two
or more semantically similar ways of communicating a piece of
information determines a specific style of communication, which in
the case of the expression of possibility characterizes it along a scale
of assertiveness. Thus, depending upon the linguistic choices made
by a speaker, and the manner in which he structures discourse about
hypothetical *situations*,[1] his communicative style may appear to be
assertive, categorical, assured, defensive, committed, uncom-
mitted, doubtful, or sceptical.

In the Introduction to this volume, Hickey (p. 2) reminds us of
Morier's distinction between *objective* and *subjective stylistics*. The
latter studies psychological facts in reference to choice of linguistic
expression. Here, though psychological facts are also considered,
we focus mainly on socio-pragmatic ones, namely those which refer
to the image which a speaker wishes to create of himself, and the
effect which he intends his act of communication to produce in an
interactional situation. Accordingly, we examine certain psychological and social facts which seem to underlie the choice of
linguistic devices in expressing assessment of the possibility of
actualizing hypothetical statements. Both psychological and social
facts indeed constrain the selection of linguistic alternatives available to speakers in any given context. To the extent that speakers
select one of these options prompted by such psychological and
social factors as their evaluation of self and their interlocutors, their
belief systems, the degree of formality of the situation, the effect
they intend to have on their audience, etc., style necessarily
becomes a question of pragmatics. This methodological approach

to the study of stylistics gives rise to the development of pragma-stylistics, the subdiscipline which motivates this volume.

Our study focuses on discourse which refers to hypothetical situations produced by six speakers of Spanish during conversations with the author. Impressionistically, the physical situation may be defined as relatively casual since the speakers have known the researcher for approximately one year, and the conversations take place in their homes. These conversations were recorded and transcribed in order to serve as the source of data for the analysis. The six speakers are Mexican immigrants who live in the predominantly Hispanic community of eastern Los Angeles, a basically stable urban community bound together by historical, social, and cultural reasons (e.g. catholicism, strong family ties). Three of the speakers E, L, and F,[2] of 20, 23, and 21 years of age, have lived in the United States for six to eight years; the other three (C, J, R), who are between the ages of 41 and 54, immigrated into the US after the age of twenty-five. While the younger speakers have had some college education in America, in the older group only R has had some. C and J completed secondary education in Mexico, and work as drivers in Los Angeles.

The goals of our study required the use of careful sociolinguistic fieldwork methodology in order to succeed in obtaining comparable data across speakers, while at the same time maintaining an atmosphere of 'social conversation' during the recordings. Crucial to a comprehensive study of stylistic differences reflected on linguistic form is spoken data ranging along a wide variety of topics and discourse genres which ensure the creation of contexts for the use of such forms, as well as the appropriateness of comparing across speakers and discourse genres.

On the other hand, the analysis of hypothetical reference in particular further requires topics which elicit both past and non-past time reference, as well as the expression of various degrees of possibility. These necessary data were obtained by introducing such topics as a) for past reference: life in Mexico if X had not come to the US, life in the US if X had chosen a different career/job/school; and b) for non-past reference: speaker's response to (i) the possibility of X dating/marrying someone from a different race/religion/cultural background, (ii) situations which would justify abortion, (iii) the possibility of having a lot of money.

Studies of the structure and function of discourse have in the last fifteen to twenty years examined both unilateral and bilateral oral texts; for instance, the structure and language of narratives (Labov and Waletsky 1967; Schiffrin 1981; Tannen 1982; Silva-Corvalán 1983), of spatial descriptions (e.g. Linde and Labov 1975; Levelt

1982), of conversation (cf. Goffman 1972; Sacks, Schegloff, and Jefferson 1974; Labov and Fanshel 1977; and various papers in Schiffrin 1984), and referential movement in various types of texts (Klein and von Stutterheim n.d.). But apparently not much attention has been paid, however, to conversational discourse which refers to hypothetical situations, nor to argumentation. Although hypothesizing is part of argumentation, especially so in essays and debates dealing with social sciences and humanities topics, we will show that not every hypothetical text is necessarily argumentative.

We define *hypothetical discourse* as a discourse passage which conveys imaginary, conjectural information, rather than facts stemming from perception and memory (cf. Klein and Stutterheim n.d.: 31). The linguistic strategies proposed to relate to stylistic differences in texts of this type, which are examined in this paper, include, on the one hand, the structure of the hypothetical oral text[3] itself, and on the other, such language devices as verb morphology, and the modal verbs *poder* 'can/may', *deber* 'must' and related expressions, namely such adverbial and adjectival items as *possible, probable, quizás* 'maybe', *puede que* 'maybe', etc.

2. The language of hypothetical discourse

To examine the pragmastylistics of hypothetical discourse, it becomes necessary to discuss briefly the modal value of verb morphology, in addition to the specific contribution of modal verbs and expressions. In this regard, we would like to propose that a crucial function of verb morphology is to contribute to the proposition (p) the meaning of 'more or less assertiveness', where *assertiveness* is defined as speaker belief or confidence in the truth of the proposition. Degrees of assertiveness are pragmatically inferred to convey degrees of hypotheticality. These two notions are in an inverse relation, such that more assertiveness is inferred to convey stronger likelihood that p is true, i.e. less hypotheticality. Assertiveness and hypotheticality correlate with verb morphology roughly as in the scale in Table 5.1,[4] which is suggested to apply in reference to non-past matter in the data examined.

In addition, counterfactuality in the past is expressed by the pluperfect subjunctive and by the conditional perfect. Both the discourse topic and verb morphology contribute to creating a hypothetical world. Furthermore, the use of verbs which either weaken the degree of assertiveness of the proposition (e.g. *creer* 'to think/to believe', *pensar* 'to think', *poder* 'may'), or refer to wishes (e.g. *querer* 'to want/to wish', *tener ganas* 'to want') serves to

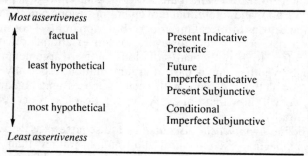

Table 5.1 Scale of assertiveness conveyed by verb morphology in reference to non-past matter

Most assertiveness		
factual	Present Indicative	
	Preterite	
least hypothetical	Future	
	Imperfect Indicative	
	Present Subjunctive	
most hypothetical	Conditional	
	Imperfect Subjunctive	
Least assertiveness		

confirm the non-actuality of the matter referred to. Finally, hypothetical worlds are created by syntactic means, e.g. conditional clauses, and temporal clauses which establish a future time frame. All these are related to the pragmastylistics of modality.

Spanish grammars (e.g. Gili Gaya 1976; Real Academia Española 1973) list *poder* 'can/may', and *deber* 'must', among the most frequently used 'modal verbs' in the language. The Academy (p. 450) specifically states that these are called 'modals' because they denote the explicit 'modus' of the sentence, while the infinitive, the 'dictum', conveys the essential content of the proposition. In a study of the meaning of these two modals, we have proposed (Silva-Corvalán 1987) that, when used in a given discourse, they convey *contextual meanings* which derive from the global interaction of the *underlying meaning* of the modal verb with syntactic, semantic, prosodic, and pragmatic factors which conform their contexts of use.

In regards to *poder*, Silva-Corvalán (1987) argues that its underlying meaning is 'does not preclude X'. In present tense affirmative form, this modal occurs in contexts which convey permission, ability, possibility, and mitigation. Of these four contextual meanings, only mitigation and possibility concern this paper. *Mitigation* refers to the fact that *poder* implies that circumstances exist which permit us to infer that some sort of obstacle has or may have to be overcome for the situation to occur. This implication of 'difficulty overcome' is illustrated by example 1.

(1)   No, no claro, vamos, de hecho esas voces que se graban, a) *tú con tu oído no las escuchas . . .* b) *solamente las puedes escuchar cuando rebobinas la cinta* y escuchas lo que se grabó.

'No, no, well, in fact some of those voices which you
record *you don't hear them* with your naked ear . . . *you
can only hear them when you rewind* the tape and listen to
what was recorded'.

From example 1 it is inferred that a certain amount of difficulty
has to be overcome for the modalized event to take place. In fact,
the speaker explicitly states that only after rewinding the tape can
certain voices be heard. Further evidence for the implication of
overcome difficulty is provided by example 5, discussed later.

In contexts of *possibility, poder* qualifies the truth of the
proposition in regards to a certain degree of probability. If
quantifiable, probability ranges between 1 if modalized p is
presented by the speaker as epistemically necessary, and 0, if the
factuality of p is epistemically impossible. Lyons (1977: 800) states
that in English, speakers can express at least three different degrees
of factuality by using such adverbs as *certainly, probably*, and
possibly, associated with decreasing degrees of probability. Likewise, Spanish has lexicalized means of expressing epistemic modality, for example the adjectives *cierto, probable*, and *posible*,
which express decreasing degrees of probability. In addition, *poder*
has become lexicalized in the expressions *puede que* 'maybe' and
puede ser que 'it may be that', which can only convey a meaning of
possibility.

It is common knowledge that *deber* can be used, as *must* in
English, in either an epistemic (i.e. possibility) or a deontic (i.e.
obligation) sense. The underlying meaning of *deber* has some points
of similarity with that of *poder*, but while *poder* 'does not preclude
X, *deber* 'favours', 'requires', or 'entails X'. That is, *deber*
communicates confidence in the outcome of p; it has connotations
of 'very likely', 'necessary', and 'appropriate'. The contribution of
deber to the meaning of modalized p appears to be, then, to require
X as essential in the light of a set of circumstances. By postulating
for *deber* a core meaning of 'requirement of X', it is possible to
account for such contextual meanings as obligation, advice, and
possibility, depending on whether a number of contextual circumstances prompt a reading of more or less forcible requirement.

Deber occurs infrequently in the data examined. *Haber que* 'be
necessary' and *tener que* 'have to' appear to occur more frequently
than *deber* in contexts of obligation. *Tener que* also occurs, albeit
quite infrequently, in probability contexts.

The probability value conveyed by the positive and negative
forms of *deber* and *poder* may be arranged on a scale as that
presented in 2, where these forms are located relative to other

modal expressions as well. *Probable/probablemente* express a higher degree of probability than *posible/posiblemente*.[5]

(2)   Scale of probability of p

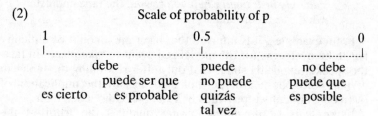

1	0.5	0
debe	puede	no debe
puede ser que	no puede	puede que
es cierto es probable	quizás	es posible
	tal vez	

3. The structure of hypothetical discourse

The fact that these oral texts refer to situations which speakers have not previously experienced, and which do not have an iconic time or spatial line of reference and development (as in narratives and descriptions, for instance) accounts for their rather loose structure both in terms of the necessary sections which must compose them, as well as with respect to the relative order of these sections in the creation of the discourse.

We have examined eighteen hypothetical oral texts produced by the six speakers described in section 1. The analysis indicates that there are at least two types of hypothetical discourse: 1) *Strictly hypothetical*: and 2) *Hypothetical with supportive argumentation*.

In the data examined, strictly hypothetical oral texts have a future time perspective and occur typically when no issue is being discussed; rather, speakers are speculating about their possible actions given a certain condition (e.g. having a lot of money, having more free time, becoming ill, retiring). As one would expect in conversational discourse, argumentation may be embedded in the development of a strictly hypothetical text, but it is not part of its main or central structure. By contrast, hypothetical oral texts which refer to past counterfactual situations incorporate argumentation in their central structure, as do oral texts which **discuss issues** either within a present or a future time perspective.

A complete hypothetical discourse with supportive argumentation may comprise the following elements: hypothetical macro-frame, hypothetical statement, argumentation, anchoring, qualification, disclaimer, and coda. Of these, the first two define a minimal hypothetical text. Strictly hypothetical discourse does not include argumentation and anchoring as part of its central structure. I proceed now to define these various elements, and to illustrate them through the analysis of some oral texts.

3.1 Establishment of a hypothetical macro-frame

We define a *macro-frame* as a body of knowledge that is evoked in order to provide an inferential base for the production and understanding of discourse.[6] This is in every case done through a question such as *¿Te imaginas cómo habría sido tu vida si te hubieras quedado en México?* 'Can you imagine what your life would have been like if you had stayed in Mexico?', or through a statement followed by a short prompting question, *Mucha gente está en contra del aborto, pero yo lo aceptaría en algunos casos. ¿Y tú?* 'Many people are against abortion, but I would accept it in some cases, would you?'.[7]

Establishing a macro-frame, then, necessarily also means establishing a discourse topic. This defines the sequence of utterances included in what we refer to as hypothetical discourse passage. In this sense, a macro-frame shares some definitional characteristics with what van Dijk (1980: 322–44) discusses in terms of macro-speech acts, and macro-structures.

3.2 Hypothetical statements

These are one or a series of utterances which present the speaker's statements about his possible actions, attitudes and beliefs given a certain state of affairs. The most frequent construction used to encode hypothetical statements is, expectedly, the conditional clause of the type 'if *p* then *q*'. If the state of affairs or condition 'if *p*' has been established in the hypothetical frame, the speaker's statements contain in nearly every case only the second part of the conditional period, 'then *q*', i.e. the assumed consequence of *p*. However, throughout the discourse speakers put forth a number of hypothetical statements dependent on certain conditions, presented by the speakers themselves, the content of which is related to the hypothetical macro-frame.

3.3 Argumentation

These discourse passages are characterized by consisting of one or a series of utterances which present reasons offered in proof, rebuttal of, or as the motivation for, a hypothesis, statement or position in regards to an issue.

3.4 Anchoring

Anchoring refers to the strategy of linking the hypothetical statements to the real world by means of illustrative narratives or exposition of relevant facts of which the speaker has direct knowledge. It appears that anchoring has a double function: communicative and cognitive. Its communicative function is argumentative and appellative, inasmuch as it supports the speaker's hypothesis and aims at convincing the listener of the possibility that the speaker is correct in its assumptions. Cognitively, anchoring hypothetical texts to experienced facts makes production and processing easier. Indeed, we have already mentioned that hypothetical discourse does not stem from perception and memory. This makes the problem of linearization, conceptualization, and linguistic encoding a harder task as compared with that of encoding narrative texts, for example (cf. Levelt 1979, 1982). Thus, speakers frequently illustrate their hypothetical statements with anecdotes about people they know to be in the sort of world which they imagine for themselves, and either state explicitly or imply that this is what they would, would have to, or would have perhaps done.

3.5 Qualifications

These are one or a series of utterances which moderate or restrict the hypothetical statements, making them less strong. Given a hypothetical statement of the form 'if p then q', qualifications take the form 'but if p then possibly also $-q$', or even a contrary hypothesis 'if $-p$ then possibly also q', or are encoded as a proviso of the form 'q, provided that x'. Qualifications are also conveyed by such verbs as *creer* 'think, believe', and *pensar* 'think', and they may be *reinforced* by means of lexical expressions of the type of *puede que* 'maybe', *probablemente* 'probably', etc.

3.6 Disclaimers

These are utterances which convey the speaker's reluctance or refusal to accept responsibility for the certainty of his conjectures about counterfactual and possible situations. Examples of disclaimers are such utterances as *No puedo yo saber/asegurar* 'I can't tell/be sure', *No sé, es difícil saber* 'I don't know, it's difficult to tell', *Así me lo imagino, ¿no?, pero no sé* 'This is how I imagine it, right?, but I don't know'.

3.7 Coda

As in oral narrative (cf. Labov and Waletsky 1967), the end of a hypothetical text may be overtly marked by means of expressions like *Eso es lo que yo pienso* 'That's what I think', *Así es como habría sido* 'This is how it would've been', *Y todo eso habría hecho* 'And I would've done all that'. However, similarly to what we have noted in the case of conversational narratives (Silva-Corvalán 1983: 765), codas are quite infrequent in conversational hypothetical texts as well.

With respect to the structural elements of a hypothetical discourse, I propose that speakers who present hypothetical statements supported by argumentation and anchoring do so in order to present an image of confidence or certainty in the truth of their hypothetical statements. Their communicative style in the discourse in question, then, is assertive. By contrast, the higher the ratio of qualifications and disclaimers to hypothetical statements, the less assured and more defensive will the speaker appear to be. Further, verb morphology and lexicon also contribute by either weakening or strengthening the degree of assertiveness of propositions within the various elements.

4. Interpreting hypothetical discourse

This section interprets the pragmastylistics of three examples of hypothetical discourse. For each example, we provide an analysis of its structure and language as a basis for our interpretation.

Example 3 illustrates the structural elements of an oral text with supportive argumentation. The issue is abortion.

(3) C: a) — ¿Pero en qué situaciones, por ejemplo, crees que aceptarías el aborto? ¿Le aconsejarías a alguien que se hiciera un aborto, en cualquier caso, un aborto?   *Hy/Fr*

B: b) Bueno, no, no aceptaría eso   *Hy/St*
c) porque me sentiría yo como, como un asesino quitarle la vida a un niño.   *Argu*
d) Ni en caso de que, digo yo,   *Qual*
e) muchos padres, pos si ven a sus hijos en problemas así, no los dejan discurrir por ellos mismos,   *Hy/St*
f) pero creo yo que   *Qual*
g) no sería capaz de quitarle a un hijo, a uno de mis hijos o, o, a cualquiera de, a mis herma- a mi hermana, o a los- en caso que hubiera alguna vez pasado ese detalle, ¿verdad?   *Hy/St*
h) Porque yo creo que   *Qual*
i) la vida, se la da a uno Dios. Y el ser que nace tiene que nacer.   *Argu*

j) Pero, bueno, eso yo no sé   *Discl*

k) si alguna vez en caso de, de que se vaya a morir la persona, ¿verdad?   *Hy/St*

l) Probablemente, eso yo creo que   *Qual*

m) ni Dios, ni Dios le permitiría a nadie, ¿verdad?, dejar morir a la madre por, por el niño, ¿verdad?   *Hy/St*

n) Pero está difícil también porque son dos, son dos seres que se quieren.   *Discl*

C: Sí, pero la madre ya está aquí ya y el-

B: o) Sí. Y luego le hace más falta a los demás hijos, especialmente si tiene familia, ¿verdad?   *Argu*

p) En ese caso, pues, todavía   *Qual*

q) podría yo, a, como le dicen los, los gringos, ¿verdad?, *bend* poquito.   *Hy/St*

(C,m54,ELA85,B160-200)[8]

C: a) — But in what situations, for instance, do you think you could accept abortion? Would you advise someone to have an abortion, in all cases, abortion?   *Hy/Fr*

B: b) No, I wouldn't accept that   *Hy/St*

c) because I would feel like, like a murderer, taking the life of a child,   *Argu*

d) And in case, I think,   *Qual*

e) many parents, well, if they see that their children are in this kind of trouble, they don't let them decide by themselves,   *Hy/St*

f) but I think   *Qual*

g) I wouldn't be able to take the child of one of my children, or, or any of, of my sister, or of- in case something like that had ever happened, right?   *Hy/St*

h) Because I think that   *Qual*

i) life, God gives it to you. And the being who is born has to be born.   *Argu*

j) But, well, I don't know,   *Discl*

k) if in a given case, if the person's going to die, right?   *Hy/St*

l) probably, that I think that   *Qual*

m) not even God, not even God would allow that to happen to anyone, right?, to let the mother die for, for the child, right?   *Hy/St*

n) But it's difficult also because they are two, they are two people who love each other.   *Discl*

C: Yes, but the mother is already here and the-

B: o) Yes. And then she's needed more by the rest of the children, especially if she has a family, right? *Argu*
p) In that case, well maybe *Qual*
q) I could, as the, the gringos say, right?, *bend* a little. *Hy/St*
(C,m54,ELA85,B160-200)

The structure of the hypothetical discourse in example 3 illustrates the following elements in its development:

a) Hypothetical macro-frame
b) Hypothetical statement 1
c) Argumentation
d) Qualification
e) Hypothetical statement 2
f) Qualification
g) Hypothetical statement 3
h) Qualification
i) Argumentation
j) Disclaimer
k,m) Hypothetical statement 4
l) Qualification
n) Disclaimer
o) Argumentation
p) Qualification
q) Hypothetical statement 5

Note that oral text 3 contains five hypothetical statements, three supported by argumentation, but no anchoring. It also incorporates five qualifications, and two disclaimers. Although it might be possible to develop a sophisticated method of quantification of the proportional number of the various elements, taking as well verb morphology and lexicon into account as an index of degree of assertiveness, we do not attempt to do it here. At this point, based simply on the larger number of qualifications and disclaimers over hypothetical statements and argumentation, plus the absence of anchoring, we interpret the style of example 3 as relatively less assertive. Thus, our interpretation of the pragmatics of example 3 is that the speaker views the issue of abortion as quite complex and is not prepared to commit himself to a categorical position. Even though he acknowledges the fact that there may be attenuating circumstances which could justify abortion (k), he qualifies the related hypothetical statement (l-m), and proceeds to disclaim responsibility in (n). However, his attitude changes slightly in response to the researcher's implication that the mother is more important than the baby, so that he ends the passage allowing for the possibility that he 'could bend a little' (q).

The language used in example 3 supports our interpretation: four of the five hypothetical statements have conditional rather than present tense morphology; two of the five qualifications are reinforced (*probablemente* (l), and *todavía* 'maybe' (p)). Note, furthermore, that hypothetical statement q is modalized (*podría* 'could'), while hypothetical statement b is not (*no aceptaría* 'would not accept'). This indicates that it is more difficult for this speaker to justify abortion than to disapprove of it, an attitude which is valued in his social group.

Example 4 presents a hypothetical discourse with anchoring. This oral text deals with the possibility of having to think about what one would do if a son or a daughter wanted to marry someone from a different cultural and ethnic group.

(4) C: a) ¿Qué harías si una de tus hijas o un hijo viniera un
            día y te dijera 'Me voy a casar con un, alguien que es
            musulmán, o budista, o con un japonés, o un iraní,
            ¿verdad?, pues-   *Hy/Fr*
     R: b) Pues no, no he pensado,   *Discl*
            c) (*Anchoring*: illustrative narrative)   *Ancho*
            tengo la experiencia de una, una supervisora que
            tenía antes.
            c1) Ella es de religión también católica y, y hace como
            unos dos años, salió la hija con un judío.   *Frame*
            Me dice exactamente así que, 'Parece, pero,
            c2) no creo que llegue a ninguna seriedad, no creo,
            no'.   *Hy/St*
            Y sí, yo le digo a fulanita, me acuerdo que es la
            única mujer que tiene, tiene tres hombres, es mayor
            que R., como dos años yo creo. Y hace unos tres,
            cuatro meses volvió a la oficina a saludarme. Y le
            pregunté, le preguntaron por su familia. Me dice,
            c3) 'Pues, fíjate que B., B. está haciendo planes ya de
            casarse'.   *Qual*
            c4) Y le digo, '¿Y cómo aceptan a este güero?'.   *Frame*
            c5) Dice, 'No sé, dice, yo creo que voy a tener que
            empezar a hacer a, a convertirlo al catolicismo.   *Hy/St*
            c6) No sé cómo lo voy a hacer.   *Discl*
            c7) Yo le digo a B. que va a ser un, un amigo muy
            difícil,   *Hy/St*

    c8) porque él es un judío, judío, de religión bien, bien
fundada, bien sedimentada, como la de
nosotros'.   *Argu*

    c9) Decía, 'No sé, voy a tener que, se, se son-, se rió,
bromeó, voy a tener que, hacerlo, hacerlo
católico'.   *Hy/St*

    c10) De allí si no lo logra es que,   *Qual*

    c11) bueno, no sé, no sé, pero ya es cuestión de B.,
pero yo no he pensado tampoco en eso.   *Discl*

    --[9]

C: d) ¿Pero tú crees que podrías aceptarlo? Tú te,
imagínate que un día venga uno [de tus hijos][10] y te
diga-   *Hy/Fr*

R: e) Yo pienso, Carmen, que,   *Qual*

    f) yo tendría que [aceptarlo].   *Hy/St*

                      (R,f43,ELA77,B262-280)

C: a) What would you do if one of your daughters or a son
came to you one day and said: I'm going to marry a,
someone who is Muslim, or Buddhist, or a Japanese,
or an Iranian, right?, well-   *Hy/Fr*

R: b) Well no, I haven't thought about it.   *Discl*

    c) (*Anchoring*: illustrative narrative)   *Ancho*
      I know the case of a, a supervisor I had before.

    c1) She is also Catholic and, about two years ago, her
daughter started going out with a Jew   *Fr*
      She says exactly this to me: 'It looks as if, but,

    c2) I don't think this will become serious, I don't think
so, I don't'.   *Hy/St*
And yes, I tell this woman, I remember she is the only
daughter she has, she has three sons, she's older than
R., about two years I think. And about three, four
months ago she came by my office to say hello. And I
asked her, they asked her about her family. She says,

    c3) 'Well, I tell you B., B.'s making plans to get
married.'   *Qual*

    c4) And I say to her: 'And how come you accept this
"güero" (anglo)?'   *Fr*

    c5) She says: 'I don't know, she says, I think I'm going
to have to start, start converting him to
catholicism.   *Hy/St*

    c6) I don't know how I'm going to do it.   *Discl*

    c7) I tell B. he's going to be a, a very difficult
friend,   *Hy/St*

       c8) because he's Jewish, Jewish, with a very strong
       religious background, very strong, like us.   *Argu*
       c9) She said: 'I don't know, I'll have to, to, she smi-,
       she laughed, kidding, I'll have to, make him, make
       him catholic.'   *Hy/St*
       c10) And then if she doesn't succeed it's because, *Qual*
       c11) well, I don't know, but it's now in B.'s hands, but
       I haven't thought about that either.   *Discl*

C: d) But do you think you could accept it? Do you,
     imagine that one day one of yours [your children]
     came to you and said-   *Hy/Fr*
R: e) I think, Carmen, that   *Qual*
     f) I would have to [accept it].   *Hy/St*
                  (R,f43,ELA77,B262-280)

The structure of example 4 is as follows:

a)   Hypothetical macro-frame
b)   Disclaimer
c)   Anchoring
      c1) 'Real world' frame
      c2) Hypothetical statement
      c3) Qualification (mixed marriages do occur)
      c4) Hypothetical frame reworded
      c5) Hypothetical statement
      c6) Disclaimer
      c7) Hypothetical statement
      c8) Argumentation
      c9) Repetition of hypothetical statement in c5
      c10) Qualification
      c11) Disclaimer
d)   Hypothetical frame (recreated)
e)   Qualification
f)   Hypothetical statement 1

In example 4 the speaker restates the researcher's hypothetical
frame in real world terms in (c1). Having established that mixed
relationships do occur and may in fact lead to mixed marriages (c3),
the speaker anchors the researcher's hypothetical frame (c4) and
her own hypothetical statement (c5) to the comparable factual
events with which she seems to identify herself at the moment of the
conversation. The speaker's answer to the hypothetical frame
recreated in (d) supports our proposal that anchoring does indeed
fulfil the communicative function of presenting, through real facts,

the speaker's own hypothetical statements and supportive argumentation. In the illustrative narrative, though realizing that mixed
marriages cause difficulties, the mother accepts her daughter's
decision. Likewise, R's final hypothetical statement (f) about her
own possible actions is that she would have to accept a mixed
marriage as well.

Anchoring creates a more assured communicative style as
compared to that of example 3.[11] Furthermore, note that the
elements in the anchoring passage are never coded with conditional
morphology. All these factors, then, lead us to propose that the
pragmatics of example 4 are that the speaker intends to assert quite
positively that a son or daughter cannot be prevented from
marrying whomever they choose. But the speaker's attitude
towards mixed marriages is one of forced acceptance. This is made
clear in the final hypothetical statement, which the speaker has
chosen to modalize with *tener que* 'to have to'. The alternative
without the modal, *yo lo aceptaría* 'I would accept it' would not
convey the same implication of resignation to outside forces
compelling her to assent to a situation which might not be approved
by her immediate community or perhaps even by her interlocutor
(whom the speaker may have judged to be catholic and conservative).

Finally, we will discuss example 5, an oral text about the
possibility of deciding to become an American citizen.

(5) E: a) ¿Entonces tú, te, te harías [ciudadana
         americana)?   *Hy/Fr*
     L: b) Tal vez sí.   *Hy/St*
         c) Pues depende de la, depende de como, de la, de la
         situación en que me encuentre,   *Qual*
         d) porque tal vez   *Qual*
         e) si en el futuro pensamos irnos a México, a vivir
         allá,   *Hy/St*
         f) pues entonces tal vez   *Qual*
         g) no podría hacerlo   *Hy/St*
         h) en caso de que nos fuéramos   *Qual*
         i) pero si con el tiempo no nos fuéramos a vivir allá y
         me quedara aquí y ya llevara varios años,   *Hy/St*
         j) yo creo que   *Qual*
         k) sí me haría   *Hy/St*
                              (L,f23,ELA72,A180-190)
     E: a) Then you, you, would you become [an American
         citizen]?   *Hy/Fr*
         b) Maybe yes.   *Hy/St*

    c) Well it depends on, it depends on how, on, on the
situation in which I find myself.   *Qual*
    d) because maybe   *Qual*
    e) if we consider going back to Mexico in the future, to
live there,   *Hy/St*
    f) well then maybe   *Qual*
    g) I couldn't do it   *Hy/St*
    h) in case we go back   *Qual*
    i) but if in time we didn't go back to live there, and I
stayed here, and several years had gone by,   *Hy/St*
    j) I think that   *Qual*
    k) I would indeed do it   *Hy/St*
                (L,f23,ELA72,A180-190)

There are three hypothetical statements, five qualifications and
no anchoring in this discourse. We interpret it to be pragmastylisti-
cally less assertive, hesitant. The speaker's attitude is characterized
by doubt about her position with respect to becoming an American
citizen. She qualifies every one of her hypothetical statements.
However, the choice of *poder* to modalize statement e, g (*no podría
hacerlo* 'I couldn't do it') and its absence in i, k (*sí me haría* 'I would
indeed do it'), where the hypothetical statement is reinforced with *sí*
'yes indeed' indicates that not becoming an American citizen
depends on an external circumstance which she cannot control, a
difficulty which she cannot overcome. Otherwise, she would have
stated *no lo haría* 'I wouldn't do it', without the modal or as she does
in k, where no further precluding circumstances are implied to exist.
This may be interpreted to convey her favouring the decision to
become a citizen, an attitude which had been hinted at earlier in the
conversation, as shown in example 6.

(6)   L: — tal vez como traicionando a México, ¿no?,
          traicionando a tu patria. Pero si te ves obligado, si
          tienes la necesidad de hacerlo, pues tienes que
          hacerlo, porque si el gobierno de México pensara que
          también él nos traiciona haciendo tantas cosas que no
          deben de hacer, entonces ellos no lo piensan, ¿por qué
          nosotros lo vamos a pensar?
                (L,f23,ELA72,A170-175)
    L: — perhaps like betraying Mexico, right?, betraying
          your country. But if you're forced to, if you have the
          need to do it, well then you have to do it, because if
          the Mexican government considered that they also
          betray us by doing so many things they shouldn't do

but then they don't think about it, so why are are we to
think about it?

(L,f23,ELA72, A170–175)

Nevertheless, despite this earlier justification, the speaker is aware
of the issue of 'betrayal of Mexico', and of its negative social value.
Consequently, both the structure and the language of her discourse
in example 5 appear to contribute to creating for her an image in
terms of approved social attributes, i.e., she claims a positive social
value for herself (cf. Goffman 1972).

5. Conclusion

The form of an oral text is determined by a number of complex
elements of the environment in which the discourse takes place
(e.g. speakers' interrelationships, degree of formality), by the topic
of the discourse, and by the speakers' belief systems and the effect
they intend to have on their interlocutors. The speaker's assessment
of these factors leads him to make a number of choices from those
made available to him by two systems: a system of principles of
discourse organization, and the language system. These choices,
paradigmatically and syntagmatically consistent, concern all language levels (phonetics, prosody, lexicon, morphology, syntax),
and the manner in which a given oral text may be structured and
developed. These two types of elements constitute a solid, objective
starting point for pragmastylistic analysis.

Many interesting questions, however, remain unanswered. For
instance, what types of oral texts incorporate anchoring? What sorts
of issues are presented with more or less assertiveness?, etc. Among
those oral texts examined here, which deal with four topics: life in
Mexico, intermarriage, abortion, and money (see section 1), we
have observed that anchoring occurs most frequently when discussing the first (in five of six texts), less frequently when the topic is
intermarriage (two of four texts), and it does not occur in
conversations about money and abortion (three texts on each
topic). Men and women in both age groups use the anchoring
strategy. It appears, then, that its occurrence may be to a certain
extent dependent upon the topic.

We have shown how discourse structure and language interact in
a complex but coherent manner in the various oral texts examined
to convey the messages intended by the speakers. Thus, we hope to
have provided some initial answers to the question which pragmastylistics puts forth: what does a text mean, what does it do, and
how does it do it?

Notes

1   After Comrie (1976), who proposes *situation* as a technical term to refer inclusively and indistinctly to actions, processes, events, states, etc.
2   Capital letters stand for the speakers' first name initial
3   *Oral text* and *discourse* are here used synonymously
4   Similar scales have been argued for in the context of studies of conditional clauses by Klein-Andreu (1986), and by Silva-Corvalán (1985). Klein-Andreu presents a well-justified six-place scale along two axes, *assertiveness* and *actuality*, which we incorporate in Table 5.1
5   Our own intuitions about these relative values were corroborated by the results of a test given to 7 native speakers of Spanish from various countries. These speakers agreed that *probable* and *deber* are more compatible with *estoy casí seguro* 'I'm almost certain', while *posible* and *puede que* are more compatible with *lo dudo* 'I doubt it'
6   This definition is based on the one given for *frame* by Levinson (1983: 281), who states that 'A frame . . . is a body of knowledge that is evoked in order to provide an inferential base for the understanding of an utterance'
7   All hypothetical macro-frames were created by the researcher. Though this may perhaps be due to the nature of our data collection procedure, the sociolinguistic recorded dyadic conversation, it seems to us that it also reflects reluctance on the part of speakers to talk spontaneously about hypothetical situations
8   Information in parentheses identifies the source of the example: speaker's first name initial, sex and age, tape number, tape side and counter number. A series of dashes in the examples stands for language material omitted from the example because it is not relevant to the specific point being made in the discussion
9   The passage omitted here deals with the topic of how couples from even the same ethnic and cultural group find it extremely difficult to have a successful marriage
10 Language material within square brackets does not have phonetic realization, but is recoverable from the context.
11 This comparison would perhaps be more reliable if both discourses dealt with the same issue

References

Bernard Comrie, 'The syntax of causative constructions: cross-language similarities and divergencies', in *Syntax and semantics VI: The grammar of causative constructions*, edited by M. Shibatani (New York: Academic Press), 1976

Samuel Gili Gaya, *Curso superior de sintaxis española* (Barcelona: Biblograf), 1976

E. Goffman, 'On face-work: an analysis of ritual elements in social interaction', in *Communication in face to face interaction*, ed. by

J. Laver, and S. Hutcheson (Harmondsworth: Penguin), 1972, pp. 319–46. Reprinted from *Psychiatry* 1955, 18, 213–31

Wolfgang Klein and C. von Stutterheim, 'Text structure and referential movement' (MS) (Nijmegen: Max-Planck-Institüt für Psycholinguistik), n.d.

Flora Klein-Andreu, 'Speaker-based and reference-based factors in language: Non-past conditional sentences in Spanish', in *Studies in Romance linguistics*, ed. by Osvaldo Jaeggli and Carmen Silva-Corvalán (Amsterdam: Foris), 1986, pp. 99–119

W. Labov and D. Fanshel, *Therapeutic discourse* (New York: Academic Press), 1977

W. Labov and J. Waletsky, 'Narrative analysis: Oral versions of personal experience', in *Essays on the verbal and visual arts*, ed. by June Helm (Seattle: University of Washington Press), 1967, pp. 12–44

Willem Levelt, 'Linearization in discourse' (MS) (Nijmegen: Max-Planck-Institüt für Psycholinguistik), 1979

Willem Levelt, 'Linearization in describing spatial networks', in *Processes, beliefs, and questions*, ed. by Stanley Peters and E. Saarinen, (Dordrecht: Reidel), 1982, pp. 199–220

Stephen C. Levinson, *Pragmatics* (Cambridge: Cambridge University Press), 1983

C. Linde and W. Labov, 'Spatial networks as a site for the study of language and thought', *Language* 51, 1975, 929–39

John Lyons, *Semantics* (Cambridge: Cambridge University Press), 1977

Real Academia Española, *Esbozo de una nueva gramática de la lenqua española* (Madrid: Espasa-Calpe), 1973

H. Sacks, E. A. Schegloff and G. Jefferson, 'A simplest systematics for the organization of turn-taking for conversations', *Language* 50, 1974, 696–735

Deborah Schiffrin, 'Tense variation in narrative', *Language* 57, 1981, 45–62

Deborah Schiffrin, (ed.), *Meaning, form, and use in context* (Washington, DC: Georgetown University Press), 1984

Carmen Silva-Corvalán, 'Tense and aspect in oral Spanish narrative: Context and meaning', *Language* 59, 1983, 60–80

Carmen Silva-Corvalán, Modality and semantic change, in *Historical semantics. Historical word-formation*, ed. by J. Fisiak (Berlin: Mouton), 1985, pp. 547–72

Carmen Silva-Corvalán, 'On the meaning of Spanish modals' (MS), University of Southern California, 1987

J. Sinclair McH. and R. M. Coulthard, *Towards an analysis of discourse* (London: Oxford University Press), 1975

Deborah Tannen, 'Oral and literate strategies in spoken and written narrative', *Language* 58, 1982, 1–21

Teun A. Van Dijk, *Texto y contexto*. First published in English, Spanish translation by J. Domingo Moyano (Madrid: Cátedra), 1980

Chapter six

Speech styles in conversation as an interactive achievement

Margret Selting

1. Introduction

Although the study of language variation has quite a long tradition in linguistics, the study of speech styles in conversation has only recently begun to attract attention. So far, the analysis of language variation and the analysis of conversational interaction have been following largely independent lines.

Both in sociolinguistics and in stylistics variation in spoken language has been primarily analysed as a dependent variable. The speaker is assumed to adapt his speech style to the extralinguistic context. This view has become most influential in linguistics and still underlies recent approaches which tend to think of the speaker as actively choosing his or her speech style. Context and speech styles still tend to be viewed as static and homogeneous entities. The interactive constitution and negotiation of speech style variation within conversational interaction is only seldom analysed.

In this paper, I shall analyse the constitution of language variation in conversation as the choice and constitution of interactively meaningful speech styles. I want to argue that the choice of speech styles in conversation and the alter(n)ation of speech styles in style shifting and switching should not be seen as the juxtaposition of preconceived linguistic varieties dependent upon or a product of extralinguistic or contextual factors but as the constitution of dynamic interactively-achieved ways of speaking by which participants signal and achieve the constitution of global and local dynamic conversational contexts interactively. The relation between context and speech styles is an interdependent and reflexive one. Choice and alter(n)ation of speech styles are to be interpreted as contextualization cues which speakers use to achieve a (new) contextualization, and which are interpreted by the recipient relying on conventional and/or interactively negotiated co-occurrence expectations on different levels. Speech styles themselves are signalled and constituted by the use and alternation of speech style signalling cues in relation to previously used speech styles as a locally established 'norm', instance of comparison, or *tertium comparationis*. In short, I want to show that:

(1) an empirical *tertium comparationis* is negotiated and constituted within conversations,

(2) speech styles are locally negotiated and constituted in conversation, and

(3) speech styles are used as one device in conversation to achieve a specific contextualization and interpretation of turns.

In consequence, all the categories of *tertium comparationis*, speech style and context have to be conceived of as dynamic and interactively accomplished ones to account for the choice and alter(n)ation of speech styles in conversation.

In section 2 of this paper, some broad developments in the concept and analysis of styles in stylistics and sociolinguistics are discussed. The view taken here is related to recent research in pragmastylistics and interpretive sociolinguistics.

In section 3, transcripts of selected sequences of a conversation between a client and a social worker in a German *Sozialamt* are presented and speech style variation is analysed in conversational context. The items used as speech style-constituting cues suggest that at least in some cases, where the alternating varieties are not very different from each other, the notion of speech style in conversation might not be definable with respect to its boundaries, internal homogeneity and frequency of selected variables, but rather with respect to prototypical kernel cues and/or increasing or decreasing density of co-occurring more peripheral cues on different linguistic levels. Boundaries between speech styles are variable and flexible. This suggests that not only contexts but speech styles too are dynamic constructs which are constituted in interactions and not just realizations of preconceived varieties of language. Furthermore, participants' orientation to the speech styles used in prior turns in their activities of negotiating and alter(n)ating speech styles is interpreted as evidence for their interpretation of previously used speech style as a *tertium comparationis* for successive choices and alter(n)ations of speech styles. This suggests that the *tertium comparationis* for the analysis of stylistic variation in conversations should also be conceived of as a dynamic and interactively accomplished construct.

In section 4, finally, the analysis is summarized and conclusions are drawn.

2. The notion of speech style: from a dependent variable to contextualization cue

In sociolinguistics, the systematic empirical investigation of speech styles began with Labov's (cf. 1972) famous studies of stylistic and social stratification of speech variables. Speech styles were defined quantitatively with reference to the probability of the occurrence of selected linguistic variables dependent upon extralinguistic context and linguistic environment. Extralinguistic context as the product of the constellation of extralinguistic parameters, such as setting, region, social class, age, sex, and social networks in interaction with speakers' self-monitoring, is thought to affect style in a unidirectional way, with changes of contextual parameters being able to cause changes of style (cf. also Auer 1986: 23). The linguistic variables constituting style were conceived of as derived from common underlying deep structure forms as a theoretically reconstructable stable *tertium comparationis*; frequency measures of linguistic variables were taken of a speaker's linguistic output in whole episodes, regardless of internal differences within episodes. Speakers were thought to adapt their speech styles according to the extralinguistic context.

Similar assumptions seem to underly the earlier research in registers in British research (cf. Gregory 1967; Ellis/Ure 1969) or in the so-called context-stylistics (cf. Enkvist 1973; Crystal/Davy 1969). More explicitly than in sociolinguistics, the assumption of homogeneity led to problems of delineation of varieties from each other and of defining the *tertium comparationis*. However, a more active and context-constituting use of style has already been considered by, e.g., Enkvist (1973: 63f.) when he points to the use of style in literature to achieve certain effects or to the choice of style to define or manipulate context. But still a kind of conventional norm or expectation, pre-existent to situations of language-use, is assumed to function as a *tertium comparationis*.

Quite a different view was taken by Riffaterre (1973, original 1971). He rejected both the postulation of a linguistic or other static *tertium comparationis* preconceived to situations or texts and the separate level analysis mostly applied in e.g., quantitative stylistic analyses. Riffaterre suggested that in each text a new pattern is constituted which functions as the linguistic context for succeeding deviations from this pattern to create stylistic effects; established expectations *within* the text thus function as the *tertium comparationis* for successive unexpected structures. According to this view, therefore, Riffaterre seems to conceive of language-use as always being the result of constituting choices. Language-users are thought of as actively constituting their textual context as a *tertium comparationis* from which they deviate in order to create stylistic effects at particular points in the text; styles themselves are viewed as basically dynamic and actively constituted entities.

A dynamic and interpretive view of speech styles and contexts as interactively negotiated and constituted constructs is relied on for the analysis later in this paper. Participants are taken actively to use differing frequencies of linguistic variables in successive turns, or even to alternate between cues on different linguistic levels, to signal different typified speech styles and thereby indexically to constitute and negotiate context.

An approach like this also underlies more recent research in stylistics such as, for instance, Sandig's (1986) conception of a pragmatic and ethnomethodological approach to stylistics (cf. also Franck 1984) or to some extent also Tannen's (1984) analysis of conversational styles. Yet, although both Sandig (1986) and Tannen (1984) believe that style is involved in all interactions and that all sorts of interactive activities can be analysed with respect to style, and although both mention the stylistic use of language variation, neither of them develops this aspect of conversational style.

Yet, if language variation is used as a means and as a resource in conversational interaction to signal and constitute social and interactive meanings, this can clearly be seen as stylistic (cf. Sandig 1986: 164). In this view, language variation will not be analysed as a subsystem or as a variety of language, but as a resource for interacting members of a speech community to constitute social and interactive meanings in discourse on the basis of shared interpretations of established syntagmatic and paradigmatic relations and contrasts within conversational situations or episodes (cf. Hymes 1974).

According to this perspective, Gumperz (1982) analysed conversational code-switching and stylistic alternations of codes in bilingual as well as other language varieties taken from 'monolingual' situations, as devices constituting conversational meanings and contexts, calling them 'contextualization cues' (idem). More or less following an interpretive sociolinguistic conception like that of Gumperz, the role of speech styles in the constitution of dynamic contexts in interaction has also been recognized by other researchers (for the German research scene in this respect compare, for instance, the analyses in Auer/di Luzio 1983; Auer 1986a; Gülich/ Paul 1983; Hinnenkamp 1987; Selting 1983, 1985). Some recent analyses suggest that the choice of speech styles and different types of alternation of speech styles, i.e. abrupt switching and gradual shifting between varieties, are used by speakers to produce global and local indexical meanings in conversations. The choice and/or negotiation of an unmarked speech style in conversation, mostly at the beginning of an interaction or conversation or after a major change in, e.g., participant relations, seems to be more related to the constitution of global contexts and interpretive frames, whereas the alter(n)ation of styles seems to be more related to the constitution of local interactive functions in, e.g., reinforcing local interactive obligations for the recipient (cf. Selting 1983, 1985). Although in these studies context has been conceived of as a dynamic construct, speech styles are generally taken to be more or less preconceived varieties of languages which participants use.

Yet if speech in conversation is looked at more closely, the question of the definition of speech styles arises again. For it is often not entire varieties which are juxtaposed; rather features attributable to different preconceived varieties are used side by side. In some cases, single cues are systematically differentiated in a conversation (cf. also Selting 1985a).

The traditional definition of speech styles with respect to the frequency of selected variables does not allow for the analysis of single or scarcely used, perhaps stereotypical, features of a marked speech style within an otherwise unmarked speech style. These seem only to be explainable with respect to a speaker's idiosyncracy, interference, etc., and not as systematic variation of speech styles.

If, however, these features are systematically differentiated and only occur in restricted conversational contexts, they may be used as single strong contextualization cues to constitute and signal these conversational contexts. The concept of contextualization cue (Gumperz 1982, cf. above) thus offers an explanation: some marked and perhaps stereotypical indicators of speech styles can be used as single contextualization cues. This in turn suggests that in the perception and interpretation of talk, at least some speech styles are conceived of as communicative idealizations constituted by some prototypical kernel features strong enough to be usable as single contextualization cues, together with other more peripheral features which tend to (but need not?) co-occur with such kernel features.[1] With respect to peripheral features, it is not always the frequency of selected variables or of features on one linguistic level, but the density of co-occurring cues on different linguistic levels, which seem to be important in many cases (cf. below).

Thus, participants' use of variation in conversational interaction suggests that they conceive of speech styles as dynamic, internally structured phenomena to be constituted in speech, not as homogeneous entities, as usually perceived in linguistic research. This is reinforced when participants in choosing and adopting styles orient the styles used in prior turns as an empirical, interactively-constituted *tertium comparationis* in conversation, rather than to any theoretical norm. This conception of styles as basically dynamic and interactively accomplished is compatible with recent developments both in cognitive science, where the notions of dynamic systems and of prototypes are well established (cf. Rosch 1973), and in ethnomethodology, where the interactive achievement of categories is a major concern (cf. e.g. Sacks/Schegloff/Jefferson 1974, Levinson 1983: chapter 6).

3. Speech styles in conversation from a German *Sozialamt*

In this section I analyse data from a conversation in a German *Sozialamt* (social security office) in the western part of the Ruhr area.[2] First, the extracts are presented and situated in a global setting. Then, formal features of speech used by the participants are analysed with respect to their use as speech style-constituting cues. Finally, I shall analyse the constitution and alter(n)ation of speech styles as signalling cues to constitute the 'global institutional' and the 'local conversational' context.

3.1 Extracts from conversation

The following extracts are taken from a conversation between an official and a client in a German *Sozialamt*, an institution where citizens in need can ask for financial and other help. A basically formal framing of these conversations is associated with their setting and the interlocutors' participant roles: the conversations take place in the office of a social worker or other official and during official consultation times. The participants take the roles of social worker/official ('Beamter'), as a member of the institution, and client, as a person in need who seeks support or who has been invited to the office to give further information concerning his or her application for support.

In spite of the basic framing of conversations as formal, different sequences are dealt with on different conversational levels, i.e. more formal or less formal, and with different forms of reciprocity, co-operative or antagonistic. Accordingly, there is no one homogeneous speech style used throughout, e.g. a 'standard' speech style that might be associated with 'formal' contexts. Rather, a baseline speech style and alterations towards opposing poles of speakers' repertoires are used to constitute and negotiate conversational levels and forms of reciprocity.

111

The participants in the conversation from which the following extracts have been taken have known each other from the client K's previous visits to the *Sozialamt*. K is a middle-aged woman dependent on social security. She was supposed to move into a new flat which she rented more than a month before the present conversation. Although the rent has been paid by the *Sozialamt*, K has not yet moved in, and although the *Sozialamt* offered her the money to buy furniture, she has not yet bought any. The official, B, now suspects that K is living with a close friend and that she is not interested in moving into her new flat. If this is true, it might have certain consequences since, according to official regulations, if a couple are living together, one has to support the other, regardless of legal status. In this case, it might mean that K's friend would have to support her and the *Sozialamt* might be able to reduce her support.

In the initial part of the conversation from which the first extract is taken, B enquires about K's ways of living, to find out with whom she is staying at the moment. This enquiry on the formal institutional level is his most important objective in the conversation.[3] (An outline of conversational development and ratios between cues are given in the margins. These will be explained in detail in the following sections.)

Extract (1)

Outline of conversational development; ratios between standard, unmarked and marked colloquial cues

1 B: ja Frau- K,. der Herr Á war vorhin hier'
   well Mrs K a little while ago Mr A was here

Conversational opening
Ratios: B: 2:5:0
         K: 3:4:0

2 K: ja, der is grád da und ich bin mit m Bus sofórt
   yes he is just there and I have by bus immediately
3 B: ja-
                               yes
4 K: zurückgekomm, er sacht ich soll herkomm,
   come back   he says I shall come here
5 B: ja, (?hörn Se
                             yes listen
6 B: ma án hier, ?) er hat mir ja gesácht daß Sie bei
   to this here he said to me   that you with
7 B: ihm warn,
   him were
8 K: (kurz) hja,
                   (short) yes
9 B: . mir is ímmer no nich klár wo Sie- sich- áufhaltn,
   to me it is still not clear where you are staying

Initiation of formal conversational level
Topic: K's ways of living (antagonistic)
Ratio: B: 1:4:0 (line 9)

10 K: ((atmet hörbar)) ((etwas langsamer)) na ich
   ((audible breathing)) ((slower))   well I
11 war auch bei- (? Herrn ?) Á' dann war ich bei B'
   was also with (? Mr ?) A then war ich bei B
12 B: Sie sóllten sich do in Ihrer *Wóhnung* ma aufhaltn,
   you should after all in your flat stay

Ratio: B: 2:3:0 (line 12)

13 K: na *wíe* denn, . ságn Se mir bítte wíe, ((atmet))
   but how then tell me please how ((breathes))
14 B: (? is do nich schwér' ?)
                   (? is after all not difficult ?)

```
15 ┌ B: . seit éinṃ Mónat, oder gút eim Monat zahln wir
   │      since one month or quite one month have we been
16 │ K:                                        ich kánn do/
   └                                          but I can/
17 ┌ B: für Sie schon ne Míete,                                    Self-defence against B's
   │      paying for you a rent                                    accusation
18 │ K:               ich háb Ihṇ doch gesacht daß                 Ratio: K: 3:2:0
   └                 but I have told you        that
19   K: ich im vorigen Monat ↓ kránk war, und da
        I in the last month      was ill    and then
20       war ich auch bei Herrn A wie ich wie ich gelégṇ
        was I   also with Mr A when I/   when I was stay-            ┌──────────────┐
21       hab-* ich wéiß ja sons nich wohín, ((atmet))                Side remark
        ing in bed after all I don't know where else                Ratio: K: 0:2:0
22       und héute vormittach war ich auch beim Árzt' ich múß       └──────────────┘
        and this morning      was I  also to the doctor I must
23       mich ↓ wáschṇ* . a is ja wohl klár, ne'                    ┌──────────────┐
        myself wash      that is no doubt clear, isn't it           Side remark
24   B: jaa' éinverstandṇ,                                          Ratio: K: 0:2:0
        yes accepted                                                └──────────────┘
25   K: (lachend) ja- also- . un deshalb ↓ kám das,*               Ratio: K: 4:3:0
        (laughingly) well so and therefore came that
26       ich weiß nur wirklich- ich wóllt auch nich mehr
        I know just really     I wanted also not again
27       herkommṇ, also ich war/ ((schnupft)) . . nich' un wenn
        come here thus I was    ((sniffs))         and when
28 ┌ K: alles ↑ drín is' ↑ fértig'* ich háb doch meine Wohnung,
   │     everything is in ready   I do have my flat
29 └ B: äh-
30   B: ja, die ham Se schon só lange' ohne sie zu bewóhn
        well you have it for so long now without living in
31       auf unsere Kostṇ,
        it at our expense
32   K: ↑ ja wenn was drín is' un un un ís jetzt* und
        well when something is in it and and and is now and         ┌──────────────┐
33 │ K: (schnell) jétz hab ich auch Angst weil die Miete no         Side-remark
   │     (fast)    now am I    also afraid because the rent         Ratio: 2:3:1
34 │ B:       (kurz) ja'
   └           (short) yes
35   K: nich bezahlt is, ạḷṣọ ich tráu mich da áu ni mehr hin,*     └──────────────┘
        has not been paid so I don't dare to go there now
36 ┌ B: . wann warn Se denn zulétzt mal in Ihrer Wohnung,
   │     when were you the last time in your flat
37 │ K: . solln die Leute-
   └     shall the people
38   B: in der neugemietetṇ die no léer is,
        in the newly rented one which is still empty
```

In later parts of the conversation, when informal topics, like K's family and an incident at a wedding party are discussed on a more informal conversational level, B tends to return to his enquiry and in these sequences switches from an informal, co-operative, to a formal, antagonistic, way of communicating. This is signalled and constituted by his choice and alter(n)ation of speech styles:

Extract (2)

```
347   B: (relativ laut) also írgndwie müssṇ wa doch mal          Conclusion from previous
          (relatively loud) now somehow must we after all        enquiry
348       allmählich Nägel mit Kópfṇ machen, entwéder Sie        Formal level
          now make nails with heads            either you        Topic: K's movement into
349 ┌ B: beziehn hier Ihre Wóhnung' . ạ̣h-                        new flat (co-operative)
    │     move here into your flat                                Ratio: B: 7:3:0
350 │ K:                            ↑ ich háb Ihṇ doch
    └                                but I told you
```

351 K: letzmal schon gesacht wenn se so weit is ich zieh   Ratio: K: 3:6:0
      last time already   when it is ready   I move

352 ⌈K: lie:bend gern da ein-
      gladly   in there

353 ⌊B: jȧȧ, . da müssṇ S sich aber
                               well there must you care   Ratio: B: 1:2:1

354 B: ganz klein wenig drum kümmern,
      a little bit for

355 K: . na ich hab mi auch gehn lassṇ- un da/ dámals wars
      well I did let myself also go and th/then was it

356 ⌈K: mit Herrn G, er hat Ihṇ ja jesächt wenn die- . aber
      with Mr G   he did say to you   if the   but   Ratio: K: 2:7:0

357 ⌊B: jaa,
                                           yes

358 K: dann- . dann hattṇ se am dríttṇ Jubiläum- die hattṇ
      then . then had they on the third a jubilee (or
                                            celebration) they had

359   am síebensten Jubiläum- die hattṇ am zéhntṇ jubiläum
       on the seventeenth a jubilee they had on the tenth a jubilee

360 ⌈K: und Ínge wárte mal' Inge wárte mal,
      and Inge wait a bit Inge wait a bit
  |
361 ⌊B: (? aha ?) wat war denn mit der Hóchzeit,   Change to informal level and
                  what was then at the wedding   everyday frame

362 B: wo die Frau Ǵ mim- . Brótmesser angeblich- irgndwo   Topic: Wedding incident
      where Mrs G with a bread knife allegedly somewhere

363 ⌈B: los gegangn sein soll, ja, ich hab das (? so ?) gehört,   Ratio: B: 0:4:1
      at went   yeah I heard that so
  |
364 ⌊K: ángeblich'   ạlso ịch-. also
               allegedly   so I   so

365 K: ich sa:ch da níx zu, aber- . äh wír wissen von unsern   Ratio: K: 2:9:2
      I say nothing about it but   we know it from our

366 K: Háuswirt' von Herrn E' . ṇe' un dér muß es ja wíssṇ,
      landlord from Mr E don't we and he must know it

367 B: ja,
                                yeah

368 K: da war Poltera : md von seiner Tóchter' . un da hat ihr
      there was eve-of-the-wedding party   and there has her
                                            of his daughter

369   Mánn wohl mit ner Ándern getanzt, ích wéiß es nich,
       husband with an other danced   I don't know it

370 ⌈K: war damals nich béi da-. gíng se lós un dann hát s   Ratio: K: 1:7:1
      was then not with them then she flew at and then she
  |
371 ⌊B: jaa, richtig, hab ich gehört,
               yes right I heard about it

372 K: sich mit- ihrm Mánn wohl áuch gehabt, un dann m äḥ-
      had herself too with her husband   and then

373   is die Polizéi gerufn worn' . un da- wissn Se' is son
       is the police were called   and then you know is such

374   kléines Haus, da geht die Tréppe so steil hoch, un da
       a small house there the stairs are so steep   and

375   hat se wohl gestandn nur, un kéin Schrítt wéiter,
       there she stood   and no step further

376   un dann ham se se nahher mítgenomm, paar Mal zur
       and then they took her later with them few times for

377 ⌈K: Áusnüchterung, ((schnupft))
      sobering up   ((sniffs))
  |
378 ⌊B: ja, die s/ . die sóll auch sehr   Change back to formal level
        yes she s/ she is also said to

379 ⌈B: eifersüchtig auf Sie sein, ne' . die Frau G, ne'   Topic: K's ways of living
      be very jealous of you   isn't she the Mrs G isn't she   (antagonistic)
  |
380 ⌊K: das kann (laut) séin,   Ratio: B: 3:0:0
                               that can (loudly) be

381 K: aber ich hab- ich hab éhrlich nix, (lachend) also-*
      but I have   I have really nothing (laughing) so

Before analysing these extracts in detail, the speech style signalling cues are dealt with.

3.2 Speech style constituting cues

The term 'speech style' is used here to refer to the use of prototypical kernel and/or co-occurring peripheral cues on different linguistic levels to signal, induce and constitute typified linguistic varieties which are paradigmatically opposed to other typified varieties in a speaker's or a community's repertoire of varieties. The relation between style constituting cues and typified speech styles is an interdependent and reflexive one: as speakers and recipients can rely on everyday knowledge of cues for certain typified styles, these cues may be used to constitute and induce such a typified style. The styles thus constituted are not necessarily clear-cut entities; they are rather taken to be interlocutors' communicative idealizations and interpretive constructs, hence their labelling as 'typified'.

Alter(n)ation of kernel and/or co-occurring peripheral cues of different typified styles in the same conversational setting is referred to here as 'style-shifting', i.e. alteration, or 'style-switching', i.e. alternation. In style-shifting, there is a gradual style alteration, in general an increase or decrease of cues for a previously used style to signal a gradual shift towards another. In style-switching, there is a sudden alternation between cues for a previously used style and cues for another, often more distant, style to signal the sudden switch from one style to another (cf. esp. Auer/di Luzio 1983 for a very similar distinction with respect to code alternations among bilingual speakers in conversations).

In the extracts, speakers B and K construct speech-styles which range between the poles of so-called typified 'standard' (Northern High German) and a typified 'marked colloquial', incorporating stigmatized cues of the Ruhr area dialect, with a so-called 'unmarked colloquial' being used as the baseline speech style by both. Yet the boundaries between these styles are not clear-cut. In most utterances, speakers use cues of more than one typified style side by side. They seem to use kernel cues and/or the density of co-occurring peripheral cues to signal their baseline style and style shifting and switching.

Prototypical kernel cues are conceived of here as the most characteristic cues of a speech style which can be used by speakers to signal and construct a particular style most clearly, and these are often looked upon (and talked about) as the most typical features of that style (cf. also Sandig 1986: 258ff.). If they are systematically differentiated by speakers, i.e. if their use is restricted to specific conversational environments or activities, kernel cues can be used by themselves as key symbols in utterances to constitute a specific style and a specific contextualization of that utterance in the conversation.

In contrast to kernel cues, more peripheral cues do not by themselves induce a particular style but seem to belong to a range of cues between, and perhaps common to, neighbouring styles. Their isolated allocation to one style is often a difficult and vague decision; it is only their density which allows the identification of styles. Density can be defined as the relative number of co-occurring peripheral cues for one style in relation to the cues for others in an utterance. If, then, the number of cues for an unmarked colloquial speech style is high and the number of cues for the standard style in the same utterance is low, the style can be typified as an unmarked colloquial one. (For examples, see section 3.2.4.)

The most important difference between kernel and peripheral cues is thus their required density to constitute a speech style: while kernel cues can be used by themselves or in low number, more peripheral cues have to be more numerous.

The difference between kernel and peripheral cues is most relevant at the poles of the continuum. In the extracts presented here, kernel cues are used to distinguish the marked colloquial style from the unmarked colloquial. Kernel cues for the standard style, which might in general be expected at the syntactic, lexical, and semantic levels, are not differentiated by the speakers here. A possible explanation could be that these speakers generally tend towards the unmarked colloquial style and shift more freely towards the marked colloquial, whereas the standard seems to be generally dispreferred.

In the analysis proposed here, speech styles can only be identified and allocated to typified styles by considering formal linguistic *and* sequential conversational criteria. In the following, three criteria are used for the analysis of styles in conversations:

(1) the systematic differentiation of kernel cues in the constitution of conversational contexts resulting in internal co-occurrence tendencies and restrictions between kernel style constituting cues, conversational levels and activities, and the form of reciprocity established or aimed at;

(2) co-occurrence tendencies between kernel cues and/or more peripheral cues on different linguistic levels, resulting in increasing or decreasing densities of style constituting cues;

(3) recipients' reactions to the choice and alter(n)ations of styles as manifestations of their interpretations of them.

In a first step, predominantly using criteria (1) and (2), the typified styles used and signalled by the speakers will be broadly identified. Following this, a more detailed analysis predominantly using criterion (3) will focus on the interactive functions of the use and alter(n)ation of styles in conversation.

3.2.1 The unmarked colloquial style

In most sequences, standard and colloquial cues are used side by side to signal an unmarked colloquial style intermediate between the poles. This style seems to be used in antagonistic and co-operative sequences on both formal and informal conversational levels. Yet the delineation of this style is most difficult as it is not the absolute, but the relative density of cues in relation to surrounding utterances which is important and which is used to signal the unmarked colloquial style versus style-shifting towards the poles. The boundaries of the unmarked colloquial itself are rather fuzzy and variable.

Speakers in the conversation analysed here use the following cues[4] in relatively low density to signal an unmarked colloquial speech style side by side with standard cues in relatively low density. (Standard orthographic forms are given in parenthesis here to ensure identification.)

(1) On the *phonological level*:
  (a) spirantization of [k]: *gesacht* [gəzɑxt] ('gesagt'), *gefracht* [gəfʁɑːxt] ('gefragt'), *vormittach* [foʁmɪtɑx] ('vormittag'), *gekricht* [gəkʁɪçt] ('gekriegt');
  (b) word-internal omission or assimilation of sounds: *meintwegn* [maentveŋ] ('meinetwegen'), *wenistens* [venɪstəns] ('wenigstens'), *Poltera:md* [pɔltʁɑːmt] ('Polterabend'), *nahher* [nɑʰheʁ] ('nachher'), *sonswo* [zɔnsvo] ('sonstwo'), *aso* [ɑzo] ('also');
  (c) dropped final consonants in monosyllabic particles, etc: *nich* [nɪç] or *ni* [nɪ] ('nicht'), *no no* [nɔ] ('noch'), *do* [dɔ] ('doch'), *au* [ao] ('auch'), *un* [ʌn] ('und'), *jetz* [jɛts] ('jetzt'), *ma* [mɑ] ('mal');
  (d) substitution of [j] for [g] by K as in *Jeld* [jɛlt] ('Geld') and *jesacht* [jəzɑxt] ('gesagt').
(2) On the *morphophonemic level*:
  (a) reduced, assimilated or deleted [ən] suffixes: *aufhaltn* [aofhaltn] ('aufhalten'), *warn* [vɑːn]

('waren'), *gegangn* [gəgɑŋ] ('gegangen'),
Angabm [ɑngɑːbm] ('Angaben'), *sagn* [zɑŋ]
('sagen'), *habm* [hɑːbm] or *ham* [hɑm]
('haben');

(b) dropped suffixes in first person singular verbs:
ich hab [ɪç hɑp] ('ich habe'), *ich brauch*
[ɪç bʁɑox] ('ich brauche');

(c) dropped final consonant in third person
singular verbforms of the verb *sein*: *is* [ɪs]
('ist') or further reduction to [ş] or [s] and
cliticization with a preceding word: *daș* [dɑş]
('das ist');

(d) reduced unstressed indefinite articles: *n̩* [n̩] or
n [n] ('ein'), *ne* [nə] ('eine'), *nen* [nən] or *ein̩*
[ɑen̩] ('einen'), *nem* [nəm] or *eim̩* [ɑem̩]
('einem'); or further reduction and cliticization
to preceding words: *son* [zon] ('so ein'), *mim*
[mɪm] ('mit einem');

(e) weakened and cliticized unstressed pronouns:
Se [zə] or *s* [s] ('sie'), *wa* [vɐ] ('wir'), *wars*
[vɑːs] ('war es'), *hadder* [hɑdɐ] ('hat er').

(3) On the *syntactic level*:

(a) dropped articles as in *komm Se nächste Mal*
(line 601) instead of *das nächste Mal* or further
reduction as in *letzmal* (line 351) instead of
letztes Mal or *das letzte Mal*;

(b) use of *wo* as a generalized embedding
pronoun as in *auf der Hochzeit wo die Frau G*
instead of *auf der* or *als*.

(4) On the *lexical level* the following idioms and expressions
seem to be used as cues for a colloquial style: *Nägel mit
Köpfn machen* (line 348), *sich mit jemandem haben* (line
370f.).

(5) On the *semantic level* a high frequency of modal and
vagueness particles seems to be characteristic of a
colloquial style. The particles used in this conversation
are: *ja, immer, noch, doch, mal, schon, denn, auch, also,
sonst, wohl*. In some cases, the particle *so* seems to be used
as an intensifier: *so lange* (line 30), *so steil hoch* (line 374):
this contrasts with the more standard form of intensifying
as in *sehr eifersüchtig* (line 378f.).

A variety of structural features may be used as cues constituting the
unmarked colloquial style. Among these cues, some assimilations
especially can be intuitively graded according to their distance from

the standard realizations in terms of the processes involved in deriving them from the standard (cf. also Auer 1986a on style shifting in Southern German speech):

e.g.:

haben	→	habm	→	ham	
[habən]		[habm]		[ham]	
nichts	→	nichs	→	nix	
[nıçts]		[nıçs]		[nıks]	
mit dem	→	mit m	→	mim	
[mıt dem]		[mıtm, mı²m]		[mım]	
hat er	→	hatter	→	hadder	
[hat²ɛɐ]		[hatɐ]		[hadɐ]	

Yet, *habm* and *ham* are both used in utterances in which the co-occurring cues suggest standard, unmarked colloquial, or marked colloquial style by B. On the other hand, K seems to restrict the use of *ham* to unmarked and marked colloquial styles. *Nix* is used by K in unmarked and marked colloquial utterances, whereas B only uses this realization once in a marked colloquial utterance. *hadder* is only twice used by B in a marked colloquial environment. Likewise, the realizations *mim* and *mit m* and other assimilations like *anne, inne*, etc., are used too scarcely to provide a meaningful contrast with respect to alternative realizations. As a consequence, these different realizations and assimilations have to be taken as free variants here; in some cases their choice seems to be motivated by accent and rhythm patterns rather than by stylistic choices.[5]

3.2.2 The marked colloquial pole

Throughout the entire conversation B's use of the items *dat* [dat] and *wat* [vat] is systematically restricted to co-operative sequences or to utterances where he seemingly wants to establish reciprocity as co-operative (cf. extract (2): line 361). In all other sequences, especially in antagonistic ones, the cues *das* [das] and *was* [vas] are used. K, however, almost always uses *das/was*; her few uses of *dat* are also restricted to very informal co-operative sequences.

Another cue which both B and K seem to restrict to co-operative sequences is the use of non-standard case[5], e.g.,

(a) use of accusative for standard dative: *von unsern Hauswirt* (extract (2): line 365); and

(b) use of nominative for standard accusative: *kéin Schritt wéiter* (extract (2): line 375).

The use of the t/d substitution and of non-standard case is thus systematically restricted in the entire conversation, with all utterances in which they occur being interpretable as establishing, or negotiating a co-operative form of reciprocity on a rather informal conversational level. The hypothesis is justified that B and K use these cues as kernel cues for the marked colloquial style.

A third cue, the separated use of pronominal adverbs like *dabei, darum, damit, danach, dazu*, etc. as in, e.g., *da müssṇ S sich aber ganz klein wenig drum kümmern* (line 353) and *sa:ch da níx zu* (line 365) seems to come quite near to a kernel cue for the marked colloquial style. Nevertheless two occurrences of this cue out of fifteen in the entire conversation are used in utterances in which the density of co-occurring cues in one case suggests an unmarked colloquial and in the other a rather standard style. On the other hand, the four uses of a non-separated pronominal adverb in the entire conversation always occur in utterances in which the speaker otherwise signals an unmarked colloquial style which still carries quite a high number of standard cues. This suggests that the non-separation of pronominal adverbs rather tends towards the standard pole, whereas the separation is in general use as a cue of the marked colloquial style. In this case, at least one occurrence of the marked colloquial cue occurring in a standard environment would have to be treated as either an exception or as a single cue compensated for or neutralized by its environment. In view of the single occurrence of this, however, the separated use of the pronominal adverb will be treated as a third kernel cue for the marked colloquial style here.[6]

Apart from the use of kernel cues, the signalling of marked colloquial speech is achieved by the use of a high density of co-occurring peripheral cues which – albeit with lower density – are also used to signal the unmarked colloquial style. For an example see lines 361–77 in extract (2).

3.2.2 The standard pole

The opposite pole to the marked colloquial seems to be the standard, especially Northern High German pronunciation. This style is almost exclusively signalled in antagonistic sequences by using the full, unreduced and unassimilated or at least syllabic, forms of lexemes and suffixes as in *auch* [aox], *nicht* [nɪçt], *vorigen* [foʁɪgən], *müssṇ* [mʏsṇ], *machen* [maxən], *wissen* [vɪsən], *Kostṇ* [kɔstṇ], *herkomṃ* [heʁkɔmṃ]. An example here is extract (2): lines 378–9.

As these cues are also used in other conversational contexts, in low density, they cannot be used as kernel cues. In fact, the standard pole at which only standard cues are used is seldom reached. In most cases, speakers move towards this pole by increasing the density of standard cues in relation to prior utterances, while still using some reduced or assimilated forms. Examples of a high density of standard cues can be seen in extract (1): lines 18–19 and 36.

3.2.4 Density of cues

In signalling and constituting speech styles on the continuum between the standard and the marked colloquial poles, speakers use the density of co-occurring cues on different linguistic levels as style constituting devices. That is, the relative number of co-occurring cues for one style in relation to the cues for others in an utterance shifts along the continuum of styles.

Consequently, the continuum of styles can be represented as follows. Typified styles are constituted either by kernel cues plus a high density of peripheral cues or by a high density of peripheral cues only. Boundaries between typified speech styles are not clear-cut.

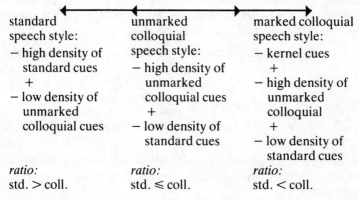

standard
speech style:
– high density of
  standard cues
+
– low density of
  unmarked
  colloquial cues

ratio:
std. > coll.

unmarked
colloquial
speech style:
– high density of
  unmarked
  colloquial cues
+
– low density of
  standard cues

ratio:
std. ≤ coll.

marked colloquial
speech style:
– kernel cues
+
– high density of
  unmarked
  colloquial
+
– low density of
  standard cues

ratio:
std. < coll.

The measurement of density thus presupposes the allocation of single cues to one style along the continuum. This is, however, in some cases an extremely *ad hoc* procedure. For instance, the difference between the variants of the pronouns of address *Sie* in its full and *Se* in its reduced form is not only one of style but also of stress. If, however, it is assumed that an isolated occurrence of the full form *Sie* can be quasi-neutralized as a stylistic cue by the use of a high density of co-occurring cues for another style, it can nevertheless be allocated as a single cue to the standard.

To exemplify the density of cues, some intuitively clear examples will be listed. Because of the above mentioned problems of allocation, the quantitative ratio of cues for one style can only be given as a sometimes quite *ad hoc* decision, leaving problems of allocation largely aside. Thus, in some examples intuitively recognizable as belonging to the standard pole, speakers use a higher number of cues for the standard than for the unmarked colloquial and no cues for the marked colloquial at all; density of standard cues is higher than in the surrounding utterances, e.g.:

example	standard cues	unmarked coll. cues	marked coll. cues
(2): 378f.	*auch, Sie, sehr eifersüchtig*	–	–
ratio:	3	: 0	: 0
(1): 25–7	*also, auch, herkomm̩, also*	*un, wollt, nich*	–
ratio:	4	: 3	: 0

Along the continuum, we find the highest number of cues slowly moving towards the colloquial and the marked colloquial cues. In signalling the unmarked colloquial, speakers still do not use the kernel cues for the marked colloquial style:

example	standard cues	unmarked coll. cues	marked coll. cues
(1):9	*Sie*	*is, no, nich, aufhaltn*	–
ratio:	1	: 4	: 0
(1):12	*Sie, aufhaltn̩*	*solltn, do, ma*	–
ratio:	2	: 3	: 0

In utterances intuitively recognizable as marked colloquial, the density is highest among the cues for the unmarked and marked colloquial styles:[7]

example	standard cues	unmarked coll. cues	marked coll. cues
(2):365–9	*wissen, wir*	*sa:ch, nix, un, wissn, Poltera:md, un, ner, Andern, nich*	*da . . . zu, von unsern Hauswirt*
ratio:	2	: 9	: 2
(2):361–3	–	*mim, irgndwo, los gegangn, wo (rel.)*	*wat*
ratio:	0	: 4	: 1

Nevertheless, even if these cases are intuitively allocatable, no absolute points seem to be definable where one style can be separated from a neighbouring one. For this reason, a higher density of cues for a specific style, especially the poles of the continuum, in relation to preceding utterances, will be analysed as shifting towards a typified style.

3.3 Choice and alter(n)ation of speech styles in conversation

The constitution and alter(n)ation of speech styles by both speakers in the extracts is now analyzed in detail with respect to their context constituting functions.

Extract (1): Extract (1), see p. 112–3, represents the beginning of the conversation. In the opening (lines 1–8), both B and K start with speech in which standard and unmarked colloquial cues are used side by side. The ratio between cues in B's utterances is 2:5:0 (*daβ, Sie : hörn, Se, ma, gesacht, warn : –*). K's ratio is 3:4:0 (*und, zurückgekommṇ, herkommṇ: is, grad, mit n, sacht : –*). In comparison with the styles used later in the conversation, both B and K start with the so-called unmarked colloquial.

A high density of unmarked colloquial cues is also used by B in line 9, where he initiates the enquiry about K's ways of living. The topic initiated here clearly constitutes a formal conversational level. B's ratio of style constituting cues is 1:4:0 (*Sie : is, no, nich, aufhaltn : –*).

In his first question on this topic in line 9, B seems to refer back to previous conversations and states his lack of knowledge with respect to K's ways of living, which seems to be implicitly opposed to his official right and obligation to know. In his further contributions, B points out the contradiction between the *Sozialamt*'s paying the rent for K's new flat and K's not yet having moved in. B's contributions all take the form of statements of facts which K interprets as accusations against which she has to defend herself. The form of reciprocity is clearly antagonistic here.

First in this enquiry, B uses predominantly colloquial cues on the phonological and morphophonemic levels, suggesting the unmarked colloquial as the basic style used. Following line 9, compare especially line 12 (*Sie, aufhaltṇ : solltn, do, ma : –*) and line 15 (*einṃ, wir, Sie : eim, zahln, ne : –*). In lines 30–1 and 36–8, however, the density of standard cues may be slightly higher (*sie, bewohṇ, unsere, Kostṇ : ham, Se : –* and *zuletzt, mal, neugemietetṇ : warn, Se, no, is : –*).

K, on the other hand, tends to use more cues of a standard speech style; she tends to pronounce the final consonants in words like *auch* (lines 11, 20, 22, 26, 33), *doch* (lines 18, 28), *und* (lines 2, 19, 22, 32) and *jetzt* (line 32). She furthermore tends to use at least a syllabic [n̩] when reducing [ən] in suffixes: *zurückkommn̩, herkommn̩* (lines 4, 27), *Ihn̩* (line 18), *vorigen* (line 19), *gelégn̩* (line 20) and *waschn̩* (line 23). Her use of predominantly unmarked colloquial cues is restricted to the utterances in lines 13 (*sagn, Se*), 21 (*sons, nich*), 23 (*a, is*) and 32–5 (*jetz, hab, no, nich, is, trau, au, ni*). In the last-mentioned utterance, she also uses the marked colloquial cue *da . . . hin* (line 35). K's tendency towards a more standard style is found in utterances in which she defends herself against B's implicit and explicit accusations. As she too uses the unmarked colloquial as basic in the conversational opening and in other more co-operative sequences like those in extract (2), K's use of a rather standard style in her self-defence might be interpretable here as her reaction against B's definition of reciprocity as antagonistic.

In contrast, the utterances in which K signals a shift towards an unmarked or even a marked colloquial style are all side remarks in her arguments to defend herself. In these side remarks, K seems to induce and set up points of shared assumptions between herself and B. In these side-remarks K, then, tries to establish or negotiate points of non-antagonistic or even co-operative reciprocity, and her style shifts towards a more colloquial signal and reinforces these attempts.

Extract (2) Later in the conversation, see p. 113–4, B alternates between the formal and the informal conversational level, sometimes trying to exploit seemingly informal topics for a continuation of his formal enquiry of K. Extract (2) represents one such occurrence in which B seems to adopt an informal conversational level for strategic purposes.

In lines 347–9, B here initiates a new phase in the conversation by explicating his conclusion from the previous enquiry: something definite now has to be done, otherwise K will have to face negative consequences. By stating this issue and his warning plainly, B defocuses his enquiry about K's ways of living and focuses on future action which K has to take in order to move into her new flat.

In contrast with the speech of extract (1), B adopts a rather mixed style in his initiation of this new phase in lines 347–9: his ratio between cues on the phonological and morphophonemic levels is 7 : 3 : 0 (*also, müssn̩, doch, mal, Köpfn̩, machen, Sie : irgndwie, wa, beziehn : –*). In addition, however, the idiom *Nägel mit Köpfn̩ machen* could be counted as a cue signalling a colloquial style, although the morphophonemic cues used in it are standard ones.

If B's speech here can be located somewhere between the standard and the unmarked colloquial, K in her following assertion that she is willing to move into her new flat as soon as possible clearly tends towards the unmarked colloquial. Her ratio between cues is 3:6:0 (*Ihn, doch, liebend : hab, letzmal, gesacht, se, is, zieh : –*). This suggests that K interprets B's utterance as the initiation of a more co-operative phase, which she herself welcomes on the level of styles by shifting away from the more standard as predominantly used in extract (1).

B in line 353–4 now clearly shifts towards the marked colloquial; this he signals by the use of the separated pronominal adverb *darum* as *da . . . drum*. His ratio between cues here is 1:2:1 (*müssn : S* as a reduced pronoun of address, *ganz klein wenig* without a preceding indefinite article : *da . . . drum*). Although B here points out K's lack of initiative, he signals a more co-operative form of reciprocity by shifting his style towards the marked colloquial.

This interpretation is confirmed by K's reaction in lines 355–6, where she admits some fault and explains her lack of initiative by reference to delay in receiving help from a friend called G. She again signals an unmarked colloquial style with a ratio between cues of 2:7:0 (*auch, Ihn : hab, mi, gehn, lassn, un, wars, jesacht : –*). Immediately following, however, in lines 358–60, K uses a higher number of standard cues again (*hattn* and all ordinal numerals are realized with at least a syllabic suffix, the only colloquial cue being *se*), but here the repeated utterance structure indicates the formulaic character of these utterances in a seemingly colloquial way.

Next, B's shift towards the marked colloquial is carried further in lines 361–2. The ratio between cues is 0:4:1 with no standard cues used at all (cf. section 3.2.4). This shift towards the marked colloquial pole of his repertoire co-occurs with his shift of topic from K's friend's jubilees or celebrations to a specific wedding party at which G's wife was involved in a particular incident. B's shift seems to signal and achieve a change of conversational level or even framing, from the institutional to an everyday one: he seems to initiate a chat rather than pursue his former topic. K adjusts to B's speech style in her reaction. In lines 364–9 she starts her story about the wedding incident in a style in which the density of unmarked and marked colloquial cues is highest compared to other utterances in the extracts given here: 2:9:2 (cf. section 3.2.4). In her next utterance, in lines 370–2, her ratio is still 1:7:1 (*auch* : dropped pronoun *ich* before the verb *war, nich, se, un, s, ihrm*, the idiom *hát s sich mit-ihrm Mánn wohl auch gehabt* : the pronominal adverb *dabei* in either a separated and reversed order *bei da* or without the first part of it; in the latter case *da* would have to be interpreted as belonging to the next utterance *da ging se los*; both possible interpretations possibly pointing to a marked colloquial cue). Until the end of this turn, the number of unmarked colloquial cues, namely 22, remains high, standard cues not being used at all. One marked colloquial cue is used: *kéin Schrítt wéiter* (line 375) with non-standard nominative case. Both K's adoption of a marked colloquial style as well as her talkativeness on this point manifest that she interprets these sequences as a sort of co-operative chat in an everyday frame which she is glad to join in.

Yet, immediately following, B shifts topic and frame again. This time he exploits talk about G's wife to point out that G's wife is said to be very jealous of K, thereby implying that K might be on too close terms with G (line 378–9). Compared to both B's and K's shifting towards the marked colloquial poles of their repertoires, B's utterance here represents a sudden switch to the standard pole of his repertoire: he only uses standard cues on the phonological and morphophonemic levels (*auch, Sie*) and the rather standard intensifier *sehr*. In a more colloquial style, the intensifier *ganz schön* might have been used instead. The entire utterance is very precisely articulated and rhythmically accentuated. This, too, contributes to the impression of a sudden switch to the standard.

This switch towards the standard signals and achieves B's return to the formal institutional framing of conversation with, once again, an antagonistic form of reciprocity. Retrospectively, his initiation of an informal everyday framing might now be reinterpreted as a strategy to make K give away facts about her way of life which she might not want to tell B. This time, however, K does not follow B's style-switch, but tries to ridicule his implicit accusation.

In this extract, B's shifting and switching and K's reactions highlight the context constituting use of style. The signalling and constitution of a co-operative form of reciprocity in lines 353–4 and the change of frames in lines 361–3 and 378–9 is achieved by alter(n)ating styles. The same content with other styles would have constituted quite different local conversational contexts: unmarked colloquial style in lines 353–4 might have constituted an accusation against which K might have had to defend herself as in extract (1); unmarked colloquial style in lines 361–3 might not have constituted a change of frame but might have suggested a direct relation between the wedding incident and K's way of life as pointed out by B in lines 378–9; marked colloquial style in lines 378–9 might have signalled a continuation of the chat in an informal everyday framing, perhaps with B teasing K. These alternative possibilities would have been interpreted quite differently by K and would have evoked different reactions.

It becomes evident here that the use and constitution of styles by each speaker is done with respect to the speech used in prior turns. In extract (1), B suggests the unmarked colloquial as the baseline. Yet K only uses this style in her side remarks; in all other sequences, she tends towards a more standard style. In extract (2), as long as the form of reciprocity is seemingly co-operative, she first uses the unmarked colloquial and then follows B in his shifting towards the marked colloquial. At the same time, B's shifting towards the marked colloquial is also a progressive process. As soon as K has signalled ratification and shifted in the same direction as B does, B carries his shifting further by increasing the density of colloquial and marked colloquial cues. The same is true of K's shifting. This suggests that in co-operative or seemingly co-operative sequences speakers choose and alter their style in relation to the previously used style as a *tertium comparationis*. Style in conversation is thus treated by participants as the result of an interactively accomplished development; convergence or a continuation of the style alteration in the next turn is used to signal ratification of a prior speaker's initiation of talk on a specific conversational level or topic. Only in antagonistic sequences is the sudden switch from one style to another used to signal the sudden divergence from a mutually achieved development. Here, too, the previously used style is looked upon as the *tertium comparationis*: switching requires some distance between styles.

4. Summary and conclusions

Speech styles have been analysed as dynamic and interactively accomplished ways of speaking and as a means of signalling and constituting dynamic interactive contexts in conversation. The analysis of the choice and alter(n)ation of styles and their functions in conversation presupposes an utterance-by-utterance and turn-by-turn analysis of co-occurring phenomena on different descriptive levels.

(1) The co-occurrence and density of formal speech style constituting cues to analyse the choice and alter(n)ation of speech styles: participants in the extracts analysed here use prototypical kernel style constituting cues and/or the density of co-occurring peripheral cues on different linguistic levels to signal and achieve their choice and alter(n)ations of styles along a continuum between the standard and the marked colloquial

poles of their repertoires. Although kernel cues and co-occurrence tendencies of peripheral cues in some cases suggest the identification of one specific typified style, boundaries between neighbouring styles cannot be drawn. In most cases, speakers use style shifting towards a typified style rather than switching between typified styles, thus suggesting a dynamic conception of the continuum with dynamic boundaries between styles. The further fact that recipients of talk design their own styles in relation to the style of prior talk in the same style, successive style alter(n)ation and style negotiation suggests that the constitution of speech styles in conversation is an interactive achievement with each prior style functioning as an empirical and interactively constituted *tertium comparationis* for successive style constitution.

(2) The co-occurrence of styles and style alter(n)ations and the sequential negotiation and constitution of global and local conversational contexts to reconstruct the context constituting functions of speech styles: the choice and alter(n)ation of styles in co-occurrence with different levels of conversation and forms of reciprocity have been analyzed as contextualization cues, as means to signal, constitute and negotiate dynamic local conversational contexts. The choice and constitution of a baseline style seems to be used to signal the global institutional framing of conversation in sequences in which formal topics are dealt with. Local style alter(n)ation, i.e. style-shifting and switching towards the poles, is used to signal and constitute local conversational levels on which topics are dealt with and on which specific forms of reciprocity are negotiated and established.

The relation between the constitution of styles and the constitution of context is a reflexive one. This is manifested by participants' interpretations of, and reactions to, talk in a specific style. In co-operative or seemingly co-operative sequences, speakers tend to converge their styles to the one constituted by a prior speaker and thus signal ratification of that speaker's activities. In more antagonistic sequences, divergence of speech style from the one used by a prior speaker seems to be used to constitute or to negotiate a redefinition of some aspect of prior activities.

If, however, formal and functional categories and criteria are interdependent and reflexive, none of them can be used as an independent variable in analysis. A separation of independent and dependent variables or factors would presuppose an independent analysis of context, context-changes, and psychological or interactive states of participants and of speech styles as discrete preconceived entities. This would not permit a description of the dynamic and reflexive relations between both sides.

Notes

I wish to thank my colleagues at the University of Oldenburg for discussing a former version of this paper in the context of our Forschungscolloquium 'Sprachvariation'

1   A differentiation between marked primary versus unmarked secondary dialectal features was also made by Schirmunski (1930) and Reiffenstein (e.g. 1976). (I am grateful to Peter Auer for these references)
2   I am grateful to the Institut für deutsche Sprache, Mannheim, for their permission to use and publish extracts from their 'Sonderkorpus Sozialamtsgespräche'
3   In the transcription of German speech conventional transcription symbols of conversational analysis are used. Standard orthography is changed (often in rather an *ad hoc* way, I must admit) to indicate speech style variation on the phonological and morphophonemic levels. For some phonetic representations see sections 3.3.1 to 3.3.3. Transcription is based on purely auditive criteria. Especially the notation of *-en* suffixes as non-syllabic [n] or syllabic [ŋ] is based on criteria like sonority and length of sound, and not on theoretical criteria.
    The following symbols are used:

x₁	= falling intonation ⎫ noted at the end of
xᴵ	= rising intonation ⎬ a unit; direction from
x-	= level intonation ⎭ last accented syllable
aber dá kam	= primary accented syllable(s) of a unit
aber *dá* kam	= extra strong accent
sí:cher	= lengthening of a sound
sicher	= lengthening of a whole word
sicher	= fast tempo in short passages
(fast) * ⎱	characterization of way of speaking, end of
(quiet) * ⎰	qualification is indicated by '*'
↑ , ↓ *	= pitch jumps to higher or lower global tone level until '*'
., .., ...	= speech pauses according to length, i.e. ca 1–2, 2–4 and 5 seconds respectively
(..)	= unintelligible short passage
(? er hat ?)	= uncertain transcription passage
al(s)o	= uncertain identification of a sound

hm		
ja		reception signals with simple falling ($_|$),
nein		rising ($^|$) or level (-) intonation
nee		
mhm		
jaa		reception signals with complex falling-rising ($^|$)
neiin		or rising-falling ($_|$) intonation
neee		
ne$^|$	=	dialogue signal to call for a reception signal
äh, öhm	=	hesitation signal according to realization
((laughs))	=	characterization of non-verbal activity
/	=	speaker's self-interruption
⌈ B:		simultaneous speaking or turn taking inside the
⌊ K:		brackets; commentaries are placed *before* points of
		overlap and do not indicate the beginning of overlap

4   The labelling of categories of cues as 'non-standard' or as variants of standard cues here and in the following sections is partly contradictory to the claim that the *tertium comparationis* is to be analysed as an empirical one. However, for reasons of space and simplicity, I here choose to present the style constituting cues in relation to the standard cues as the *tertium comparationis*. More adequately, however, each typified style and each cue would have to be analysed and presented as a variant in its own right in relation to paradigmatic alternatives

5   In contrast to an approach like Ammon's (1985), in which the degree of dialectality is measured by allocating each single feature to a definite level of dialectality between standard and broad dialect as established by the linguist's (re)construction of the system or grammar underlying each variety, the approach adopted here aims less at the reconstruction of homogeneous systems and more at the reconstruction of speakers' conceptions of these systems as it is revealed in their language-use in conversations

6   In speech evaluation and recognition experiments, both Mihm (1985) and Steinig (1976) found the [s]/[t] substitution and the use of non-standard cases to range among the most easily recognized and most stigmatized features of the Ruhr area dialect (cf. also Mihm 1985a). This explains why these features can also be most effectively used as kernel cues. According to Mihm (1985a), however, the separate use of pronominal adverbs is less stigmatized (cf. idem.: 187)

7   As, for example, kernel cues co-occur with a high density of unmarked colloquial cues but a high density of unmarked colloquial cues does not by itself increase the probability of a kernel cue co-occurring, a kernel cue could be defined as a cue hierarchically superposed on unmarked colloquial cues for the constitution of the marked colloquial style and implicating the occurrence of such cues. This reasoning would amount to postulating implicational scales like those suggested by DeCamp (1971) and Bickerton (1973), albeit on the level of styles within a speaker's continuum of styles. Yet the relation between kernel and peripheral cues here is not taken to be an automatically triggering one.

Speech styles in conversation

References

Ulrich Ammon, 'Möglichkeiten der Messung von Dialektalität', in
W. Besch and K.-J. Mattheier (eds) *Ortssprachenforschung* (Berlin:
E. Schmidt), 1985, pp. 259–82
Peter Auer, 'Kontextualisierung', in *Studium Linguistik* 19, 1986, 22–47
J. C. P. Auer, 'Konversationelle Standard/Dialekt-Kontinua (Code-
Shifting)', in *Deutsche Sprache* 2, 1986a, 97–124
J. C. P. Auer and Aldo di Luzio, 'Three types of variation and their
meaning', in L. Dabène, M. Flasaquier and J. Lyons (eds), *Status of
Migrants' Mother Tongues* (Strasbourg: ESF), 1983, pp. 67–100
Derek Bickerton, 'The nature of a creole continuum', in *Language* 49, 3,
1973, 640–69
David Crystal and Derek Davy, *Investigating English Style* (London:
Longman), 1969
Nikolas Coupland, 'Accommodation at work: Some phonological data
and their implications', in *International Journal of the Sociology of
Language* 46, 1984, 49–70
David DeCamp, 'Toward a generative analysis of a post-creole speech
continuum', in D. Hymes (ed.) *Pidginization and Creolization of
Languages* (Cambridge: Cambridge University Press), 1971, pp. 349–70
Geoffrey Ellis and Jean Ure, 'Language varieties: Register', in A. R.
Meetham (ed.), *Encyclopedia of Linguistics, Information and Control*
(London: Pergamon), 1969, pp. 251–9
Nils Erik Enkvist, *Linguistic Stylistics* (The Hague: Mouton), 1973
Dorothea Franck, 'Stil und Interaktion', in B. Spillner (ed.): *Methoden
der Stilanalyse* (Tübingen: Narr), 1984, pp. 121–35
Michael Gregory, 'Aspects of varieties differentiation', in *Journal of
Linguistics* 3, 1967, 177–98
John J. Gumperz, *Discourse Strategies* (Cambridge: Cambridge
University Press), 1982
Elisabeth Gülich and Ingwer Paul, 'Gottesdienst: Kommunikation-
Institution-Ritual. Linguistische Überlegungen zum Problem von
horizontaler und vertikaler Kommunikation and zur institutionellen
Vermittlung des Rituals', in K. Ermert (ed.) *Gottesdienst als
'Mitteilung'. Loccumer Protokolle* 24, 1983, 84–141
Volker Hinnenkamp, 'Foreigner talk, code-switching and the concept of
trouble,' in K. Knapp, W. Enninger and A. Knapp-Potthoff (eds),
Analyzing Intercultural Communication (Berlin: Mouton/de Gruyter),
1987, pp. 137–80
Dell H. Hymes, 'Ways of speaking', in R. Bauman and J. Sherzer (eds)
Explorations in the Ethnography of Speaking (London: Cambridge
University Press), 1974, pp. 433–51
William Labov, *Sociolinguistic Patterns* (Philadelphia: University of
Pennsylvania Press), 1972
Stephen C. Levinson, *Pragmatics* (Cambridge: Cambridge University
Press), 1983
Arend Mihm, 'Prestige und Stigma des Substandards. Zur Bewertung des
Ruhrdeutschen im Ruhrgebiet', in A. Mihm (ed.): *Sprache an Rhein*

und Ruhr: dialektologische und soziolinguistische Studien zur sprachlichen Situation im Rhein-Ruhr-Gebiet und ihrer Geschichte (Stuttgart: Steiner-Verlag-Wiesbaden-GmbH), 1985, pp. 163–93

Arend Mihm, 'Zur Entstehung neuer Sprachvarietäten. Ruhrdeutscher Kasusgebrauch und seine Erklärung', in A. Mihm (ed.) *Sprache an Rhein und Ruhr: dialektologische und soziolinguistische Studien zur sprachlichen Situation im Rhein-Ruhr-Gebiet und ihrer Geschichte* (Stuttgart: Steiner-Verlag-Wiesbaden-GmbH), 1985a, pp. 245–76

Ingo Reiffenstein, 'Primäre und sekundäre Unterschiede zwischen Hochsprache und Mundarten', in *Opuscula slavica et linguistica. Festschrift für Alexander Issatschenko* (Klagenfurt), 1976, pp. 337–47

Michael Riffaterre, *Strukturale Stilistik* (München: List), 1973

E. H. Rosch, 'On the internal structure of perceptual and semantic categories', in T. E. Moore (ed.) *Cognitive Development and the Acquisition of Language* (New York: Academic Press), 1973, pp. 111–44

Harvey Sacks, Emanuel Schegloff and Gail Jefferson, 'A simplest systematics for the organization of turn-taking in conversation', in *Language* 50, 1974, 696–735

Barbara Sandig, *Stilistik der deutschen Sprache* (Berlin: de Gruyter), 1986

Viktor Schirmunski, 'Sprachgeschichte und Siedlungsmundarten', in *Germanisch-romanische Monatsschrift* 18, 1930, pp. 113–22 and 171–88

Margret Selting, 'Institutionelle Kommunikation: Stilwechsel als Mittel strategischer Interaktion', in *Linguistische Berichte* 86, 1983, 29–48

Margret Selting, 'Levels of style-shifting. Exemplified in the interaction strategies of a moderator in a listener participation programme', in *Journal of Pragmatics* 9, 1985, 179–97

Margret Selting, 'Ebenenwechsel und Kooperationsprobleme in einem Sozialamtsgespräch', in *Zeitschrift für Sprachwissenschaft* 4, 1, 1985a, 68–89

Margret Selting, *Verständigungsprobleme. Eine empirische Analyse am Beispiel der Bürger-Verwaltungs-Kommunikation* (Tübingen: Niemeyer), 1987

Wolfgang, Steinig, *Soziolekt und soziale Rolle* (Düsseldorf: Schwann), 1976

Deborah Tannen, *Conversational Style. Analyzing Talk Among Friends* (Norwood, NJ: Ablex), 1984

Chapter seven

Discourse control in confrontational interaction

Jenny A. Thomas

1. Outline

In an earlier article (Thomas 1985) I argued that many features of
the exchange system which conversational analysis presents as
purely *structural* configurations can be seen to be *motivated* and to
have interpersonal significance. For example, many pre-sequences
(cf. Levinson 1983: 345–64) can be more powerfully explained in
pragmatic terms – as devices which can be used to affirm or,
possibly, to negotiate power relationships, role relationships, etc.
In this paper I shall focus on other levels of discourse organization
(particularly, but not exclusively, on levels above the adjacency
pair) and pursue the argument that by incorporating within
traditional ethnomethodological descriptions of conversation insights from recent work in interpersonal pragmatics, it is possible to
move towards a more predictive and explanatory model of discourse organization. Drawing my examples principally from 'unequal encounters'[1], I shall try to show that certain forms of
metadiscourse[2] offer privileged access into the way in which
discourse is organized. In particular, I shall demonstrate how three
categories of surface level discourse markers are used in such a way
that the discoursal options of a subordinate interactant are severely
constrained. The strategies I describe are not exclusive to unequal
encounters or to confrontational interaction, but they do occur
more frequently in such situations and, because of the power
relationship obtaining between the interactants, have a highly
predictable perlocutionary effect.

My principal source of data is an interview between a chief
inspector of police and a detective constable who is being severely
censured[3]. In the course of the interview, the detective constable is
told that he is to be returned to uniformed duties and by the end of
the proceedings he is in tears. To illustrate the degree to which my
findings are generalizable across other unequal encounters, I shall
also refer to transcripts from two separate interactions between a
headmaster and teenage girls who had been caught playing truant

and who subsequently lied about their actions. In addition, I shall refer to transcripts of hearings in magistrates' courts taken from Harris (1981). The names of all the participants have been changed.

In previous papers (Thomas 1984, 1985) I have suggested that many concepts which are central to pragmatics, concepts such as size of imposition, rights and obligations, social distance, etc., are not necessarily *givens*, tacitly recognized *a priori* by the participants in an interaction. For example, a parent and a head teacher might have diametrically opposed views as to which of them has the ultimate right to determine a child's course of studies; a parent might consider it a trivial matter to transfer a child from one class to another, whereas a head teacher might see it as a major imposition, involving time-tabling difficulties and the setting of undesirable precedents, and so on. Their relative rights and obligations, the perceived size of the imposition, etc., may be established, negotiated, modified, asserted or reinforced in the course of the interaction.

In this paper I shall argue that pragmatic concepts of relevance, rights and obligations and size of imposition have *discoursal* equivalents and I shall introduce the notions of discoursal relevance, discourse rights and obligations and the concept of discoursal imposition. I shall further argue that, like their pragmatic equivalents, these values are not necessarily given but may be established by means of talk.

2. Introduction

Keller (1979) argues that it is possible:

. . . to identify special signals used by speakers as part of their conversational strategies, and . . . discover in this fashion much of the underlying structure of this type of discourse.

Stubbs (1983: 16) writes in similar vein:

. . . in the course of conversation, it is quite usual, and passes unnoticed, for an utterance to step outside the conversation . . . such utterances are simultaneously conversational acts *in* the linear sequence of discourse and also acts at a higher metalevel, which comment on the lower level. The routine nature of such utterances has been taken as an argument that such comments from conversationalists give interesting access to the way they themselves understand the conversation, and therefore should have privileged status as data.

In this paper I shall describe one such group of conversational strategy signals (which I term discourse control acts) which offer insights into the way in which a dominant speaker may deliberately limit the discoursal options of a subordinate interlocutor. I shall argue that in order to explain the effectiveness of these discourse control acts, it is necessary to turn to pragmatic theory, in particular to recent work on interpersonal pragmatics, such as that of Brown and Levinson (1978 and 1987) and Leech (1977 and 1983).

3. Discourse control acts

Fotion (1979) makes what I think is a very valuable distinction between controlling talk and controlled talk. The purpose of controlling talk is to 'control, direct or guide' the 'real' (i.e. message-bearing[4]) talk:

> When we have some reason for speaking it usually takes some time for us to say it. To tell even about a simple event often takes several speech acts. . . . Given, then, that most of our language uses will be composed of sequences of speech acts, the need for controlling or guiding these sequences will quite naturally arise. In order to bring about sequence-control, some use of language *other* than the sequences controlled is required. So the need arises for making a distinction between *controlling uses* of language (or controlling talk), on the one hand, and the *controlled uses* (or talk) on the other. In a narrative about one's overseas trip, the controlled talk would be the narrative itself. The controlling talk would normally precede the narrative and would be brief, but could, under certain circumstances, reach conversational proportions . . . it could be brief if the narrator had said, 'Let me tell you what happened to me on my trip,' and the listener-to-be had acquiesced with a nod.
>
> (Fotion 1979: 616–17)

Bunt and Rosenberg (1980: 95) make a similar distinction and introduce the term 'dialogue control act' to refer to:

> . . . communicative actions bearing on the communication as such, rather than on the information transfer that is to be accomplished. . . . Generally speaking, dialogue control acts have the function of creating conditions for the main dialogue to take place without communicative problems.

I wish to build on the distinction these writers have made and distinguish three different sorts of act which I shall call collectively 'discourse control acts'. Fotion and Bunt and Rosenberg were chiefly interested in the way in which speakers organize or 'package' their talk in an orderly manner; how, to a greater or lesser degree, they define the speech event, set up expectations on the part of the addressee as to how the discourse will develop and is to be interpreted, and generally make the discourse easier for the addressee to process. What interests me, on the other hand, is an aspect of 'controlling talk' which neither of these articles discusses; namely, how controlling talk can be used in order to constrain the contributions an addressee, particularly a subordinate addressee, may make. It is in order to describe the various ways in which the discoursal options of the subordinate participant can be restricted that I have distinguished three separate, though related, discourse control acts. The principal function of the first set (discoursal indicators) is to define the purpose and boundaries of the discourse. By means of the second set (metadiscoursal comments) the dominant participant is able to keep the subordinate participant within these pre-defined limits and the third set (interactional controllers) is used to elicit a particular form of feedback. It will become apparent that while discoursal indicators serve to constrain in a rather *general* way the range of acceptable contributions that a subordinate participant can make, metadiscoursal comments and interactional controllers constrain in a very *specific* manner both the form and substance of the contingent utterance.

4. Discoursal indicators

Discoursal indicators are best thought of as the discoursal counterpart of the Illocutionary Force Indicating Device, since they are surface level markers of the speaker's discoursal intent. They are used principally in order to establish the purpose and nature of the talk and to define the topic boundaries of the interaction.

There is another form of discoursal indicator which does not, in fact, occur in any of the unequal encounters data but which has been described by, among others, Atkinson (1985), in relation to political discourse[5]. Typically, it takes the form of a politician's saying, 'I have three points to make . . .', a tactic which has the effect of creating discoursal space, of allowing the speaker to make a specified number of points before he or she can legitimately be interrupted. I have seen this ploy used extraordinarily effectively by a speaker at a conference who, having been told that he must restrict his comments to two minutes, nevertheless managed to hold the floor for more than twenty simply by announcing that he had 'quatre points à faire'. Each time the chairman attempted to interrupt him, he reiterated that he had 'quatre points'. A second illustration of the effectiveness of this tactic occurred recently during the *Today* programme[6]. Roy Hattersley, who had stated that he had three objections to raise concerning a Conservative Party election poster, was cut off by Timothy Raison after having made only two. Raison was allowed to continue uninterrupted with a long counter-argument, but as soon as he had finished, the presenter turned to Roy Hattersley and said, 'I believe you had three objections, Mr Hattersley.' Hattersley made his third point and the interview ended immediately. Neither the presenter nor Hattersley took up any of the points Raison had made; his contribution was tacitly 'disallowed' by both of them. Not only had Raison wasted a turn but he had been made to appear rather boorish into the bargain.

It is perhaps because a dominant speaker has little reason to fear being interrupted and does not, therefore, need to create space to the same degree, that this particular discoursal indicator does not occur in the police demotion interview or in asymmetrical discourse in general. Indeed, in the entire police exchange there are only six instances of overlapping speech initiated by B (the subordinate interactant) which might be interpreted as attempted interruptions and none of them is successful. The inspector generally talks down the police constable, as in the following examples (A is the Chief Superintendent, B is the detective constable):

Example 1

A   well you know but I'm saying ⎡ that's what that's what they ⎤
B   ⎣ no I'm not saying that at all ⎦
A   said that's what they said
B

Example 2

A   Well you have got some form of redress it's quite open to
     you to go
B
A   and see mr er fuller ⎡ detective chief ⎤ superintendent or
B   ⎣ oh yeah yeah what ⎦
A   indeed to see the chief constable if you wish
B

Of the five clear instances of attempted interruptions on the part of the Superintendent[7], on the other hand, four are successful, in that the Superintendent takes over the speaking turn and prevents the constable from taking it back, e.g.:

Example 3

A ⌈ no no that's I'm ⌉
   saying
B   I can't help sir what the young lads in the ⌊ department may ⌋
                                          think
A   that this is what your supervisors say ⌈ about you ⌉ just a
   moment
B   ⌊ indistinct ⌋

It is important to bear in mind that, as with all discourse control acts, the effectiveness of the 'space-making' discoursal indicator lies not just in the act itself (though I would maintain that even in equal discourse, as in the Hattersley example, it is fairly effective), but in the act PLUS the context of utterance[8] (including, of course, the relationship obtaining between speaker and addressee). The degree to which one interactant feels free to trespass on the discoursal space created by another is at least partly a function of the power relationship obtaining between them.

4.1 Establishing the purpose of the interaction

Of far greater significance in the unequal encounters interviews is the fact that not only are there occasions when the dominant speaker makes it abundantly clear in the surface structure of his/her utterances what he or she intends their illocutionary force to be (a characteristic feature of asymmetrical discourse, as was shown in Thomas 1985), but that he or she also makes quite clear the way in which the discourse is intended to develop. It is this form of discoursal indicator which I shall discuss at some length here. It corresponds in part to what Fotion rather infelicitously terms the 'master speech act'[9]:

> Such an act has the function of supervising, controlling, directing, 'guiding' . . . other speech acts . . . when the speaker issues the master speech act 'Let me tell you what happened to me on my trip' the controlled talk which follows is understood as emanating from it. As a result, the master speech act creates an expectancy on the part of the listener as to what is in store for him linguistically.

> (Fotion 1979: 617)

This discoursal indicator, then, by stating the purposes and defining the boundaries of the interaction, also, in a rather less obvious way, creates discoursal space for the dominant (or would-be dominant) speaker. More importantly, it has the effect of simultaneously limiting the discoursal options of the subordinate interactant. As Candlin *et al.* (1983) have shown in relation to dentist-patient communication, once the dominant speaker has introduced the topic for discussion, it becomes very difficult for the other participant to introduce and warrant a different topic. To do so without violating interactional norms and appearing impolite requires a degree of communicative competence which by no means all speakers possess:

> . . . patients can encounter difficulty in identifying and employing appropriate communication strategies and in making contributions which are always and only allowable ones.
>
> (Candlin *et al.* 1983: 61)

It should be noted, moreover, that Candlin *et al.* are discussing interactions where it is to be supposed that the dominant speaker (doctor, dentist) has no conscious desire to restrict the discoursal options of the other. It goes without saying that the subordinate participant's problems are considerably exacerbated when the dominant speaker has precisely this aim.

It might be supposed that the use of discoursal indicators would also have the effect of restricting the contributions which the dominant speaker can make, but, as we shall see below, this is not the case. The dominant speaker, whilst insisting that the subordinate remain within the previously defined limits, does not necessarily do so him/herself.

In the police data there are two very obvious discoursal indicators of this type, which establish the purpose and nature of the talk which will ensue and which alert B to what he may expect:

Example 4
    A   Right number one then um. I want to see you in the first instance about um the inquiry over the cassettes.

Example 5
    A   Okay that's that part. The next part that I want to deal with is your suitability to remain as a as a CID officer.

4.2 *Establishing the nature of the speech event*

In an earlier article (Thomas 1985: 780–1) I have argued that the felicity conditions for the performance of a particular illocutionary act may be negotiated in discourse. In a similar way, a dominant speaker may establish the basis for (or legitimize) a particular speech event by a 'rehearsal of known facts'. In chat shows on radio or television, interviewees may be presented with 'B' information[10], not in order to establish their identity or to enable them to confirm or deny the facts (as might be the case in a court of law), but for the benefit of the audience. The 'rehearsal of known facts' in the absence of an audience or jury can serve to establish the basis for the speech event, as in the following example from the beginning of the police interview:

Example 6

A: Now you will recall that um, I did see you on a particular day and ask you where they were?

B: That's right, Sir, yes.

A: And you were unable to give a satisfactory explanation and in fact I understand they were found in your locker?

A: That's right, yeah, found them in there, Sir.

However, there is no reason to suppose that the dominant speaker's rehearsal of the facts will be in any sense neutral, objective or faithful. For example, when summarizing earlier talk, the dominant speaker may distort, if not the 'propositional' element of what has been said, at least the author's interpersonal, discoursal, or social intent. A useful framework within which to begin discussing this is provided by Leech (1976) and Leech and Short (1981). Leech (1976: 6), discussing the question of faithfulness in reporting utterances, refers to a report being 'to a greater or less degree FAITHFUL or UNFAITHFUL to its original' and later (page 14) proposes that the relationship between equivalent direct and indirect speech reports is that '. . . a direct speech report refers to the reported utterance in the formal mode, while an indirect speech report refers to it in the content mode'. Elaborating this in a later work (Leech and Short 1981: 318–34), the authors suggest that the continuum from 'narrative report of action' through 'narrative report of speech act' and indirect speech to direct speech, similarly represents an increasingly strong claim to faithfulness on the part of the narrator.

However, it is not possible to transfer Leech and Short's model, designed to handle literary discourse, to naturally-occurring spoken or written discourse, without modification. When Leech (1976) refers to 'content' mode he is (perhaps legitimately in the context of that article) concerned only with semantic content, and Leech and Short, when they speak of 'faithfulness' are concerned principally with the accurate representation of the words uttered by the original speaker or with the accurate representation of the original speaker's intended speech act. They do not consider the faithfulness with which other pragmatic aspects of an utterance, namely the interpersonal and textual, may be represented.[11]

Consider the following example, taken from a British television programme called *Bergerac* – a police series set in Jersey. In this episode, the storyline concerns the making of a film about the Nazi occupation of the Channel Islands. The scene takes place at the top of a cliff, where a supposedly famous, but extremely unpleasant German actor who plays the part of an SS officer is talking to Timothy, the floor manager, who in turn is receiving instructions by means of a walkie-talkie from the film's director, stationed at the foot of the cliff. (The sections which are spoken over the walkie-talkie are shown in italics).

Example 7

1	Actor:	What's the hold up now, Timothy?
	Floor Manager:	We're nearly there, Sir. Now, on 'action' if you just move to the cliff edge, that'll be fine. Then we cut and bring in Greg.
5	Actor:	The double is unnecessary. I always do my own stunts.
	Floor Manager:	Ah. Right. *Tim to Carlton. Tim to Carlton. He says he'll do it himself.*
	Director:	*For God's sake, Tim, tell the bloody eejit he can't.*
10	Floor Manager:	Carlton says he appreciates the offer, Sir but
	Actor:	tell him to roll or I leave. Come on, man, let's get on with it.
	Floor Manager:	*Carlton, he insists.*
	Director:	*With luck we'll have a fall and kill the hun,*
15		*but we couldn't afford a death clause.*
	Floor Manager:	Carlton's just a tiny bit worried about your insurance, Sir.

In the extract we have four examples of reported speech by Tim, the floor manager: lines 7–8, line 10, line 13 and lines 16–17.

    A1   I always do my own stunts.
Is reported as:
    A2   He says he'll do it himself.
    B1   Tell the bloody eejit he can't
Is reported as:
    B2   Carlton says he appreciates the offer, Sir
    C1   Come on, man, let's get on with it!

Is reported as:
   C2   He insists
   D1   We couldn't afford a death clause.
Is reported as:
   D2   Carlton's just a tiny bit worried about your insurance,
         Sir.

Utterance A2 reports the A1 faithfully enough and C2 is a reasonably accurate narrative report of speech act of C1. But B2 and D2 are very different. While each reported utterance represents the *force* of the original moderately well, the *interpersonal* aspect, in this case, the attitude of the original speaker (or author[12]) towards the addressee is not reflected faithfully. On both occasions the reported message conveys far more politeness and deference than the original. Furthermore, D2 lacks *textual* faithfulness, in that only part of the original utterance is reported – the least discourteous element is foregrounded.

In the police data, it comes through very clearly that when the dominant participant is occupying the discourse role of 'spokesman'[12], he or she has considerable freedom to distort messages in this way. There are times when the Detective Chief Superintendent appears to be reporting verbatim and without comment the opinion of the group:

Example 8
. . . throughout that time, whilst you were a very cheerful type of kind of a fellow and so forth and on the face of it you're enthusiastic, um you appear to lack confidence since you've been back and have not really come up to expectations.

At other times, however (when the Constable appears reluctant to accept the decision without question), the Chief Superintendent is clearly putting what is in the report into his own words, possibly changing the force of what was written and certainly altering the interpersonal message from 'direct transmission of the facts' to 'personally offensive':

Example 9
The young lads in the department think you're a bit of a bloody joke.

Similarly, in rehearsing known facts in order to establish the 'felicity conditions' for a speech event, the dominant participant may well impose a particular ideological or personal interpretation on the events. Thus the Headmaster in the school data explicitly presents the little girl's behaviour as 'setting out to deceive me quite deliberately'; he does not ask her about her motives or listen to her attempt to give an alternative interpretation.

I am not concerned here with the rights and wrongs of these particular cases, but they do illustrate the general point which I want to make, namely, that a subordinate interactant presented with such a rehearsal of his/her alleged misbehaviour may want to challenge, not the account of the events which took place, so much as the interpretation and/or slant which the dominant participant has placed on those events. Erroneous facts are relatively easy to challenge, tendentious presuppositions are not. Like 'upshots' and 'reformulations' (see Thomas 1985) they are difficult to challenge for three reasons. In the first place, to identify them at all demands a cognitive development which is beyond most children and many adults. Secondly, they are difficult to challenge discoursally, since to do so involves interrupting the flow of conversation. Finally, they are difficult to challenge without violating the politeness norms of an institution. Weiser (1974) discusses some of these questions, when she postulates a Gricean-type maxim, namely, 'maintain smooth flow':

> If you imagine that a person using a sentence containing presupposed and non-presupposed material is in effect saying, 'Assume that part and respond to this part', then it becomes clear that you are not cooperating if you respond instead to the presupposition . . .

> My intuition is that . . . flow-breaking responses are more difficult to make, especially between people not well acquainted or outside the academic community. There is an expectation felt . . . as a subtle but very real pressure, that both participants will maintain the flow.
>
> (Weiser 1974: 727)

4.3 Establishing discoursal relevance

Now I would not, of course, wish to suggest that discoursal indicators, particularly of the sort which establish the purpose of the interaction ('I'm ringing you about the . . .') are only present in unequal discourse. Indeed, Bunt and Rosenberg (1980: 98) have shown that various forms of discoursal comments[13] account for 50 per cent ±10 per cent of 'moves' in exchanges between 'visually separated interactants', such as people talking on the telephone. (They do not give figures for face-to-face interactions, but lead one to suppose that in such circumstances the percentage would be considerably lower.) What I would claim, however, is that if one speaker is in a position of authority *vis-à-vis* the other, the use of discoursal indicators severely constrains in advance the range of the subordinate participant's allowable/warrantable contributions.

It is generally accepted in pragmatics (cf. Brockway 1981: 67) that utterances are relevant or irrelevant only in context. However, it is the dominant party in an interaction who has, to a very great extent, the power to define the context, and hence the prerogative of determining what is and what is not 'discoursally relevant', that is, 'relevant to the topic in hand'[14]. It might well be argued that 'defining the context', establishing the purpose and scope of the interaction, is the prerogative of every first speaker and to some extent, of course, this is true[15]. What is different in 'unequal encounters' is that the dominant participant uses a whole range of devices to keep the subordinate to the topic(s) which he or she has selected. The context as defined by the dominant speaker becomes the yardstick against which judgements of relevance are made, and the subordinate's contributions allowed or disallowed.

5 Metadiscoursal comments

Discoursal indicators, then, allow the dominant participant to control an interaction by creating discoursal space for him or herself and by restricting the options of the subordinate interactant in a fairly general way (they are perhaps best seen as mapping out the path which the interaction is to take).

Metadiscoursal comments have several functions. They can be used by the dominant participant in order to keep the subordinate from wandering from that previously established path, by disallowing contributions which do not contribute to the dominant participant's discoursal or social goals. They can be used by the dominant participant to make new stages in the development of the interaction, or to signal that it is to end. Finally, they can be used in order to mark or legitimize the fact that the dominant speaker is going to go beyond his/her own pre-established boundaries.

5.1 Disallowing subordinate speaker's contributions

There are many ways in which a dominant participant can dismiss a contribution he or she considers irrelevant. He or she can, for example, interrupt the current speaker (cf. section 4 above) or simply ignore what the subordinate says or fail to take up his/her point. And whereas a dominant speaker appears to have no difficulty in re-introducing a point which has not been dealt with to his/her satisfaction, a subordinate speaker cannot readily do so without interrupting the flow of conversation. There are four clear examples of this in the police data. In the example which follows, the constable complains that he has been treated unfairly, whereupon the Superintendent abruptly changes the subject:

Example 10
    A: What's been done to me, it's not right.
    B: For God's sake, if this happens, why don't as I said to you
          just now, go and get your uniform, come and see me, let's
          talk it out.

To qualify as a metadiscoursal comment, however, the dismissing of the subordinate's contribution must be overt.

Harris (1980: 26), as I have already remarked, also comments on the unusual number of 'references to speech acts' in asymmetrical discourse, although some of the illustrations she gives might better be seen as metadiscoursal comments, making explicit reference to the nature of the *speech event* (Example 11) or to the discourse rights associated with that particular speech event (Example 12).

Example 11
    [Magistrate to defendant.]
    'Now we're not having an auction.'

(Harris 1980: 168)

Example 12
    [Magistrate to defendant.]
    I'm not here to answer questions – you answer my questions.

(ibid. p. 136)

Once the purpose of the interaction has been established, the dominant speaker can dismiss as irrelevant contributions which he or she does not welcome, by reference to that purpose ('We're not here to talk about that'), by reference to discourse rights (Example 12) or by interjections or backchannels ('turn-disruptive' moves) which have that force[16]:

    No, no, no, no, don't interrupt me.[17]
    I wonder if I might continue with the programme without you
    chipping in.[18]
    I'd just like to make two points before you interrupt.[19]

Brockway (1981) in her discussion of markers of relevance and irrelevance (typically yes/no/well/but) suggests less obvious ways in which a dominant speaker may dismiss another's contributions, as well as warranting his/her own. Many examples of this are to be found in the 'police data', for example:

Example 13
  A   I'm so pleased I really am sir I've never had such a good
        time for basic police work as I've had in the last I'm
  A   staggered . . .
  A   absolutely and utterly
  B   well all right then if you say that I
        didn't intend to carry out your appraisal today and I still
        don't but

5.2 Marking new stages in the interaction

Examples 14, 15, and 16 show the dominant speaker controlling the interaction by marking new stages in the discourse.

Example 14
  A   Okay that's that part. The next part what I want to deal with
        is your suitability to remain as a CID officer.

Example 15
  A   I didn't intend to carry out your appraisal today, and I still
        don't intend to, but let's have a look at that.

Example 16
  A   Let's look at the future shall we? Let's really look at the
        future, let's acce accept the fact that you're going to be put
        into uniform, okay? Let's just look at that for a moment.

Finally, Example 17 offers an example of the dominant participant's determining that the exchange is to end:

Example 17
  A   . . . well you you er . off you go now and just think about it
        . . . and do come back and see me . and discuss it, will you?
  B   Yeah I will . I'll go off and have a think.

Examples 15 and 16 are also instances of the powerful speaker's going beyond his own pre-established bounds, and it is significant that even a dominant speaker feels obliged to mark such imminent digressions. The effect of 'calling one's own violations' in this way is that it then becomes very difficult for one's interlocutor (particularly a subordinate interlocutor) to complain without infringing the Politeness Principle (cf. Leech 1983, Chapter 6) and the Maxim of Quantity. In the following (invented) exchange, for example, B's utterance seems discoursally ill-formed:

Example 18
    A: I know we agreed not to discuss your work today, but I'd
          like to talk about it briefly.
    B: (*?) We agreed not to discuss it today.

It would, of course, have been perfectly possible for B to have
replied, 'That's right, we did', but pragmatic principles (cf. Leech
1983: 132 and 138) would predict that in circumstances where the
power difference and/or social distance between speaker and
hearer are great, the speaker would invoke the agreement maxim:
'Minimize the disagreement between self and other. Maximize the
agreement between self and other'. We have ample evidence from
the police interview that Barry does operate this maxim: when a
series of assertions made by the Superintendent about A/B events,
which in equal discourse would elicit at most a back-channel
response and more probably a non-verbal acknowledgement, here
receive very full verbal response from the Detective Constable.
What Leech does not point out is that the agreement, or what I have
called 'orientation to one's interlocutor's goals', may operate on
several levels[20]. The fact that the two interactants' *social* goals are
inimical (the Superintendent is going to transfer Barry to uniformed
duties and Barry does not want to be transferred) does not prevent
Barry from exhibiting the maximum possible relevance to the
Superintendent's *interactional* goals. Example 19 is particularly
revealing in this regard, in that Barry manages to display the
maximum degree of agreement with A's assertion, without
admitting responsibility for having put the cassettes in the locker in
the first place. In other words, although Barry's contribution is
highly relevant *interactionally* (demonstrating his attentiveness and
displaying a high degree of lexical or semantic relevance and
politeness), he does not orientate to the Superintendent's *discoursal* goals (if we assume that the Superintendent is seeking confirmation or denial of Barry's guilt):

Example 19
    A   Right, number one then, um, I want to see you in the first
         instance about um the inquiry over the cassettes.
    B   Yes, Sir.
    A   Now you will recall that um I did see you on a particular day
         and ask you where they were
    B   That's right, Sir, yes.
    A   And you were unable to give a a satisfactory explanation
         and in fact I understand they were found in your locker?
    B   That's right, yeah, found them in there, Sir.

147

5.3 Warranting dominant speaker's contributions

Baker (1975) has shown how what I have called metadiscoursal comments can be used systematically to constrain the next contribution. She also points out (1975: 40–1) that 'but-clauses' can serve as signals of imminent violations of conversational maxims. They may thus be used (by the powerful participant) to warrant a contribution which goes beyond his/her previously defined limits, just as metadiscoursal comments may be used to dismiss as irrelevant the contributions of the subordinate. Other ways in which relevance may be overtly signalled (e.g. *after all*, *actually*, *now*, *anyway*, *well*, *still*) are discussed by Bird (1979: 150) and by Brockway (1981: 40–1) and similarly include utterances which indicate that S is trying to make relevant an utterance, the relevance of which is not immediately apparent. Such markers are typically the prerogative of the dominant participant and are never in these data used successfully by the subordinate.

Some examples of the use of markers of discoursal relevance by the Superintendent to warrant his own contributions follow[21]:

. . . but let's have a look at that . . .
. . . well you know, but I'm saying . . .
. . . now look, you're a bit upset at the moment . . .
. . . yeah well, yeah well, what you're basically saying
. . . well, there you are Barry, I've spelt it out to you

The Detective Constable, on the other hand, uses such markers more as hedges:

Well I've never had any comments other than that.

Or as markers of the imminent violation of politeness norms (in this case, the only instance on Barry's part of a direct contradiction):

But I think it is, Sir.

There are no instances of Barry's successfully using these markers to make his contributions discoursally relevant. He is invariably interrupted almost immediately:

Example 20
A   I can't comment on that, but if people want to look in books
and find out from my DS and my colleagues the work and
the prisoners I've had, I just don't believe
$\begin{bmatrix} \text{it and} \\ \text{mm} \end{bmatrix}$ I'm afraid $\begin{bmatrix} \text{sir I'm just} \\ \text{yeah well yes well} \end{bmatrix}$
B

A   absolutely ⌉
B   what you're ⌋ basically saying is that um detective inspector
    jessop
A
B   is wrong

6 Interactional controllers

So far in this chapter, I have tried to show how discoursal indicators
and metadiscoursal comments can be used to structure an interaction in such a way that the discoursal rights and opportunities of
the subordinate participant are restricted. In Thomas (1985) I
showed how 'upshots' and 'reformulations' severely *constrained* the
range of possible responses a subordinate participant could make
without violating politeness norms. Their use generally resulted in
his/her retracting or mitigating a previous contribution or backing
down in some other way, often by retreating into silence. Interactional controllers also contribute to the generally oppressive
nature of 'unequal encounters' but have the opposite effect to
upshots and reformulations. Instead of silencing a subordinate,
they are used by the dominant participant in order to secure a
particular 'on-record' response.

The subordinate participants in the interactions under discussion
are, in general, extremely compliant. In particular, they demonstrate a high degree of surface-level co-operation[20]: they observe
the Politeness Principle by giving very full and direct responses
whenever they can express agreement, whilst expressing disagreement only indirectly. The Superintendent and the Headmaster, in contrast, go bald-on-record in the performance of even
the most face-threatening acts.

Thus Barry and Helen and Hannah (after she has conceded
defeat), appear to be Gricean paragons, displaying by their use of
very full 'go-ons' and back-channels a high degree of orientation
towards the Superintendent's/Headmaster's interactional goals.
The number of go-ons which the subordinates give is in itself
significant (the dominant participants give almost none). A high
proportion of the dominant participants' contributions are verbally
responded to, in both the school and the police data and this
replicates the findings of other discourse analysts who have

investigated asymmetrical discourse. Thus Fishman (1978), examining the manifestations of 'powerless speech' exhibited by women in male-female interaction, reports that:

> Throughout the tapes, when the men are talking, the women are particularly skilled at inserting 'mm's', 'yeah's', 'oh's', and other such comments throughout streams of talk rather than at the end. These are signs from the inserter that she is constantly attending to what is said, that she is demonstrating her participation, her interest in the interaction and the speaker. How well the women do this is also striking – seldom do they mistime their insertions and cause even slight overlaps. These minimal responses occur between the breaths of a speaker and there is nothing in tone or structure to suggest they are attempting to take over the turn.
>
> (Fishman 1978: 402)

I want to propose three reasons for the very high degree of orientation on the part of the subordinate participants to their superiors' interactional goals. The first reason has already been hinted at. Researchers (e.g. Abbeduto and Rosenberg 1980) have come up with the unremarkable finding that responding as fully as possible to the other participant's turns is taken as 'an indication that subjects were active conversational participants.' Since all the subordinate participants are anxious to avoid or minimize punishment, it is not very surprising that they should try to give at least the appearance of being maximally co-operative, and in orientating so completely to the dominant participants' *interactional* goals, they can in some degree compensate for their inability to go along with their *social* goals.

The second two reasons relate to the use of interactional controllers, the first set designed very specifically to force feedback when it is not forthcoming, the second more generally involving a high degree of what I shall term 'discoursal imposition'.

6.1 Forced feedback

As we have seen, very full feedback is usually volunteered by the subordinate participant. However, when no *verbal* acquiescence is proffered, the dominant participant forces it by the repeated use of tag questions or 'right' or 'OK' with questioning intonation. This is particularly noticeable in one of the Headmaster/child interactions, in which the child is pinioned against the wall and is nodding frantically at everything the Headmaster says. The Headmaster nevertheless uses no fewer than ten elicitations of feedback.

The same phenomenon recurs throughout the police data, but again two instances are particularly striking. In the first example, the Constable has already given extremely full feedback, yet he is nevertheless forced to give still more:

Example 21

A   . . . you'll probably find yourself um before the Chief Constable, okay?

B   Yes, Sir, yes, understood.

A   Now you er fully understand that, don't you?

B   Yes, Sir, indeed, yeah.

The second remarkable instance of forced feedback in the police data occurs when Barry, who has already indicated his inability to respond[22] by shaking his head in disbelief at what the Superintendent has said to him, is forced to answer by the Superintendent's saying:

What do you have to say about that?

6.2 Discoursal disambiguation

Part of the explanation for dominant speakers forcing feedback from their subordinates even when some form of feedback has already been volunteered relates to the notion of 'discoursal ambivalence'. Leech (1983: 23) points out that it is very much the norm for utterances to display 'ambivalence and multiplicity of function'. He is referring here to pragmatic ambivalence, but the same holds true for ambivalence of discourse function. Is a contribution a 'go-on', an 'agreement' or both? And just as a dominant speaker may force his or her subordinate to go on record with the intended pragmatic force of an utterance, so he or she may force the subordinate to disambiguate *discoursally* ambivalent utterances and oblige him or her to distinguish, say, an indication that he or she is attending, from an indication that he or she understands, or an acknowledgement of the accuracy of a fact from acquiescence with what the dominant speaker is saying. The subordinate is being required, in other words, to indicate co-operation with the dominant speaker's discoursal or social goals, rather than purely interactional ones.

6.3 Discoursal imposition

In previous sections I have suggested that the pragmatic concepts of ambivalence and rights and obligations have discoursal equivalents and that denying one's interlocutor the possibility of exploiting these and other forms of indirectness is typical of 'unequal encounters'. In this final section, I want to show how the fourth pragmatic parameter, size of imposition, also has a discoursal counterpart, which I shall call discoursal imposition.

Schegloff and Sacks's (1974) notion of adjacency pairs (where A is the first pair part and B a contingent and related second pair part produced by a conversational interactant), can usefully be reformulated (cf. Abbeduto and Rosenberg 1980) as obligating illocution A and perlocution B:

> . . . for Schegloff and his colleagues, an adjacency pair is composed of any two turns that are related in that the first determines the content and/or form of the second. . . . These researchers have in mind such pairs as question/answer and request/refusal. The concept of the adjacency pair, however, can be reinterpreted so that the first turn of the pair performs a given illocutionary act (with intended perlocutionary effects) and the second is a response indicating the perlocutionary effect it achieved.

> Schegloff and his co-workers have limited the concept of the adjacency pair to include only those pairs, such as question/answer, where the illocutionary act performed by the first turn obligates the listener to indicate its perlocutionary effect. However, other illocutionary acts do not obligate the listener to respond[23]. For example, although the intended perlocutionary effect of an assertion is that the listener believes some proposition to be true, the listener is under no obligation to indicate that this, or some other perlocutionary effect was achieved.

> (Abbeduto and Rosenberg 1980: 407–8)

Even Abbeduto and Rosenberg's reformulation perpetuates, in my view, a fallacy typical of conversational analysis, namely, that perlocution B follows obligating illocution A automatically and inevitably, as if the obligating nature of the illocution lay in the language alone. However, I do think that there is some truth in the contention that some illocutions are inherently more 'obligating' than others. In fact, one might postulate a 'hierarchy of obligating-ness' running from 'highly obligating' to 'minimally obligating'[24]. At the 'highly obligating' end would be greetings, summonses which name the addressee, direct questions and direct requests. The more direct the illocution, the more obligating it would be, since it is more difficult for the addressee to pretend not to have understood. At the less obligating end would be illocutions such as assertions about 'A' events or phatic communication.

If, however, we were to build into Abbeduto and Rosenberg's model some description of the relationship obtaining between Speaker and Addressee, the model becomes more powerful and the degree to which an illocution constrains a particular response becomes more predictable. The size of discoursal imposition is thus determined by the degree of 'obligatingness' of an illocution + the power of S over A.

Even a 'minimally obligating illocution' directed by a superior to a subordinate thus becomes 'obligating' and this helps to explain the frequency with which the subordinates in the interactions I have described give such full feedback. Conversely, as we have seen, powerful interactants have few qualms about ignoring 'obligating illocutions' directed at them by their subordinates. The frequency with which one interactant responds to non-obligating illocutions (even to extremely indirect ones which could be ignored without any obvious impoliteness) might be taken as a marker of unequal power relationships.

Notes

1 'Unequal encounters' are here defined as interactions which take place within social institutions with a clearly-defined hierarchical structure (such as schools, the police, the law courts, etc.) in which the power to discipline or punish those of lower rank is invested in holders of high rank (head teachers, inspectors, judges, etc.)
2 'Metadiscourse' (Stubbs 1983: 16)
3 Taken from a BBC TV documentary series *Police*, filmed over several months with the Thames Valley Police Force
4 'Message-bearing' here includes both the interpersonal and speech act functions
5 A major shortcoming in the work of conversational analysts is, in my view, typified by Atkinson's over-emphasis on a particular linguistic strategy, at the expense of other features of the activity-type. See also note 8
6 The *Today* programme, BBC Radio 4, 8 a.m. 22.5.83
7 There are another three instances of overlapping speech initiated by the Inspector, but in the case of two of them it is not possible to say whether the last two (which occur after pauses at transitionally relevant points) are attempted interruptions or merely simultaneous starts
8 It is difficult to imagine, for example, a person at a conference speaking from the floor and announcing that he or she has eighty-three points to make and holding the floor successfully

9   Note that Fotion's 'master speech act' is totally different from van Dijk's 'macro speech act' (van Dijk 1977: 238–47). The former *precedes*, the second *succeeds* the series of speech acts or stretch of discourse in question. The 'macro speech act' is what an exchange, stripped of all polite interpersonal and interactional content, boils down to. The 'macro speech act' can thus be seen to resemble my 'upshot' (see Thomas 1985: 773–6) more than it resembles Fotion's 'master speech act', but van Dijk proposes it only as a possible analytical category for the discourse analyst. He is not concerned, as I am, with how it might function in interaction or with the way in which interactants might respond to it

10 Labov and Fanshel (1977). 'A' events refer to information which is known to the speaker, 'B' events refer to information which is known to the addressee and 'A/B' events refer to information known to both parties

11 Of course, it would be a mistake to believe that the propositional, interpersonal and textual 'strands' of an utterance can be separated out unproblematically. For example, there are many occasions on which pragmatic force is assigned on the basis of the perception of the interpersonal. This is particularly true in the case of *related* speech acts (such as ordering/requesting/inviting) which might be distinguished solely or principally on the basis of the relationship between speaker and addressee

12 On the discourse roles of 'author', 'spokesperson', etc. see Thomas (1986: 86–148) and forthcoming (b)

13 Their categories are different from mine

14 See Thomas (1986: 54–78)

15 On the control exerted by the initiator of a conversation see, for example, Ochs (1979: 50), Scollon and Scollon (1981: 23)

16 In the entire interaction, there is not a single instance of *supportive* back-channelling from the Superintendent and the same is true of the Headmaster in the 'school data'

17 Appendix 2, line 6

18 Robin Day *Question Time*

19 ibid

20 On levels of co-operation, see Thomas (1986: 25–35, and forthcoming (b))

21 Others are found at staves 119, 120–2, 202

22 Abbeduto and Rosenberg (1980: 424) describe 'communicative distress' as a signal given by a speaker that he or she is unable to communicate

23 I disagree with Abbeduto and Rosenberg here. I think *all* utterances impose some, however minimal, obligation on an addressee to respond

24 Of course, the degree of 'obligatingness' inherent in the illocution alone might also vary from language to language. In German, or Russian, for example, the obligation to respond *verbally* to thanks (danke/bitte) is very high, whereas in (British) English it is optional

References

L. Abbeduto and S. Rosenberg, 'The communicative competence of mildly retarded adults' *Applied Psycholinguistics* 1, 1980, 405–26

J. M. Atkinson, *Our Masters' Voices*, (London: Methuen), 1984

C. Baker, 'This is just a first approximation, but . . .' *Papers From the Chicago Linguistics Society* 11, 1975, 37–47

G. Bird, 'Speech acts and conversation – II' *Philosophical Quarterly* 29, 1979, 142–52

D. Brockway, 'Semantic constraints on relevance', in H. Parret *et al.* (eds), 1981, 57–78

P. Brown and S. Levinson, 'Universals in language usage', in E. N. Goody (ed.) *Questions and Politeness* (Cambridge: Cambridge University Press), 1978

P. Brown and S. Levinson, *Politeness: Some universals in language usage* (Cambridge: Cambridge University Press), 1987

H. C. Bunt *et al.*, 'Dialogue control acts', *Institute for Perception Research Annual Progress Report* 15, 1980, 95–9

C. N. Candlin, J. Burton and H. Coleman, *Dentist-Patient Communication Skills: Working Papers* 1–4 (Lancaster: University of Lancaster Department of Linguistics and Modern English Language/Institute for English Language Education), 1980

P. Cole, (ed.) *Syntax and Semantics* 9: *Pragmatics* (New York: Academic Press), 1978

P. Cole and J. Morgan, (eds) *Syntax and Semantics* 3: *Speech Acts* (New York: Academic Press), 1975

T. A. van Dijk, *Text and Context: Explorations in the Semantics and Pragmatics of Discourse* (London: Longman), 1977

P. Fishman, 'Interaction: the work women do' *Social Problems* 25, 1978, 397–406

N. Fotion, 'Master speech acts' *Philosophical Quarterly* 21, 1971, 232–43

N. Fotion, 'Speech activity and language use' *Philosophia* 8 (4), 1979, 615–38

N. Fotion, 'I'll bet you $10 that betting is not a speech act,' in H. Parret *et al.*, 1981, 211–23

H. P. Grice, 'Logic and conversation', in P. Cole and J. Morgan (eds), 1975, 41–58

H. P. Grice, 'Further notes on logic and conversation' in P. Cole (ed.) *Syntax and Semantics* 9 (New York: Academic Press), 1978, 113–27

H. P. Grice, 'Presupposition and conversational implicature' in P. Cole (ed.) *Radical Pragmatics* (New York: Academic Press), 1981, 183–98

S. J. Harris, 'Language Interaction in Magistrates' Courts', unpublished Ph.D. thesis, University of Nottingham, 1981

J. Heritage and D. R. Watson 'Formulations as conversational objects', in G. Psathas (ed.) *Everyday Language – Studies in Ethnomethodology* (New York: Irvington), 1979, 123–61

D. Holdcroft, 'Speech acts and conversation – 1' *Philosophical Quarterly* 29, 1979, 125–41

E. Keller, 'Gambits: conversational strategy signals' *Journal of Pragmatics* 3 (4), 1979, 219–38

W. Labov and D. Fanshel, *Therapeutic Discourse* (New York: Academic Press), 1977

G. N. Leech, 'Being precise about lexical vagueness' *York Papers in Linguistics* 6, 1976, 149–65

G. N. Leech, 'Language and tact' *LAUT Series A* Paper 46, University of Trier, 1977

G. N. Leech, *Explorations in Semantics and Pragmatics* (Amsterdam: Benjamins B.V), 1980

G. N. Leech, *Principles of Pragmatics* (London: Longman), 1983

G. N. Leech and M. H. Short, *Style in Fiction* (London: Longman), 1981

S. Levinson, 'Activity types and language' *Linguistics* 17 (5/6), 1979, 365–99

S. Levinson, 'The essential inadequacies of speech act models of dialogue', in H. Parret *et al.* (eds), 1981, 473–89

S. Levinson, *Pragmatics* (Cambridge: Cambridge University Press), 1983

E. A. Schegloff and H. Sacks, 'Opening up closings', in R. Turner (ed.) *Ethnomethodology* (Harmondsworth: Penguin), 1974, 233–64

R. Scollon and S. Scollon, *Narrative, Literacy and Face in Interethnic Communication* (Norwood, New Jersey: Ablex), 1981

C. M. Scotton, 'The negotiation of indentities in conversation: a theory of markedness and code choice' *International Journal of the Sociology of Language* 44, 1983, 115–36

M. Stubbs, *Discourse Analysis* (Oxford: Blackwell), 1983

J. A. Thomas, 'Cross-cultural pragmatic failure' *Applied Linguistics* 4 (2), 1983, 91–112

J. A. Thomas, 'Cross-cultural discourse as unequal encounter' *Applied Linguistics* 5 (3), 1984, 226–35

J. A. Thomas, 'The language of power: towards a dynamic pragmatics' *Journal of Pragmatics* 9 (6), 1985, 765–83

J. A. Thomas, 'The Dynamics of Discourse: A Pragmatic Analysis of Confrontational Interaction', unpublished Ph.D. thesis, University of Lancaster, 1986(a)

J. A. Thomas, 'Complex illocutionary acts and the analysis of discourse' *Lancaster Papers in Linguistics* 11, 1986(b)

J. A. Thomas, *Pragmatics: an Introduction* (London: Longman), forthcoming (a)

J. A. Thomas, *The Dynamics of Discourse* (London: Longman), forthcoming (b)

A. Weiser, 'Deliberate ambiguity' *Papers from the Tenth Regional Meeting of the Chicago Linguistics Society*, 1974, 723–31.'

Section III

Style in Literature and Learning

Since there are no stylistically neutral texts, every use of language in the real world, written or spoken, must manifest one or more styles. Nevertheless, it might be claimed that the very concept of style assumes a special significance in the area of creative literature, for that is where – in one sense at least – it finds its 'highest' expression. How a reader responds to a literary work may, in fact, be the very test of its 'texture' or even its value, and such response constitutes the subjective aspect of style mentioned in the Introduction, while the linguistic surface of the text, being the stimulus of any response, represents the objective side of the same phenomenon. Whereas stylistics is sometimes divided into 'literary' and 'linguistic', pragmatics has not yet been applied extensively or in great detail to the study of creative writing. However, there is no intrinsic reason why this should not be done, for the pragmatics of literary style is analogous to the pragmatics of any other style or class of styles.

The three chapters in Section III focus on what texts (in general or in particular) mean, what they do, how they do it and indeed what people can do with them. They discuss conversation, and particularly dialect, in fiction, the interpretation of certain kinds of word-group and the problem-solving activity involved in readers' responses to a poem presented in various stages.

Following in a fairly natural way upon the chapters in Section II, Raymond Chapman examines the language of conversation, not in the real world, but in fiction. His purpose is to explain how a reader differs from a participant in a living conversation, how an author uses fictional speech to convey both the implied and the overt content of a conversation and especially how dialect is used in a novel, for 'the value of dialect in the novel is probably less synaesthetic than pragmatic'. In these cases, he concludes, it is less important to show how the characters actually speak than how their speech manifests their relationships and attitudes to each other.

The focus of Claes Schaar's study is one particular kind of

157

linguistic structure, namely that which by analogy he calls an 'inscription'. The textual elements he has in mind function like inscriptions or epigraphs in actualizing meaning not deducible from the horizontal environment alone; they are words or groups of words whose environment provides no clues, or no satisfactory clues, to their interpretation: only the 'infracontexts', implicit contexts, help in this process. The object of the investigation is to elucidate how a reader responds to such inscriptions (the pragmatic element) devised, as they are, in order to stimulate such a response (the stylistic element).

Also concerned with readers' responses to a text, Nils Erik Enkvist and Gun Leppiniemi provide an empirical, data-based study of literary text comprehension, in order to discover what readers actually experience as they read. According to this approach, a text is a problem to be solved and the text comprehension or text processing is a form of problem-solving. One of their findings is that 'Neither communicative success nor text coherence depends on syntactic well-formedness', while another, perhaps more unexpected, finding is that the method used proved attractive to the informants and the whole process was 'suggestive for the development of teaching methods'.

Chapter eight

The reader as listener: dialect and relationships in *The Mayor of Casterbridge*

Raymond Chapman

The representation of speech through written language is a major part of the novelist's craft. Alice thought that a book without pictures or conversation was a dull book. We may learn in time to do without the pictures, but we cannot well conceive of a novel without dialogue. It advances the plot by showing how the characters grow and relate to each other in changing circumstances, and it gives information which might become tedious if confined to narrative. Additionally, and most importantly, it builds up the characters themselves: it establishes them as 'people' in a way that narrative and description alone can never do.

To say this is not to fall into a simplistic theory of mimesis, or to take a Bradleyan position which postulates some additional reality beyond the text in which hypotheses about the characters can be formed. It is fundamental to the tradition of that genre which has been subsumed under the word 'novel', diverse though the entities contained within it may be. We cannot proceed far in the criticism of the novel unless we agree with Hough's statement that 'Literature is meaningful fiction, an imaginary presentation that has nevertheless some meaningful relation with the real world'.[1] One of the criteria for this criticism is the skill with which the author differentiates his characters through dialogue, building up idiolects within his imaginary structure and not relying solely on the name-tags attached to speeches for identification. The novelist is far more than a straight reporter; yet his art includes what Fowler calls 'a clear instance of structural overlap between two distinct situations of discourse, the language of life and the language of fiction'.[2]

If the novel is in any sense related to life, what the characters say must convey the implied as well as the overt content of their conversation. Their relationships, like those of the real people who create, read and analyse the text, are not limited to verbal communication: yet those relationships are bound to affect what is said, and in turn to be affected by it. A verbal message can of course be transmitted neutrally, without any addition to its semantic meaning, as in news bulletins and the issuing of formal instructions in a technical process. In conversation, however, the message is seldom if ever totally neutral. The novelist therefore must be prepared to use more in dialogue than is needed simply to convey information about the objective facts which frame the speeches and form their surface content. To create in the reader the experience which has been imagined for the characters, other signals must be built in. Spoken exchanges are controlled not only by the need to communicate facts and opinions but also by the relationship between the persons, which creates linguistic *register*. This has been conveniently defined as 'variation in the selection of linguistic items for various purposes'; 'a set of contextual features bringing about a characteristic use of formal features'; 'a variety of the use of language as used by a particular speaker or writer in a particular context'.[3]

Register is more easily identified and described in some languages than in others. The 'polite' forms of Japanese have a specific morphological structure for use in certain situations; the choice of the second person singular rather than the formal plural in addressing one person in many European languages can create both problems and advantages for the speaker. English marks of register are harder to define and to teach to foreigners, but are readily accepted by native speakers.[4] A more intimate situation can be shown by the use of slang, by laconic sentences, and particularly by intonation. The same group of words said in different ways can convey completely different implications. Thus 'Do come in and sit down' is a neutral imperative sentence in writing but is transformed by spoken intonation into either a friendly welcome or a weary command to a troublesome child. The question, 'Do you want another drink?', can be said so as to indicate a relaxed situation or an explosive one.

The features which determine implicit rather than semantic meaning are stylistic. They give a connotative sense to the actual words used, adding to the denotative meaning and perhaps even superseding that meaning – what is actually being said may be different from what appears to be said. Some such features are easily accommodated in written form. The choice of words, the use of more colloquial syntax, the omission or inclusion of polite formulas, can all be transferred to writing with a guarantee of recognition by the intelligent reader. Others are less easily accessible: stress requires either typographical aid such as italic print or capital letters, or verbal comment additional to the spoken words. Intonation, gesture, facial expression, bodily movement, and the elusive 'atmosphere' of a conversation can be conveyed only by authorial comment. A point between prolonged comment and lack of direction can be reached through 'phonically-descriptive verbs' such as 'mutter', 'gasp', 'chuckle', 'squeal'.[5] These, together with deviant spelling and accepted typographical conventions, aid the writer's task of conveying an auditory experience through the written code – of helping the reader to 'hear' what is meant by marks on a page. The process gives an added dimension to the truth that, 'as readers of literature we are involved first and foremost in a response to language'.[6]

The novelist must convey these relationships and nuances through dialogue as far as possible. Narrative becomes tedious if it contains excessive description of how the characters sound and what they are implicitly communicating to one another. The author becomes intrusive and manipulative; and although some novelists have chosen to draw attention to their art and the unreality of their creations, even they must in general keep up the illusion that the characters have some kind of reality. Dialogue in a novel makes sense if it obeys the rule which governs coherence in living speech: 'the fact that some segments of language are only interpretable as rejoinders or replies to preceding speech events brought about in the most obvious cases by some other speaker'.[7]

The illusion depends on acceptance of the agreement about sight-sound correspondence in language. An alphabetical system allows a regular relationship between the letters and the phonemes known to users of a language, even if the correspondence is unbalanced and imperfect. English, with a much greater number of phonemes than letters, has a less tidy relationship than is possible in Italian or Welsh, but its speaker can accept the visual presentation of speech without much difficulty. Members of a literate society make the switch very easily, reading a play-text or taking notes of a lecture with equal facility. The novelist, however, cannot rest on the basic convention; he has to convey a great deal more than is permitted or needed in referential writing.

The relationship between the writer and the reader of fictional dialogue is unusual and complex. The reader's position is different from that of a party to a living conversation. In social speech there is at any given moment a speaker and one or more listeners. The listeners may be called *addressees* if the speaker's words are directed to them. The roles will continually change as the conversation takes its 'turns', unlike a lecture or a sermon where the addressees will keep the same relationship to the speaker throughout the discourse. In fictional dialogue these changing roles are assumed by the characters, as different persons in turn are imagined to be addressed by a speaker. The reader has a somewhat curious part in these exchanges. He is the ultimate addressee, the unseen and silent participant in the work of creation. The author may indeed apostrophize the reader directly, a manner more assumed by the Victorian than by the modern novelists. Yet even if the author chooses to remain remote and withdrawn, a god contemplating his creative work dispassionately like Joyce's image of the artist, the reader is still an essential part of the work, the target of all the dialogue. In this sense, the reader 'listens' to a number of different speakers whose words the author projects towards him.

There may, however, be another party to a conversation. Someone may be within hearing as a *receiver*, having no direct part in the exchanges but passively aware of all that is said.[8] The receiver may be a chance listener or a deliberate eavesdropper; in either case he has a general impression of the whole conversation, without the power to direct and change its course, or to take the turn of speaker. He stands outside its framework yet within its receptive area. The reader bears this relationship to what is supposed to be said in a novel. He takes in the situation as a whole but cannot influence it. He thus occupies a dual role, as both the author's ultimate addressee and also the receiver in an imaginary situation which is not supposed to be directed towards him at all. He is the author's target, the characters' unseen listener. Thus a character may change from S (speaker) to A (addressee) and back again. As S he or she may relate to more than one addressee at a time, as A^1, A^2 . . . The reader, ultimate addressee and never speaker, may be designated A^n, while he stands towards every speaker in the novel as R (receiver).

In some episodes a fictional character may stand as R rather than A in a passage of dialogue. The unseen auditor is a useful fictional device for giving a detached view of a conversation. Here the reader shares the position of the listening character; his own role as R is emphasized and seems to be brought closer to the action of the novel. The freedom of the R character to return to participation as S or A adds, perhaps not always consciously, to the reader's sense of being drawn into the story as well as standing outside it. The character as R, as a deliberate or chance eavesdropper, may be amused, plotting, imperilled or simply uninvolved. Examples of each type in turn can be found in Arabella and her companions overhearing Jude's grandiose plans in *Jude the Obscure*; Mrs Sparsit spying on Louisa and Harthouse in *Hard Times*; Jim Hawkins hiding in the apple barrel in *Treasure Island*; Helen and Rachel in the hotel garden in *The Voyage Out*.

Those who hear a conversation, as A or as R, react to it in a complex way. They will of course be aware of the overt message, the ideas and information which are being conveyed. In proportion to their linguistic awareness, their sensitivity and their interest in the background situation, they will be conscious also of other elements. The relationship of the participants, social or personal, their feelings about each other and about the subject of conversation, will appear through the prosodic features of speech such as stress and intonation, and through things which are not specific speech-features at all. Pauses, silence, gestures, and facial expressions play their part as much as lexical and syntactic choices.

Thus the listener, whether acting as A or R, has a heuristic problem to solve, unless he is a passive recorder with no personal interest in what is happening. To be really 'within' the conversation he needs to know the implications as well as the surface of what is being said. This problem is familiar to everyone in life and is projected into fictional dialogue by the critically aware reader. Both as A^n in his total encounter with the text, and as R in his imaginary contact with the characters, he is deprived of much that would help him to solve the problem with real people. There is no visual aid, except imagination and whatever information the author chooses to give. There is no actual hearing, so that penetration beneath the surface requires the same authorial aid. The passive experience of reading fiction therefore would be silent, solitary and confined to the semantic value attached to certain signs on a page. The true experience of the reader is more dynamic, with the semblance of being auditory, personally involved, and able to go past denotation to connotation and thus to relationships.

The degree to which the author assists the transition from passive to dynamic reading depends on skilful use of conventions, to which the reader must respond sensitively. If the author gives too much, the result is fussy, contrived and lacking in verisimilitude. If too little, interest may flag and the author's conception of felt life in the characters will not be conveyed. With some knowledge of the social background of the novel, it is possible to make heuristic use of the spoken words alone. Thus in Trollope's story 'The Journey to Panama' a youngish woman travelling alone is completely put down by an older, married woman. Discussing the latter's daughter, Miss Viner suggests that, 'If a lady knows what she is about, she need not fear a gentleman's attentions.' The reply is apparently sweet, but devastating:

> 'That's just what I tell Amelia; but then, my dear, she has not had so much experience as you and I.'

The suggestion that a single woman is as 'experienced' as an older,

married woman effectively closes a conversation in the England of
1860. The excess of authorial aid can be illustrated from Theodore
Dreiser, who lacked in stylistic finesse what he possessed in
observation and power:

> He continued his wry smile and mental examination, the
> while he said, 'We thought you would be showing up today or
> tomorrow. Did you have a pleasant trip?'
> 'Oh, yes, very,' replied Clive, a little confused by this inquiry.
> 'So you think you'd like to learn something about the
> manufacture of collars, do you?' Tone and manner were
> infiltrated by the utmost condescension.
> 'I would certainly like to learn something that would give me a
> chance to work up, have some future in it,' replied Clive genially
> and with a desire to placate his young cousin as much as
> possible.
>
> (*An American Tragedy*, ch. 5)

The temptation to make the implicit part of dialogue known by
explicit comments is one to which most novelists succumb at least
from time to time. D. H. Lawrence had a splendid ear for speech,
but he also liked to intrude his authorial presence, as in this passage
from chapter 13 of *The Rainbow*. Ursula Brangwen is starting work
as a teacher and is now sharing the lunch period with the depressed
and embittered Brunt and Miss Harby:

> 'Will it be so terrible?' she said, quivering, rather beautiful,
> but with a slight touch of condescension, because she would not
> betray her own trepidation.
> 'Terrible?' said the man, turning to his potatoes again. 'I
> dunno about terrible.'
> 'I *do* feel frightened,' said Ursula. 'The children seem so –'
> 'What?' said Miss Harby, entering at that moment.
> 'Why,' said Ursula, 'Mr. Brunt says I ought to tackle my
> class,' and she laughed uneasily.
> 'Oh, you have to keep order if you want to teach,' said Miss
> Harby, hard, superior, trite.
> Ursula did not answer. She felt non valid before them.
> 'If you want to be let to *live*, you have,' said Mr. Brunt.
> 'Well, if you can't keep order, what good *are* you?' said Miss
> Harby.

The reader is enabled to share much of the implicit relationship
which would be felt in a living conversation. There is direct
comment on the manner of speech: 'with a touch of condescension',
'hard, superior, trite'. There is attention also to the entirely

non-verbal signals: 'she laughed uneasily', 'did not answer'. The resources of typography are used to show heavy stress: *do, live, are.* Taken in its total context, the passage does not in fact present too much authorial presence because the reader is already close to the situation and can feel that these aspects of the dialogue are part of his own reception as R.

One of the features of speech which go beyond neutrality is the use of dialect or other substandard pronunciation. Lawrence hints at it in the spelling *dunno* for 'don't know'. Both in life and in fiction, the receipt of such speech is part of the heuristic process. It gives information about the speaker's social status, and thus about his relationships with others of a similar or different status. It may identify the speaker as a stranger or a native, according to the fit between the dialect and the geographical situation. Turner sees dialect as often acting in the same way as register, 'to divide speakers as well as speech'.[9] Leech prefers to distinguish the 'register scale' from the 'dialect scale', related as 'intersecting axes' so that the work of an author would have to be plotted with reference to both scales.[10] The debate could interestingly be continued, but for the present purpose it is enough to note that dialect is a clear signal beyond the meaning of the words used. When it appears in fiction, it may bring the reader as R closer to the characters about whom he is reading: 'hearing' what A^1 is supposed to be hearing as well as sharing the spoken message.

Once a system of orthography has been established in a language, it is not difficult to give some impression of dialect in writing. If normal spelling is used for narrative and for unmarked speech, deviant spelling readily shows deviant pronunciation. Indeed, the effect may be greater than that of dialect heard in real speech, which would be scarcely noticed in many situations if the message were clearly conveyed. Dialect obtrudes only when it is unexpected, either in the situation or from the speaker using it: and in such cases it may well show or create a special relationship between S and A. Its appearance in writing is always deviant and unexpected and thus fulfils Enkvist's criterion for style as measured by difference from a 'norm'.[11] It is likely to increase the interest felt towards its user, to foreground S in the view of the reader as R and to suggest either isolation from, or kinship with, other characters who share in turn the functions of S and A.

Now it is of course true that the 'normal' or unmarked speech implied by orthography is not homogeneous and, in the case of English, is not always the Received Pronunciation which might theoretically be equated with it. In reality, few of the normal-spelling speakers would be RP speakers, and even these would show considerable differences of idiophone and voice quality. The warning that 'Standard English' is itself a dialect, that is 'an amalgam of syntax and lexis' not to be equated with RP, is particularly relevant in dealing with fictional dialogue.[12] All that normal spelling suggests is that the sounds made by S do not convey any implication to A, or set up any relationship, above what is actually being said. The appearance of deviant spelling removes this neutrality and gives S a special role which may be humorous, contemptuous or intimate in relation to A.

The reader, both as R and as A[n], meets dialect through the eye and shares its effect with A[1], who is supposed to be receiving it through the ear. Because the signals received through writing are more subject to conventional expectation than those received through speech, he is more aware of them as deviant. The rapport with A[1] may not be close: if A[1] inhabits a dialect area, even though not a dialect speaker, he or she is less likely to take conscious note of dialect unless other factors in the situation make it prominent. The reader's immediate response is that of R, receiving speech which seems deviant and to some extent distanced. It may need an effort of the imagination to come back into the contextual situation and receive dialect as A[1], A[2] etc. are hearing it – to change from the neutral role and borrow other ears. It is a necessary transition for a satisfactory reading of the text, and one which the author can assist.

A sample of written dialect from the first chapter of *The Mayor of Casterbridge* may serve for illustration. Michael Henchard has just 'sold' his wife and daughter to a passing sailor; one of the bystanders comments:

> 'Serves the husband well be-right,' said the staylace vendor. 'A comely respectable body like her – what can a man want more? I glory in the woman's sperrit. I'd ha' done it myself – od send if I wouldn't, if a husband had behaved so to me! I'd go, and 'a might call, and call, till his keacorn was raw; but I'd never come back – no, not till the great trumpet, would I!' (14)[13]

This shows that it is not difficult to convey in writing the impression of dialect. Deviant spelling and syntax, with unusual lexical items, bring the reader into a 'listening' situation which recognises a particular mode of speech. No such rendering can be complete without a full phonetic transcription, which would of course defeat the communicative purpose and alienate most readers. The same can happen with excessive use of deviant spelling; the Yorkshire speech of Joseph in *Wuthering Heights* is sometimes baffling and can break the flow of reception.[14] Certain literary conventions for depicting dialect have developed, resting on normal expectations and reaction to deviance as a stylistic feature. The rolled lingual /r/ of Scots speech is shown by repetition of the written letter *r*. Cockney is suggested by dropping the initial *h* and the final *g* in words ending with *-ing*. While the serious dialectologist may reasonably object that these are crude and inadequate renderings, the convention moves even farther from reality when deviant spelling to suggest substandard speech is actually closer than orthography to standard pronunciation. By the normal, if loose, correspondence of sound and letter in English, *sez* and *wot* represent the educated pronunciation better than *says* and *what*.[15] No matter: the convention is accepted that characters who would misspell words would also have substandard speech.

It is therefore not difficult for an author to foreground a character by signalling speech different from the norm. Although the desire to re-create auditory experience through writing, with ingenious use of onomatopoeia, may be an interesting experiment in literature, the value of dialect in the novel is probably less synaesthetic than pragmatic. A character can be isolated from others, put in a comic or embarrassing social situation, by building in the right signals. This is fairly superficial and generally applies only to a single episode. The reader of a serious novel expects to be introduced to the deeper relationships which are shown in life by register. In critical terms, the success or failure of the novelist to do this makes the difference between denotation and connotation, and conse-quently decides how far the encounter with the text will be an imaginative and enriching experience. Too much signalling can be counter-productive; too little may fail to make the point. Is it possible to design an ideal ratio of deviance to normality? To ask such a question leads towards the excess of naturalism. Surely the novelist desires to gain the attention of the reader as A^n and share with him the significant factors in the imaginary situation, rather than to create a completely mimetic experience.

The purpose of dialect in serious fiction is not simply to establish the status of certain characters and their loose relationship to others, though these may be part of its function. It may also suggest the more delicate and shifting relationships of particular encounters and conversations. If the framework of imagination is to mesh with the framework of reality, without ceasing to be an artistic structure, a character will respond variously to other characters and the response will alter, and perhaps alter back, as events develop. Connotation in style has been described as 'choices being made with an eye to what has already been said and what will be said later';[16] and this may be particularly important with regard to the specific 'saying' of dialogue. The control of dialect signals may be one way of showing the reader what is 'really going on': to suggest what A^1 is hearing beyond the actual semantic content of the words spoken.

The author's skill may bring the reader close to the auditory experience of A^1. What is more important is to enable him to share the relationship in which that experience is contained. It is possible to build some auditory factors into the written code without explicit commentary. The same signals can be used to build in register factors, supplementing or obviating the author's intervention. The use of dialect features may be less important for the imaginative 'ear' of the reader than for his pragmatic response to the contextual situation. Again, the use of too many deviant spellings and unfamiliar items may prevent communication on this level as on others; but the author may need partially to contradict the clarity principle for the sake of effect. The use of dialect in fiction may to some extent destroy Leech's first maxim of this principle – 'retain a direct and transparent relationship between semantic and phonological structure (i.e. between message and text)', with allowance for the written code standing for the phonological. However, Leech also recognizes the type of clarity which creates a message 'perspicuous or intelligible in the sense of conveying the intended illocutionary goal to the addressee'.[17]

This brings us close to the art of fictional dialogue, related both to a character as A^1 and to the reader as A^n. The author takes the risk of partially obscuring the text in order to make the conversational situation more realistic and more effective. The text may be less important than the hidden message: what is said may be less important than the manner of its saying, because it is the unspoken relationship that is most significant. This is certainly sometimes true in life, where speech may be phatic, threatening, reassuring, etc., with only minimal importance attached to the actual words used. Text obscurity may actually make the intended contact more efficient in social speech, where attention is directed to the implicit rather than the explicit message, though not in scientific and technical communication where clarity of text is the essential aim.

The manipulation of dialect signals may depend less on the desire to make as accurate a transcription as normal letters can provide than on the importance of those signals in the immediate context. It is not how the characters 'really' speak that matters, but rather how their speech shows them to stand in relationship to others. When Hardy introduces a minor character in *The Mayor of Casterbridge* who is a magistrate, he gives him the 'normal' speech of standard spelling in contrast to the illiterate constable, Subberd:

'What can we poor lammigers do against such a multitude!' expostulated Stubberd, in answer to Mr. Grower's chiding. ''Tis

tempting them to commit *felo de se* upon us, and that would be
the death of the perpetrator; and we wouldn't be the cause of a
fellow-creature's death on no account, not we!'

'Get some help, then! Here, I'll come with you. We'll see
what a few words of authority can do. Quick now; have you got
your staves?' (323)

In the hierarchy of English society at the supposed time of the
novel, Mr Grower's real equivalent would not have stood very high,
high, and would almost certainly have had a detectable Dorset
accent. Hardy is concerned with his superior relationship to
Stubberd, not to his abstract status, so he foregrounds the constable
with deviant syntax, dialect lexis, and malapropism. The effect is to
heighten the reader's experience, and to keep him within the text
instead of speculating about 'background' social realities.

The novels of Thomas Hardy provide excellent material to
illustrate the suggestions which have been developed. He was much
concerned with the representation of dialect, at a time when social
awareness of varieties of speech was increasing. His method was not
based on scientific phonetic principles, which were in any case not
far advanced during his most productive period as a novelist, but he
had a good understanding of what was in question. He could both
describe and represent the speech-differences which would be most
striking to his readers, and he regarded dialect as a serious factor in
the world of his novels. He was careful to avoid the excessive
deviance which hindered understanding in the work of Emily
Brontë and the poems of his own Dorset contemporary William
Barnes, whom he liked and admired. When he was criticized by the
Athenaeum reviewer for the dialogue in *The Return of the Native*, he
defended himself in words which show that he was concerned with
impression rather than precision and was prepared to draw on all
aspects of speech and not only the phonological:

An author may be said to fairly convey the spirit of intelligent
peasant talk if he retains the idiom, compass, and characteristic
expressions, although he may not encumber the page with
obsolete pronunciations of the purely English words, and with
mispronunciations of those derived from Latin and Greek. In
the printing of standard speech hardly any phonetic principle at
all is observed; and if a writer attempts to exhibit on paper the
precise accents of a rustic speaker he disturbs the proper balance
of a true interpretation by unduly insisting upon the grotesque
element; thus directing attention to a point of inferior interest,
and diverting it from the speaker's meaning.[18]

Hardy's concern for the effect of dialect on the reader, rather than as a show of virtuosity in translating the auditory code into the written, is made abundantly clear in his fiction.[19] His awareness of dialect was well used in the service of his best qualities as a novelist: his sensitivity to both social and personal relationships, and his capacity for conveying the feelings of his characters towards each other. The fictional world which he created for his people was 'Wessex', a wide area of south and south-west English with its centre in the Dorset of his youth and later years. Although his mother is said to have discouraged his use of dialect when he was a child, he retained enough of an accent for his wife to notice it on their first meeting, when he was thirty.[20] Wessex was his particular which held the universal, and he was anxious not to let the localizing at which he was so skilful be a limitation on the human dimension of his characters. Deeply aware of the continuity and flow of life, he knew also that changes were flooding into his world, prefiguring a new age which, if not Utopian, at least brought new challenges and was inescapable in the light of evolutionary understanding.

In such a world, the use of dialect was taking on a significance which it had never before possessed. It was becoming more a mark of social inferiority, to be consciously eschewed by those like Ethelberta Chickerel and Grace Melbury who have 'bettered themselves', and not to be heard from those like Paula Power who come from a superior background of wealth. It remains a distinguishing, shared and comforting feature of the 'workfolk' who make up the majority of the rural population. Some, like Tess, can switch from dialect to standard speech according to circumstances. Hardy's comment on her shows that he was well aware of dialect as a sign of register:

> Mrs. Durbeyfield habitually spoke the dialect; her daughter who had passed the Sixth Standard in the National School under a London-trained mistress, spoke two languages: the dialect at home, more or less; ordinary English abroad and to persons of quality.
>
> (*Tess of the D'Urbervilles*, bk 1, ch. 3)

In the earlier, serialized version of the novel, the words after *mistress* are, 'used it only when excited by joy, surprise, or grief'. Whether in social or emotional relationship, the effect of dialect is strongly felt. Hardy's concern for the pragmatic response to dialect, rather than for a phonetic rendering, is further shown in his preface to the 1912 edition of *The Mayor of Casterbridge*. Referring to criticisms of the speech attributed to Farfrae he explains:

It must be remembered that the Scotchman of the tale is represented not as he would appear to other Scotchmen, but as he would appear to people of outer regions.

In taking Hardy to illustrate the heuristic effect of dialect in fiction, *The Mayor of Casterbridge* (1886) is chosen as a text in which relationships are particularly sensitive, shifting and uncertain. At its centre stands the Mayor himself, Michael Henchard, a man of no education whom we meet first as an itinerant rural craftsman, seeking for work, who abandons his wife and child in a mock sale when drunk. Sobered by his act, he abstains from drink, comes to the country town of Casterbridge, establishes his own business and eventually becomes mayor. The advent of Farfrae, a clever young Scot, is the beginning of his downfall. Without any villainous intent, Farfrae prospers by his skill, acquires Henchard's business, and marries Lucetta who has come to live in Casterbridge after a previous intimate acquaintance with Henchard in Jersey. Henchard's wife and supposed daughter also come to the town after a long absence. He remarries his wife, who dies not long afterwards, and discovers that the girl, Elizabeth-Jane, is really the daughter of Newsom, the sailor to whom he had sold his wife. After the death of Lucetta, Farfrae marries Elizabeth-Jane. Henchard dies alone, destitute and embittered.

The brief analysis which follows is not presented as anything approaching a detailed study of the use of dialect in this novel. It offers simply a few examples of how the general observations which have previously been made may be illustrated from an actual text. Not all conversation is loaded with implicit meanings, either in a novel or in life. The dialect features which are heard may not have bearing on the business of direct communication. Yet the way in which Hardy varies the intensity of his dialect signals in relation to different situations and personal encounters can be seen as significant. The reader is not to suppose that the characters' accents are fluctuating in an objective sense (though emotion and stress may bring out latent dialect qualities, as Hardy notes in the earlier description of Tess quoted above). Rather, the force of dialect reveals how the character as S stands towards A^1 at the moment of speaking, and thus how the silent reader as R should respond to the text at this point. The author is inviting him as A^n to share the position of A^1 and offering him the means to do this. When there is no strong implicit message, dialect signals may be reduced or removed altogether from characters who at other times have them: the neutrality of regular spelling presents the neutrality of the explicit statement.

1. Strangeness or isolation

A character may be shown as an outsider in the eyes of those around him. This is most marked in the case of Farfrae, who shows strong dialect features when he first arrives in Casterbridge. He explains to Henchard that he is not the expected applicant for the post as manager:

> 'It is true I am in the corren trade – but I have replied to no advairrtisement, and arranged to see no one. I am on my way to Bristol – from there to the other side of the warrld, to try my fortune in the great wheat-growing districts of the West!' (52)

The signals here are strong, though confined to three words; suggestions of different vowel quality and of the rolled *r* show Farfrae to be a stranger from Scotland – an identity emphasized by his surname. His speech strikes oddly on Henchard's ear, and there is no need for a detailed transcription. As the acquaintance of the two men develops, Farfrae's accent is less apparent. When he talks to Elizabeth-Jane there is only the hint of Scots speech:

> 'O no, I don't want to go back! Yet I'll sing the song to you wi' pleasure whenever you like. I could sing it now, and not mind at all.' (108)

When he begins his alienation from Henchard the accent seems to grow stronger – a sign that Henchard is newly aware of his partner's alien quality and is now irritated by it:

> 'You're no yoursel' the day?' Donald inquired.
> 'Yes, I'm very well,' said Henchard.
> 'But ye are a bit down – surely ye are down?' (115)

When he first meets Newsom, the sailor hears the Scots accent to which the people of Casterbridge have become accustomed:

> 'A great deal of trouble and expense would be saved ye? – and 'tis a convenience when a couple's married not to hae far to go to get home!' (363)

Yet only a few pages earlier, he shows no such signals in speaking to Elizabeth-Jane:

> 'Ah, I doubt there will be any good in secrets! A secret cast a deep shadow over my life. And well you know what it was.' (352)

The reader is not supposed to assume that Farfrae's accent comes and goes unpredictably. Rather, it shows his relationship to those

with whom he speaks, according to the significance which awareness of his accent plays in the total situation between them. The
reader is brought closer to A¹ by detecting strange elements in the
speech of S.

2. Social differences

Henchard's speech varies considerably according to his role as S.
He might generally be understood, as a man of no breeding and
formal education, to have quite a strong Dorset accent. But on his
first appearance in the novel, his speech is in marked contrast to that
of another countryman whom he meets. Henchard is the first
speaker:

> 'Then is there any house to let – a little small new cottage just
> a builded, or such like?'
> 'Pulling down is more the nater of Weydon. There were five
> houses cleared away lass year, and three this; and the volk
> nowhere to go – no, not so much as a thatched hurdle.' (4)

While Henchard's syntax shows some substandard features, his
interlocutor has the signals of heavier accent through deviant
spelling of common words. Henchard is depicted as a superior
character – not in point of refinement but of potential interest in the
story which he is to dominate.

When Henchard is successful and becomes mayor, he speaks
almost without a trace of dialect. Hardy actually removed a passage
in strong dialect, spoken when Henchard is mayor, in the course of
revision.²¹ He is 'heard' as a man of authority, the exact sound of
whose speech is irrelevant to the respect in which he is held. So too
when he talks with his wife and supposed daughter. When he has
fallen and is working as a journeyman for Farfrae, his speech sounds
rougher as a sign of how people now regard him. The dialect signals
become liberal:

> 'A fellow of his age going to be Mayor, indeed!. . . But 'tis
> her money that floats en upward. Ha-ha – how cust odd it is!
> Here be I, his former master, working for him as man, and he
> the man standing as master.' (264)

The contrast is marked by the way in which, during his prosperity,
he censures Elizabeth-Jane for her use of dialect words:

> 'Bide where you be', he echoed sharply. 'Good God, are you
> only fit to carry wash to a pig-trough, that ye use such words as
> those?' (148)

Elizabeth-Jane accepts the rebuke and tries to improve her speech. There have been few dialect signals previously in her conversation: her accent has no effect on those around her, but Henchard in his new gentility becomes aware of it. Thus again the reader shares the experience of A^1, feeling the status in local society of S equally with the overt message received.

3. Emotional pressure

It is reasonable to suppose that a latent accent may grow stronger when there is an emotional element in the situation. In fictional dialogue, the effect is not so much realistic, carefully measured to show the amount of increase, but rather to allow the reader to enter into the situation. When Henchard is poor and wretched, he hears from Elizabeth-Jane of the death of Lucetta; stronger dialect is shown in his speech, including the word 'bide' which he had once censured her for using. Farfrae, embarrassed and moved by Henchard's plight, reverts to the strong accent of his first appearance – 'It's the way of the warrld' (260). Even in conversation with Lucetta the signals are apparent:

> 'I couldna sing to-night! It's Henchard – he hates me . . . I would understand why there should be a wee bit envy; but I cannot see a reason for the whole intensity of what he feels.' (279)

While it could be argued that emotion has caused reversion, so that these speeches represent what A^1 'really hears' in each case, the effect on the reader is not so much to share with A^1 as to receive impressions which go beyond the sounds of speech. In the imagined situation, expression and manner would show more than was being said, and set up a feeling of sympathy or hostility between S and A^1. The reader, having only the words on the page, is brought into the secret without excessive authorial comment.

4. Ease of intimacy

The complete absence of dialect features from the speech of those who might realistically be assumed to have them can be taken as a sign of intimacy and relaxation. When Henchard converses normally with his returned wife Susan, with Elizabeth-Jane and with Farfrae, none of them shows dialect beyond occasional usage of forms like 'ye'. Farfrae usually has scarcely any accent in speaking to Lucetta; and the latter, befitting her status as a woman of substance, has no dialect features. As in life, the characters are not aware of speech peculiarities in those whom they know well and see daily: it is only in tense situations that there is a sense of differences, so that the messages become loaded with other elements.

It is, however, possible for dialect itself to function as a mark of intimacy and alienation at the same time. The ordinary people of Casterbridge and the surrounding area speak with strong dialect. The effect is to distance them, not so much from the principal characters in themselves as from the tragic action. As often in Hardy's fiction, they act as a kind of chorus, playing some part in the plot but unaffected by it and free to comment upon it. The fact that their speech is visually more deviant than that of those who directly suffer, sets them apart in the reader's consciousness. Yet it also gives them a sense of cohesion and sharing among themselves: detached from the rest, they know the ease of a spoken code which makes no excessive demands because its very deviance is familar and unnoticed.

Examples are frequent throughout the novel. A combination of deviant syntax, lexis, and spelling serves to foreground the speech of those whose lives were settled before Henchard or Farfrae came to Casterbridge, and will continue whatever happens to them. Sometimes the choric function is strongly marked. After the death of Susan Henchard, the townspeople discuss her and her husband. One of their number has stolen the coins left to close the dead woman's eyes; his deed is defended, against the majority opinion, by the philosophic observations of Solomon Longways:

> 'I say it to-day, and 'tis a Sunday morning, and I wouldn't speak wrongfully for a zilver zixpence at such a time. I don't see noo harm in it. To respect the dead is sound doxology; and I wouldn't sell skellintons – leastwise respectable skellintons – to be varnished for 'natomies, except I were out of work. But money is scarce and throats get dry. Why should death rob life o' fourpence?' (137)

The encounter with a principal character may be no more direct. A dialect speaker will enter into conversation, but still seem distanced from the other. When Henchard demands that the choir shall sing a 'cursing psalm' against Farfrae, their leader replies:

> 'I know the Psa'am – I know the Psa'am . . . but I would as lief not sing it. 'Twasn't made for singing. We chose it once when the gipsy stole the pa'son's mare, thinking to please him, but pa'son were quite upset.' (269)

The consistent use of dialect for a group of characters gives them a shared identity from which their individual characteristics can emerge, without threatening the primacy in the text of the principal characters who have more personal idioms. The reader is addressed directly by the author, being given signals which are supposed to be less apparent to the characters themselves. The reader as A^n knows more about roles and relationships than the words of dialogue alone would convey.

5. Specific role

A particularly interesting use of dialect is in the character of the woman who aids Henchard's downfall by serving him 'furmity' with rum in it. Years later she is brought before him, as mayor and magistrate, for offences in the street in Casterbridge. In her early appearance she is a strong dialect speaker, like the members of the 'chorus':

> 'I can mind a man doing something of a sort – a man in a cord jacket, with a basket of tools; but, Lord bless ye, we don't gi'e it head-room, we don't, such as that.' (24)

When she appears in court, she defends herself by giving evidence of Henchard's offence. Her speech loses almost all traces of dialect:

> 'A man and a woman with a little child came into my tent . . . they sat down and had a basin apiece. Ah Lord's my life! I was of a more respectable station in the world than I am now.' (231)

She has assumed a new temporary role: no longer simply a coarse woman accused in court but an avenging voice from the past that hastens Henchard's tragedy. It is not that her voice changes, but the listeners become unaware of its peculiarities as they concentrate on her actual words. The explicit message is what dominates the situation; the change of style shows the implicit feelings of those present by foregrounding what is explicit, and regular spelling assumes a kind of deviance. The reader, signalled to as A^n, shares the tension of A^1 as he acts as R towards the whole conversation. The tension is heightened as the woman concludes with an almost formal indictment:

> 'It proves he's no better than I, and has no right to sit there in judgment upon me'

and as Henchard responds with a trace of dialect in his shame:

> 'No – 'tis true . . . 'Tis as true as the light.'

These are only brief selections from a single text. They and other examples need to be studied in full context to get their real effect.

The critic must also be alert to the literary fashions and conventions which may govern presentation, such as the tendency of Dickens and others to give perfect standard English to virtuous and innocent characters like Oliver Twist, irrespective of supposed environment. There is perhaps enough here to suggest that visual signals of deviance can show more than the words which are being spoken, just as in life various factors of speech can make the implicit more important than the explicit. The reader, passive as R, is required also to be active in response as A^n, to read the signals and learn about relationships and situations. The signals, whether of dialect or of other features, have a heuristic function. The recurrent features which form stylistic evidence may be occasioned by the pragmatic needs of an imaginary human situation.

The reader of a novel is doing much more than simply following a story. He is entering into a nexus of attitudes and relationships which must affect all that is supposed to be said between the characters. The reader comes to the text with living experience, aware of pragmatic elements in his own encounters, even if he cannot isolate or name them technically. Concentration and sympathy without direct involvement may sharpen his reception of such features. The reader approaches the text with experience; he may leave it with greater sensitivity to fresh experience of that even more complicated nexus which is at the heart of human life and which so often shows itself by what accompanies human speech.

Notes

1 G. Hough, *An Essay on Criticism* (London: Duckworth), 1960, p. 44
2 R. Fowler, *Linguistics and the Novel* (London: Methuen), 1977, p. 114
3 W. A. Bennett, *Aspects of Language and Language Learning* (Cambridge: Cambridge University Press), 1968, p. 50; R. Fowler 'Linguistic theory and the study of literature', in R. Fowler (ed.), *Essays on Style and Linguistics* (London: Routledge & Kegan Paul), 1970, p. 14; A. E. Darbyshire, *A Description of English* (London: Edward Arnold), 1967, p. 23
4 R. Chapman, 'Developing awareness of register in English', *System*, 10, 2, 1982, 113–8
5 G. N. Leech, *Principles of Pragmatics* (London: Longman), 1983, pp. 212f.
6 R. Carter (ed.), *Language and Literature* (London: Allen and Unwin), 1982, p. 4
7 W. Edmondson, *Spoken Discourse* (London: Longman), 1981, p. 15
8 G. N. Leech, (1983), p. 13; cf. J. Lyons, *Semantics* (Cambridge: Cambridge University Press), 1977, vol. 1, p. 34
9 G. W. Turner, *Stylistics* (Harmondsworth: Penguin), 1973, p. 166

10   G. N. Leech, 'Linguistics and the figures of rhetoric' in R. Fowler (ed.), *Essays on Style and Language* (London: Routledge & Kegan Paul), 1966, p. 138

11   N. E. Enkvist, *Linguistic Stylistics* (The Hague: Mouton), 1973, p. 21

12   M. Stubbs, *Language and Literacy* (London: Routledge & Kegan Paul), 1980, p. 125

13   References in parentheses after quotations from *The Mayor of Casterbridge* refer to pages in the 'Wessex' edition (London: Macmillan), 1920

14   Joseph speaks much more 'broadly' than his equals and this suggests that Emily Brontë intended his use of dialect to be more than representational: he has a sinister role in the plot

15   Allowance must sometimes be made for changes in educated pronunciation: older speakers would often have said [seiz] and [mɔt]. It is literary convention that causes the reader to react to these forms, even if they now represent standard speech

16   P. M. Wetherill, *The Literary Text* (Oxford: Blackwell), 1974, p. 96

17   Leech, (1983), pp. 66,100

18   *Athenaeum*, 2, 1872, p. 654

19   R. W. V. Elliott, *Thomas Hardy's English* (Oxford: Blackwell), 1984; R. Chapman, 'A true representation: speech in the novels of Thomas Hardy', in B. White (ed.), *Essays and Studies* (London: John Murray), n.s. vol. 36, 1983

20   E. Hardy, *Some Recollections* (Oxford: Oxford University Press), 1979, p. 33

21   N. F. Blake, *Non-Standard Language in English Literature* (London: Deutsch), 1981, p. 167

Chapter nine

Inscriptions in *Paradise Lost*: five variants of a vertical context system

Claes Schaar

Time and space are, as usual, limited, and I am not sure that it would be a very profitable task to examine in detail the discussion of the meaning of 'context' over the last few years. As far as I can see, there is no startling news in this field after Enkvist's articles of 1976 and 1980, though readers who want to update and/or supplement their knowledge may glean a point or two from Derrida, Genette, Suleiman and Crosman's essay collection, Riffaterre and Said.[1] For my own part it is sufficient, as a beginning, to posit the existence of an essentially reader-based coherent non-linear structure surrounding a word or a group of words. Just as, in epigraphy, an inscription is only seemingly 'out of context', so there are textual elements which work like inscriptions in actualizing meaning not deducible from the horizontal environment. The obvious difference, that an inscription is surrounded by a void, will, I hope, prove to be less important than it seems to be. A special kind of similarity is of greater interest: the interpreting epigrapher fills the void, the constructor of a vertical context system (see below) does so too, on a concrete, pragmatic level, up to a point unassisted by the actual linear context, for which he or she substitutes another one on an infralevel. The linear, or horizontal, environment is, in a sense, non-existent. So in both cases, *mutatis mutandis*, voids are filled with the aid of the reader's knowledge, susceptibility and experience. We are dealing with poetry and therefore not with meaning only – whatever definition of the term we use – but also of course with overtones and 'haloes'. The infralevels provide sounding-boards for the words in Milton.

What happens from the point of view of style, more exactly, is that the poetic discourse increases in density and becomes more forcible, a phenomenon which was described quite early by one of the most influential of the Greek rhetoricians, Demetrius. Of the various details which make a style forcible (*deinós*) he refers particularly to 'what is distantly hinted at' (*hyponoóumenon*) and which thus demands an effort on the part of the reader. Longinus in his treatise on the Sublime emphasizes everything in style that induces wonder. These notions suggest ideas in Baroque literary theory. Tesauro discussing the marvellous explains the device 'allusione' as one which makes the ingenious mind move towards strange and distant matters. His contemporary Pallavicino similarly stresses the effect on the reader of features in literature which strike him as marvellous and far removed from the ordinary paths taken by the mind. Such devices and their effects were intimately connected with the Baroque doctrine of wit, aptly analysed by J. Mazzeo in a well-known essay. The marvellous 'was expected to furnish some remarkable new similitude or insight and arouse wonder'. Nor should we forget the element of obscurity and hence difficulty in this context. Augustine had a good deal to say about obscurity as an important element of style. Obscurity in the style of Scripture, for example, is a challenge which whets our appetite for more insight and knowledge. It is easily seen that these phenomena are pragmatic in that the effects involved depend on the reader's responsiveness and ability to pick up echoes. It is very much a question of the relation between signs and those who use them.[2]

In this paper I use some terms I have used before, but not from habit or because of their somewhat technical character. 'Infracontext' indicates words or word-groups in some text or texts which are suggested by similar details in a text we study. Recognition is thus an essential factor. In many cases it is a question of allusions, but since allusions proper are, by definition, deliberate, since we can seldom say with absolute certainty what similarities on points of detail are deliberate or not (what is half-conscious, subconscious, and so on?), and since I am interested in the reader rather than the author, I prefer my own term. The result of the semantic relationship between the different textual strata is a 'vertical context system' which, if I may quote myself, may 'include allusions in the proper sense of the term, overt or covert, and all conceivable borderline cases down to reminiscences and faint echoes of various kinds, quite irrespective of authors' awareness. The only relevant criterion is that associative richness is conveyed infracontextually, or else that the surface context [the text primarily studied] provides intensification, and that in the majority of cases meaning of some kind is imparted to surface context by infracontext'.[3] The point is that, in the humanities as in the sciences, a descriptive model is supposed to cover as much material as possible without leaving loose ends lying about. Anyway, within the field of stylistics described above I shall attempt a rough typology, distinguishing between five special groups.

In the first group a single word emerges, supported by an infracontext operating steeply underneath a bulge containing a variety of uses, a mixed bag. As an example of this phenomenon, we choose the word 'baleful' as employed in the first book of *Paradise Lost* about Satan, whose pride, arrogance, and punishment are described before the poet turns his attention to the fallen angel himself, tormented by the thought of 'lost happiness and lasting pain' (55). Then there is a glimpse of the evil spirit himself, concentrated on his eyes: 'Round he throws his baleful eyes', which expressed 'huge affliction and dismay/Mixed with obdurate pride and steadfast hate', and which take in the dismal scene around him. We are not now concerned with other instances of the word 'baleful' in Milton (such as 'the baleful streams' for the four infernal rivers at *Paradise Lost* 2.576, or the 'baleful drugs' in *Comus* 255). These uses are reminiscent of the instances in the mixed bag containing examples of the word in Shakespeare, for example all those parts of *Henry VI* where the semantic area is vaguely represented by the word 'pernicious' (Schmidt)[4]. In *1 Hen. VI* 2.1.15 Talbot describes the opportunity to take the French unawares, thus quitting their 'deceit/Contrived by art and baleful sorcery'. In the same play, York refuses to lay down the conditions of the truce with France; anger chokes his voice 'By sight of these our baleful enemies' 5.4.122, where 'baleful' means 'causing destruction' as well as 'hateful'. In *2 Hen. VI* 3.2.48 the King addresses Suffolk, bearing the news of Gloucester's death: 'Thou baleful messenger, out of my sight!' (=harbinger of disaster). Again in *3 Hen. VI* 2.1.97 in a similar context, announcing the death of the Duke of York, Richard speaks of this and other catastrophes as 'our baleful news'. Turning to *Titus Andronicus* 2.3.95 we find Tamora describing 'the barren detested vale' into which she has been enticed: 'the trees, though summer, yet forlorn and lean,/O'ercome with moss and baleful mistletoe:/Here never shines the sun; here nothing breeds/Unless the nightly owl or fatal raven', etc. The description forms part of the 'weird garden' tradition exemplified in Tasso's account of the dismal forest outside Jerusalem in the *Gerusalemme Liberata* 3.56 or the infernal garden in Marino's *Sospetto d'Herode* 44, inspired by the weird forest surrounding the Palace of Mars in Boccaccio's *Teseida* 7.31. Against this background, 'baleful' in *Titus Andronicus* would correspond to Italian 'funesto', 'infausto', or 'nocente'. Similarly translatable are the friar's words in *Romeo and Juliet* 2.3.7ff., where he says his first task before sunrise will be to fill up his osier cage with 'baleful weeds and precious-juiced flowers', preparations for supplying the sleeping-potion in act IV. The 'baleful-herb' group and the various associations involved also suggest the

Greek adjective *lygrós*, as in Homer's *phármaka lygrá* (*Od.* 10.236), Circe's baleful drugs bringing forgetfulness and casting a spell over her guests. In Spenser, 'baleful' is common (40 cases) and used in all sorts of contexts (with 'bowre', 'house', 'mansion', as a small group by itself), but not in the way Milton uses it in 1.56.

Leaving these bulges in Shakespeare and Spenser we climb down into the narrow shaft provided in some passages in Euripides in order to find infracontextually relevant instances.[5] The adjective *skythrōpós* covers a semantic area which can be roughly characterized by 'angry-looking', 'menacing', 'sullen', 'of sad countenance', in Latin a combination of 'torvus', 'minax', and 'tristis' (Ovid, characteristically, says 'torva forma minantis' in *Pont.* 2.8.22). In *Medea* 271 Creon, banishing Medea, whom he has come to fear and hate, addresses her with the words *se τεn skythrōpòn kai pósei thymouménēn*, aptly rendered in A. S. Way's edition by 'black-lowering woman, wroth against thy lord'. *Skythrōpón*, highly suggestive, calls up Medea's dangerousness and fearful record, a menace to the people around her. A somewhat different atmosphere surrounds the word in *Hippolytos* 1152, where the chorus announces the arrival of one of Hippolytos' attendants, who approaches *skythrōpòn*, 'with sorrowful and ill-boding countenance'. He brings the tidings of the youth's violent death, and the word suggests not only the expression of sorrow and fear, but signals the whole subsequent story of doom and tragedy. A similar function of the word, even more obvious, is met with in *The Phoenician Maidens* 1333, where the messenger announcing the deaths of Creon's sister and her two sons has *skythrōpòn ómma kai prósōpon*, 'eyes and face expressing despair and sorrow', the messenger being about to tell a story of horrors. The words also evoke the tragedy, unavoidable and bringing with it other tragedies. In a fourth instance from Euripides, the tragedy of Alcestis' death forms the context of characterizing the way in which the servant watches Hercules entering (*Alcestis* 774). Here the word suggests not only despair but the servant's anger and menacing looks as he watches Hercules, unfamiliar as yet with the tragedy that has befallen Admetus' house. The word in these various contexts in Euripidean tragedies, in short, suggests the same feelings that are concentrated in Satan's 'baleful eyes': hatred, fear, sorrow and despair, and also anticipating, by their expression, coming disaster, as in fact we know will later overtake Satan and his comrades. This adds an element of Sophoclean irony to the word, if we are prepared and allow it to be suggested by 'baleful' in Milton. It adds to the significance and the stylistic effect of the word in *Paradise Lost* irrespective of its immediate surroundings. The prerequisite for this effect, of course, is that we are intensely (not vaguely) aware of the contexts in Euripides.

In the second type of 'inscription' we have to do with a combination of words which derive their full meaning from contact with a set of phrases in several contexts in a homogeneous body of literature: patrology. The inscription viewed in such a light has a double function: it aids interpretation, and simultaneously carries forceful connotations throwing this interpretation in important relief. The relevant words in *Paradise Lost* are met with in 8.107ff., where they form part of Raphael's comment on the swiftness of his descent to Eden: 'The swiftness of those Circles attribute,/Though numberless, to his Omnipotence,/That to corporeal substances could adde/*Speed almost Spiritual*; mee thou thinkst not slow,/Who since the Morning hour set out from Heav'n/Where God resides, and ere mid-day arrived/In Eden, distance inexpressible/By Numbers that have name.' According to Fowler, the idea that speed is spiritual 'depends on the ancient and medieval belief that the spheres were moved by intelligences or spirits'. Fowler[6] refers to Ficino's Commentary on Plotinus' *Enneads* (2.1–3) which establishes an analogy between the movement of the heavens and that of the soul in thought. Fowler's interpretation is indeed reasonable in view of Raphael's words, 'The swiftness of those Circles', etc. However, a more relevant comment on Milton's text was made by Pearce: 'It is God's Omnipotence which gives to the circles, though so numberless, such a degree of swiftness.'[7] In a vertical context it is an important and well-known theme in patrology that one of the properties of the angels is their incomprehensible speed, thus in fact a prerequisite for the movements of the intelligences, one of the order of the angels. The theme is first found in the earliest of the Latin Fathers, Tertullian, who stresses that the speed is such that angels and demons can be simultaneously present wherever they wish: 'Omnis spiritus alis est: hoc est angeli et demones. Igitur momento ubique sunt. Totus orbis illis locus unus est' (*Apologeticum*, 22.8). Later, Anselm of Canterbury stressed the angels' willingness and readiness to serve God: 'Per te millia millium, ad complenda Patris mysteria, alacri discursu meant inter caelum et terram, quasi apes negotiosae inter alvearia et flores, disponentes omnia suaviter; populus accinctus, nesciens labem et inobidentiae moram' (*De Christo, Meditatio* 3). In some Greek patristic texts, the theme of obedience and submission to God's will is a marked feature of the theme. In the *De Fide Orthodoxiae*, John of Damascus provides a chapter on the angels and their nature, in which he stresses their strength and their being prepared to do the will of God, and 'how they find themselves at once wherever the divine wish orders them due to the speed of their nature' (2.3). Also Gregory of Nazianzus in *Orationes* pays attention to the nature and tasks of the angels. They are servants under the will of God, who by the strength of their own nature but also with [God's] help (*epiktērō*) have their powers, traversing all regions and finding themselves at once everywhere and in all places owing to the urgency of their business and the lightness of their essence (*kouphórēri phýseōs*) (28.30). Obviously this stress on speed due to obedience as found in patrology puts a certain construction and emphasis on Raphael's words. 'Speed almost Spiritual' works epigraphically, and the reader who can interpret it uses an infracontextual key that opens the door to an understanding of the horizontal context rather than the other way round. The phrase derives additional dignity and authority from the infracontexts. Regarded as an inscription, the words explain 'The swiftness of those Circles' and above all elucidate and stress 'Omnipotence'. It is as the willing servant of God that Raphael appears, ready to do his bidding in his spiritually swift manner; the very mention of this feature of his mission is indicative, and not absolutely necessary for the description as such. The speed indicates the urgency of Raphael's business and of, as it were, God's personal involvement. Raphael is indeed, as R. M. Frye observes from a different point of view, an instructor for Adam and Eve, a 'guardian angel *par excellence*'.[8] A pity that Adam could not take a hint from patrology!

The third type is bound up with the idea of vacillating interpretation. Depending on whether this vacillation (or these alternatives) is recognized or not, the relevant words work like an inscription, otherwise they form part of a less informative, ordinary horizontal context. This type is particularly interesting from a stylistic and pragmatic view and also fairly infrequent. An example is the invocatory lines at 1.20f., where the Holy Spirit 'with mighty wings outspred/Dovelike sat'st brooding on the vast abyss'. 'Brooding', says Fowler, renders the Hebrew word in Genesis 1.2 translated as 'moved' in the Authorized Version ('And the Spirit of God mouved vpon the face of the waters'), but in patristic texts is rendered as 'incubabat', for instance by Jerome: 'incubabat sive confovebat'. Now the Hebrew word in Genesis 1.2 (< *rich(ch)aph*) has been variously interpreted. According to the *Targum* of Onkelos and Ibn Ezra it means 'produced wind' (to dry up the waters), a meaning referred to, in addition to 'incubabat', also by some of the commentators in the *Critici Sacri* (a Variorum Bible commentary of 1698). A third suggested meaning, probably the right one, is 'flutter' or 'hover', undoubtedly the sense in Deuteronomy 32.11: 'As an Eagle stirreth up her nest, fluttering ouer her yong'. This would seem to be the meaning in *Paradise Lost* 7.235, 'His brooding wings the spirit of God outspred,/And vital virtue infus'd, and vital warmth/Throughout the fluid mass'. Milton no doubt thought of 'incubabat' in 1.21, but the rendering 'flutter', 'move the wings rapidly' is conceivable (*LXX* at Genesis 1.2 provides *epephéreto* Vulg. 'ferebatus'), in which case 'sat'st' means 'remain in a certain state', hover over the same place.[9] Several editors of *Paradise Lost* discuss the meaning; it seems that to them, either 'brood' or 'hover' is a likely alternative. Some modern exegetes similarly regard both meanings as possible and even as amounting to the same thing (hover – protect – keep watch over – brood), though König on etymological grounds regards 'flutter', 'hover' as the only acceptable sense.[10] The sense and stylistic value of 'brooding' taken as an inscription depends first, paradoxically, on our associating the word on the spatial level with other passages later in the poem. Contact with 2.927ff. brings the meaning 'hover' to the fore by contrast: the Holy Spirit hovering effortlessly over the abyss, bringing forth new life, stands out in contrast to Satan trying to bring evil into the world and almost failing when 'Fluttring his pennons vain plumb down he drops/Ten thousand fadom deep' into the abyss of Chaos (2.933f.). Again, the sense 'incubabat' with the same idea of 'life-giving' emerges by contrast with the sterility motif in 1.351ff. where the host of the fallen angels, recently compared to locusts, are a multitude 'like which the populous North/Pourd never from her frozen loins, to pass/Rhene or the Danaw', devastating barbarian hordes. The motif of sterility can be defined with more precision, for the frozen loins of the North suggest its male counterpart, the *semen frigidum* doctrine: Satan's icy cold, sterile and deadly sperm. This ambiguity of Milton's brooding thus does not come to the fore on the basis of the immediate horizontal context.

The fourth type is concerned less with vacillating than with complex interpretation. As an instance I choose 7.374, a detail in the account of the creation. The sun is described at some length, and 'the gray/Dawn, and the Pleiades before him danced,/Shedding sweet influence'. Before these lines the poet speaks in fairly general terms of the creation of sun and moon, then of the host of the stars; then of Venus, then of Venus and the origin of light, and then of the sun. After the lines on the Pleiades comes the moon, its borrowed light, its movements, etc.; then back to the stars. Thus: sun, moon, stars, Venus, stars, sun, Pleiades, moon, stars; and then the creatures of the earth. There is then in part a tendency towards a chiastic arrangement, suggestive of the circular movements of all created beings praising God. We may ask ourselves why, of all the constellations, the Pleiades have been selected, a nebulous cluster of notoriously feeble brilliancy. According to Aratus,[11] 'single they can be perceived but dimly' (255f.), and, more precisely, 'they are equally small and dim' (264: *hai men homōs olígai kai aphengées*). Cicero in his translation of Aratus (*Aratea* 37) repeats this piece of information: 'Hae tenues parvo labentes lumine lucent', as does Manilius (*Astron.* 4.522): 'Pleiadum parvo referens glomeramine sidus'. It is unlikely that Milton took a view different from these authorities, and the reason that he mentions the Pleiades instead of brilliant constellations like Ursa Major, Corona, or Via Lactea has of course something to do with the 'sweet influence' they shed, words derived from Job 38.31 in the Authorized Version: 'Canst thou bind the sweete influences of Pleiades?' Obviously the Pleiades (*kīmā*, originally 'group', 'assembly') are a good power, a life-giving force, and the interpretation in Job derives from medieval renderings of Hebrew *ma*^{a}*dannōth* as 'delights' (e.g. fine food, dainties, various kinds of physical pleasure), taken over during subsequent centuries by various Christian exegetes and resulting in the 'sweet influences' of the Authorized Version.[12] Munsterus provides 'Numquid tu ligabis suaves influentias Pleiadum'. The 'influentiae' were probably regarded as celestial forces producing flowers and fruits in spring and summer. According to Aratus, Zeus bids the Pleiades announce the beginning of summer (heliacal rising) and their cosmical setting in late autumn is a sign of the sowing-season. Vatablus, Castalio, Clarius and Grotius in the *Critici Sacri* speak of the Pleiades as a sign of spring, Clarius adding that they were a signal for seafaring people to set sail. It is likely that these meanings of *ma*^{a}*dannōth* were current in Milton's day.[13] In view of these semantic factors the epigraphic quality of the Pleiades dancing before the sun and 'shedding sweet influence' emerges quite clearly by contrast with the second half of Job 38.31, 'canst thou loose the bands of Orion?', and from the meaning it acquires in the vertical context system in *Paradise Lost* 1.300 ff. on the defeated angels lying stunned in the Underworld. In this passage Satan's defeated legions are compared with autumnal leaves and scattered sedge, 'Afloat, when with fierce Winds Orion armd/Hath vext the Red-Sea Coast', whose waves drowned the Egyptian army in pursuit of the Israelites. It appears from the infracontextual pattern – the meaning of the Hebrew word for Orion, *K*^{e}*sîl*, later commentators' identification of Orion with Nimrod, the giant hunter, the classical traditions concerning the function of Orion, and the cluster of meanings surrounding these traditions – that Orion has many features in common with Lucifer, the godless rebel. In the 'autumnal-leaves' paragraph in *Paradise Lost* the evil Orion-Lucifer is a power bent on destruction, including his own; in the creation passage the Pleiades are a power bringing life and fruitfulness and signalling beneficial and useful activities. Like Christ, they stand out as members of the sharpest possible antithesis. So the function of the Pleiades in the creation passage emerges first of all from the infracontextual pattern underneath *kīmā*, to which we are directed by way of the passage in Job 38.31; then from the close contrast *kīmā-kᵉsîl*, Pleiades-Orion in the Job verse, a contrast which becomes apparent only when the complex and esoteric infracontextual pattern behind *kᵉsîl* is taken into account. The meaning of the sweet influences of the Pleiades may seem simple enough, but a full and satisfactory interpretation and the intensification it provides can only be made on the basis of contexts to be found far from the immediate environment of the word-group.

The fifth type, finally, is one in which the inscription, if interpreted rightly, sheds an unexpected light on the passage from which it detaches itself. This passage is found in 4.610ff., Adam's description of evening and of the repose in store for the weary, so that they can begin another day with renewed vigour. With some of the rhetorical theorists this kind of praise does not rate very high; Quintilian for instance (3.7.28) co-ordinates praise of sleep with other types of an indifferent character: 'Et somni et mortis scriptae laudes et quorundam a medicis cibarum' ('praise of certain kinds of food'). Adam's words are preceded by a passage on evening, a well-known topos in classical poetry which seems here, on the face of it, to be a praise of the beauty of the hours when night approaches: the setting sun, twilight, silence, wakeful nightingale singing amorous descant, sapphires on firmament, Hesperus leading starry host, rising moon with peerless light and silver mantle. However, appearances may be deceptive: the approach of night also means imminent danger, as indeed it does in Milton's text. Ambrose wrote a hymn ('Te lucis ante terminum') sung at the end of the last service (*completa*), in which God is asked to preserve man from nocturnal temptations, guard his house from the enemy, and allow his holy angels to live in it. The beginning of the hymn is quoted in *Purgatorio* 8.13, and in this canto, as in Milton's poem, temptation is near – in Dante in the shape of a serpent – but the souls' prayer is heard by God, who sends two angels for their protection. This infracontextual detail is thus not irrelevant to the interpretation of Milton's night description. Again, the mention of the nightingale and her descant evokes a sinister classical myth, and the moon is associated with Satan directly at 1.287, where his shield is compared to a moon, and 596, where Satan in his defeat is correlated with the solar eclipse 'behind the moon'; indirectly at

1.440, where the moon is a demon goddess, and 2.665, where the moon is eclipsed by the Lapland witches' charms. The moon of course is also a feature of black magic, as it is via an infracontext for 1.784f. on the sorceress Canidia and her power over the moon in Horace's fifth Epode. Also, the moon 'Apparent Queen unvaild her peerless light' suggests Satan's sudden and amazing appearance in 10.449f. where, among his followers, 'At last as from a Cloud his fulgent head/And shape Starr-bright appeerd, or brighter', etc.

The description of sleep and rest, from l.611 onwards, contains a detail which carries on these suggestions of something seemingly charming and beautiful, but which simultaneously hints at a deeper and more sombre reality. 'God hath set/Labour and rest, as day and night', says Adam, 'and the timely dew of sleep/Now falling with soft slumbrous weight inclines/Our eye-lids'. The words call up the account of Adam and Eve after the fall, embracing until 'dewie Sleep/Oppressed them, wearied with thir amorous play' (9.1044f.). In classical texts the dew of sleep has sometimes a menacing note indicating magic, danger, and/or death. In Apollonius Rhodius' *Argonautica* 4.156ff., where Medea by her magic, chanting her incantations, plunges the giant serpent into deep sleep, she sprinkles his eyes with the dew of her magical brew, enabling Jason to steal the golden fleece unhindered. In the *Aeneid* 5.854ff. Somnus in disguise brings bad dreams to Palinurus, Aeneas' helmsman, and sprinkles over his temples the dew of Lethe, shaking a bough steeped in the river Styx – forgetfulness and death. He then hurls him into the sea, the victim damaging helm and stern in his fall. Giambattista Marino in his *Sospetto d'Herode* 48 describes weird Crudeltà winging her way to the palace of Herod, the mass-murderer, spreading death and destruction. This account colours the subsequent stanza, particularly if read in the light of Virgil's lines, which were no doubt imitated by the Italian poet. Crudeltà arrives during the night when sleep, Night's companion, gliding on silent wings, 'Sparse le tempie altrui d'acque lethali', sprinkled men's temples with lethal dew (interestingly, 'lethali' means 'bringing death' as distinct from 'leteo', bringing forgetfulness, a word derived from the name of the river of The Underworld, Lethe). In English epic, the dew of Morpheus appears in close proximity to magic and danger in *The Faerie Queene* 1.1.36, where the 'sadde humour' loads the travellers' eyelids and Morpheus' messenger 'on them cast/Sweet slombring deaw, the which to sleep them biddes'. After his guests have fallen in a deadly sleep, Archimago repairs to his study and his magic art and mighty charms, troubling sleeping minds and calling up a host of evil spirits. There are many instances of a 'neutral' use of the dew-of-sleep formula (in *Il Penseroso*, for example), but association of the passages in *Paradise Lost* with those discussed above puts a certain construction on the deceptively harmless dew of sleep falling with soft slumbrous weight on Adam and Eve's eyelids. If read horizontally it ranges itself with other details of a night-and-sleep description of great beauty. If we look beneath the verbal environment, detaching the words and transforming them to an inscription, a meaning and a stylistic quality of a very different kind emerge, as indeed they do if the preceding lines, on night, are also so regarded. The 'marvellous' comes to the fore.

A feature of these inscriptions, important from a theoretical point of view, seems to be that they function properly only in concentration, within fairly narrow limits. They are words or small word-groups, whose horizontal environment provides no clues, or unsatisfactory ones, to the interpretation in a wide sense of the term. The larger the word-groups, the greater the interpretative and stylistic part played by the linear context, and the lesser the importance of infracontexts such as those discussed above. It would be an interesting problem to try and find out just how wide the limits can be drawn for a word-group to function epigraphically.

Notes

1 N. E. Enkvist, 'Die Funktion literarischer Kontexte für die linguistische Stilistik', in *Stilistik* 6, 22, 1976, 78–85; 'Categories of Situational Context from the Perspective of Stylistics', in *Language Teaching Abstracts* 13, 6, 1980, 75–94; J. Derrida, 'Signature Event Context', in *Glyph* 1, 1977, 172–97; G. Genette, *Narrative Discourse* (Oxford: Basil Blackwell), 1980; S. Suleiman and I. Crosman, *The Reader in the Text* (Princeton: Princeton University Press), 1980; M. Riffaterre, *Semiotics of Poetry* (London: Methuen), 1978; E. Said, *The World, the Text, and the Critic* (Cambridge, Mass.: Harvard University Press), 1983

2 Demetrius, *Peri Hermeneias* (*On Style*) 5.254; Longinus, *Peri Hypsous* (*On the Sublime*) 1.4; Emanuele Tesauro, *Il Cannocchiale Aristotelico*, 1670 (repr. 1968), p. 618; Sforza Pallavicino, *Trattato dello stile e del dialogo*, 1662, 10.4. Tesauro's and Pallavicino's treatises were first printed in 1654 and 1646, respectively, Augustine discusses obscurity and difficulty as virtues of style in *De Doctrina Christiana* 4.8.22. Joseph Mazzeo's essay ('A Seventeenth-Century Theory of Metaphysical Poetry') is published in his *Renaissance and Seventeenth-Century Studies*, New York, 1964; the quotation is from p. 34. In the same book Mazzeo refers to Augustine's views on style on pp. 16f.

3 The quotation is from *The Full Voic'd Quire Below. Vertical Context Systems in 'Paradise Lost'*, Lund, 1982, pp. 19f. I have earlier

described the model in two articles, 'Vertical Context Systems' (*Style and Text. Studies Presented to Nils Erik Enkvist*, Stockholm, 1975, pp. 146 ff.) and 'Linear Sequence, Spatial Structure, Complex Sign, and Vertical Context System' (*Poetics* 7, 1978, 377 ff.)

4 Alexander Schmidt, *Shakespeare-Lexicon* I, Berlin and Leipzig 1923, repr. Berlin, 1962, p. 73

5 Euripides had a considerable reputation in the Renaissance, probably because he was said by Aristotle to be the most tragic of poets (*Poetics* 13, 10)

6 Alastair Fowler, edition of *Paradise Lost*, Harlow, Essex, 1968, repr. 1982, p. 401

7 Many of the excellent comments on *Paradise Lost* (1733) by Zachary Pearce, Bishop of Rochester, were incorporated into Thomas Newton's Variorum edition of the poem in 1749. The quotation is to be found in Newton 2, p. 75

8 *Milton's Imagery and the Visual Arts. Iconographic Tradition in the Epic Poems* (Princeton: Princeton University Press), 1978, p. 179

9 *OED sit* 7†

10 *Die Genesis*, erklärt von Eduard König (Gütersloh: C. Bertelsmann), 1925, pp. 142–3. This interpretation is accepted by most later exegetes

11 In his poem on astronomy, the *Phaenomena*, written 276–274 BC

12 *The Anchor Bible*, introduction, translation and notes by Marvin H. Pope (Garden City, New York: Doubleday & Co. Inc.), 1965, p. 254

13 Some later Orientalists feel that *ma^adannōth* is related to a Persian word with the sense 'jewels', 'jewelry', and that the Job passage means 'Canst thou knit together the jewels of the Pleiades?' In reality there is evidence that neither this meaning nor those mentioned above are the correct ones, but that *ma^adannōth* is a metathesis, oral or scribal, of *ma^anaddôt* in the sense 'chains', 'fetters'. 'Can you bind the chains of the Pleiades?' is in all probability the right rendering, corresponding to the second half of the verse: 'Can you loose the fetters of Orion?' See *The Book of Job. Commentary, New Translation and Special Studies* by Robert Gordis (New York City: The New Theological Seminary of America), 1978, p. 450

Chapter ten

Anticipation and disappointment: an experiment in protocolled reading of Auden's 'Gare du Midi'

Nils Erik Enkvist and Gun Leppiniemi

Despite the vogue of *Rezeptionsästhetik*, reader-response criticism, and other movements emphasizing the role of the reader in literary communication, empirical, data-based studies of literary text comprehension have been relatively rare (cf. e.g. Fairley 1979, Stalker 1982 and van Peer 1986). Indeed the usefulness of such empirical studies has been called in question. They have been characterized, and even dismissed, as a 'vestige of superannuated scientism', which 'will have to assume a more modest and ancillary function'. To go on citing Robert Holub,

> Continuing on its present course, empirical reception theory is bound to remain an isolated and ridiculed branch of literary endeavor. Purged of its absolutist notions about objectivity and applied in a judicious manner, on the other hand, empirical studies could become a boon rather than a bane for our understanding of the literary text and its reception.
>
> (Holub 1984: 145–6.)

The experiments and analyses reported on in the present paper have, if anything, confirmed our belief that Holub is justified in his scepticism, for two obvious reasons at least. To begin with, responses to literary texts of course vary – and should vary – from one individual to the next. They are more properly a matter of individual response and criticism, and perhaps of explications of how a critic was affected by his background and prejudices, than of empirical mass registration and statistical treatment. Secondly, reliable responses to literary texts are difficult to get at. Either they must be elicited with more or less persuasion from heterogeneous groups of captive informants, or then they are volunteered by people who can be regarded as exceptional: their very volunteering implies that they have special interests and sensibilities.

The present experiment grew from a far humbler endeavour, namely, finding out what happens when a captive group of students are compelled to verbalize their experiences of a poem given to them incrementally, bit by bit. It should perhaps be said at once that, quite apart from the theoretical interest of these experiments, most of the informants claimed to like them and said they gave a fine start towards reading and understanding a poem. Whatever else the experiments did or failed to do, at least they compelled a group of readers to contemplate a poetic text. Therefore they seem to us suggestive for the development of teaching methods. As to the data themselves, our scepticism is derived mainly from the heterogeneity of the responses and from the well-known difficulties inherent in all evaluations of relatively free, minimally cued protocols. All the same there is every reason to agree with Irene Fairley's claim (Fairley 1979: 336) that subjective and introspective data can be analysed with explicit, reproducible, and in that sense objective, methods. A case in point is van Peer 1986. But if the data are too fuzzy for reliable, and preferably discrete, classification, they are hardly worth subjecting to rigorous statistical analyses.

We do, then, wish to share our experiences, perhaps to warn and perhaps to inspire, and more to show an example of weakly cued protocol studies than to claim findings of major theoretical or psycholinguistic import.

To a hearer or reader, a text is a problem, and text comprehension involves problem solving. Understanding a text – or, in the terms of the text, establishing its interpretability – is not a quality or function of the text alone, but a result of an interplay between the text, the situational context, and the receptor (including his linguistic skills, his knowledge of the world, his purpose and his judgements of relevance, as well as his text-processing capacity at the relevant moment, which may vary with his alertness, sobriety and a number of other transient influences).

A simplistic model of text comprehension might start by positing that the receptor must first analyse the text intelligibly: he must segment the text into letters and graphemes or phones and phonemes, morphemes, syntactic units, and textual as well as discoursal units. This presupposes a command of the linguistic and discoursal background of the text; two of the important processes involved are pattern recognition and parsing. Then the receptor must assign meanings to the linguistic and discoursal structures. He must understand what is meant by discoursal devices such as politeness signals and turntaking signals, and he must understand the basic semantic meanings of the structures and lexical items: he must for instance understand that *This room is hot* means something like 'the temperature in this room is high'. Further, he must interpret the function of the structures in their communicative setting: he must for instance grasp that *This room is hot* can under certain circumstances be uttered in the sense 'will somebody please open a window'.

Intelligibility thus involves recognition of phonological/orthographic and syntactic patterns. Comprehensibility involves assigning referents to the units identified. Interpretability refers to those qualities of the text which enable us to interpret its function in the relevant situation. Those fond of neat classifications can say that intelligibility involves syntax, comprehensibility, syntax plus semantics, and interpretation, syntax plus semantics plus pragmatics.

In actual fact, however, text processing does not proceed linearly and unidirectionally from patterns through meanings to functions. Experienced receptors will, on the contrary, process texts simultaneously both bottom-up, from signals to meanings and functions, and top-down, from established or expected functions and meanings to signals. In this view, text comprehension results from heterarchic rather than hierarchic processes, whose ordering and ranking may well vary from one person to the next. Thus there are situations in which the spoken or written form of an utterance can be greatly distorted, but where the receptor will nevertheless understand it perfectly because his interpretation is guided by his experience-based expectations of how people behave and what they say in a certain situation or predicament. Further, even if a text proves impervious to semantic comprehension in that the receptor fails to get its referential message, it is still not meaningless: it will all the same be interpreted as a symptom of the speaker's or writer's abilities, attitudes, and mental state. If, for instance, a professor comes into a classroom and starts lecturing in a language unkown to his audience, his hearers will at once interpret his behaviour as owing to his being in the wrong classroom or perhaps as rude, absent-minded, or crazy. Messages, says Deborah Tannen, are always accompanied by metamessages, which can be even more important than the message proper (Tannen 1986). And when a message could trigger off several interpretations we assign priorities to them through judgements of their relevance (Sperber and Wilson 1986).

Discourse interpretation, then, involves both a referential and a symptomatic element, a message and a metamessage; and these are understood through an interplay of syntax, semantic knowledge, and pragmatic knowledge referring both to the world-at-large and to the specific communicative situation. Neither communicative success nor text coherence depends on syntactic well-formedness. There are many modern poems, whether Dada, Concrete, or Algorithmic, and many advertisements and many utterances in impromptu speech which fail to meet traditional specifications of syntactic well-formedness. They may still work nicely and effectively in actual communication. Therefore the interpretability of a text cannot be measured in terms of the well-formedness of its linguistic structures. Those wishing to define interpretability in terms of a single, holistic definition might go on to suggest that a text is interpretable to those who can, under the relevant circumstances, build around it a text world in which that text makes sense. Such a text world can be conceived of as a highly constrained, specific instance of a more comprehensive class of worlds which are 'possible' in the sense of being projections of a person's store of knowledge and experience. And 'makes sense' could then be explicated both as 'might be true' (as science fiction 'might be true' in its particular text world which is different from ours) and as 'could be subjected to principles of relevance in discoursal behaviour'. Such 'potential truth' or 'conformance to discoursal interpretability principles' provides the mortar that holds together the bricks – units of meaning[1] – out of which the receptor builds his text worlds. 'Potential truth' takes the student of text worlds into truth-conditional semantics, 'discoursal interpretability' to theories of relevance such as those of Grice or of Sperber and Wilson.

This construction of a world around the text is an incremental process. A receptor does not wait for a complete text before he begins his interpretation. As soon as he has started hearing or reading the text, he begins forming sets of anticipations as to what is to come next, using all the means at his disposal: phonotactics, graphotactics, syntax, his experience of lexical frames and collocations, as well as his knowledge of the world and of the speaker/writer and his view of the situational context. The process builds on complex heterarchic interplays of bottom-up and top-down processing. The resulting anticipations are then confirmed or disappointed, and the entire process of anticipation, confirmation and disappointment is an essential aspect of text comprehension. At each point of the text, meanings consist of two components: available meaning and anticipation. In other terms we might say that the available meaning defines a state of affairs, and the anticipation is in the nature of a projection from the known into the so-far-unverified, whether that be certain and predictable, uncertain, or improbable.

If text comprehension is problem-solving, then problem-solving strategies should be applicable to processes of text comprehension as well. In studies of problem-solving, commonly cited strategies include breadth-first (where the problem-solver contemplates a number of possible paths towards the solution), depth-first (where he tries to advance along one single specific path as far as that will take him), and means-end (where he tries to go from his current situation towards a plausible goal, and at the same time from this plausible goal back towards the current situation, hoping that the two paths will meet). The heuristics of judgement under uncertainty have also been classified under headings such as the representativeness heuristic, the scenario heuristic, and adjustment from an anchor (Kahneman *et al.* 1982: 20). Thus if we see a man in oily overalls on board a luxury yacht we expect him to be a crew member rather than the owner or a passenger because his appearance is more representative of a sailor. The scenario heuristic enables us to predict that, in all probability, the couple sitting at the next table in a restaurant will pay their bill before they leave. And the adjustment-from-an-anchor strategy enables us to guess that a new Cadillac costs more than $10,000 if a new Ford costs $8,000. Should we wish to model such problem-solving and inferencing processes we must provide our model with the necessary background knowledge first to identify states of affairs, and then to project inferences and anticipations beyond what has actually been given to us as fact.

These were some of the background considerations that prompted our actual experiments with protocol studies of incremental text comprehension.

For practical reasons the poems we used for our experiments in incremental, protocol-documented reading had to be short. The poem given to the largest number of informants was W. H. Auden's 'Gare du Midi', and we shall therefore report on readings of this poem only.

The poem was presented to groups of students at three different universities:

1. A preliminary test was given to participants of an advanced, predominantly postgraduate seminar to students of English as a foreign language at Åbo Akademi (the Swedish-language university of Finland); participants had a very good to near-native command of English and considerable experience of reading literature in several languages: 7 informants.
2. The test proper was given to groups of students at two universities in the United States:
    Indiana University—Purdue University at Indianapolis, IN:
    a. L105, 'Appreciation of Literature': Freshmen, no prerequisites, heterogeneous group, 2 sections, 68 informants (scripts 1–68).

    b. L115, 'Literature for Today': freshmen, non-English majors, 13 informants (scripts 69–81).

    c. L115, same but a weekend class with older, part-time students, 13 informants (scripts 82–95).

    d. L202, 'Literary Interpretation': sophomore-level course for non-English majors with some prior literary courses, 7 informants (scripts 96–102).

    e. L301, 'Survey of British Literature I': junior-level course for majors in English and in Education with concentration in English, 19 informants (scripts 103–120).

Purdue University in West Lafayette, IN:

    f. English 627A: postgraduate seminar in discourse analysis, mainly for English majors with some participants from Education, 11 informants (scripts 121–131).

Thus the total number of protocol scripts analysed from the test proper was 131. Some scripts had been discarded because of illegibility or paucity of comment.

The scripts were obtained as follows. The text of the poem was xeroxed onto an overhead transparency. Informants were requested to write down anonymously their responses to a poem which was in advance stated to consist of eight lines. The instruction was: 'Please state, after each passage, your expectations and your disappointments. End with a summary of your experiences.' As many of the American informants failed to understand the meaning of 'Gare du Midi', the phrase was explained. After these preliminaries, the poem was presented by uncovering the transparency in chunks as marked in the following:

        (1) Gare du Midi.
  (2)   A nondescript express in from the South,
  (3)   Crowds round the ticket barrier, (4) a face
        To welcome which the mayor has not contrived
        Bugles or braid: (5) something about the mouth
        Distracts the stray look with alarm and pity.
  (6)   Snow is falling. (7) Clutching a little case,
        He walks out briskly to infect a city
  (8)   Whose terrible future may have just arrived.

At each juncture between the chunks, there was an interval of five minutes during which informants were supposed to write down their comments. At the end of the experiment, which, including the preliminaries, required approximately one class period, the informants were invited to comment on the whole poem.

To anticipate comments we should state at once that this kind of incremental, protocol-documented reading obviously does not simulate what happens in a normal reading. A normal reading can be faster and takes place in the reader's own tempo. The reader can chunk the poem as he wants to. He can read more of the text at one go and then return if he wants to. Another problem was that, for practical reasons, the test had to be administered by several different persons on several different occasions. This may have introduced some uncontrolled variables into the test administration. Though the general instructions were the same, protocols make us suspect that informants interpreted 'Gare du Midi' variously as 'South Station' or 'railway station in the South of France' and not always as 'a station in a French city for rail traffic to and from the South'. It is hard to judge the possible effects of such uncontrolled variables in test administration.

After various attempts at classifying the responses in the protocols into groups, the following categories were adopted:

physical setting, time, place, weather: 'Sort of a foggy, misty, dark morning' (44), 'maybe this train is at an amusement park' (168).

mood, comments on the tone of the poem in terms of positive, negative, neutral: 'a dismal tone is set . . . the entire poem has switched from joyful and exciting anticipation to despair and coldness' (106), 'originally the mood seemed happy and festive but becomes gloomy and leaves a feeling of disaster impending' (80).

character, the physical or mental characteristics, feelings, reactions, occupation and status of people in the crowd, the visitor arriving on the train, the mayor, the citizens and others: 'I would guess the visitor to be a political figure who has arrived to assume his position within this city' (73).

action, forecasts as to what will happen, reflections on events, either in general terms: '. . . something will occur that will be life changing for someone in the poem . . .', or in specific ones: '. . . I expect a beautiful woman to pull in a car, pick up one of the three men and drive off at a fast pace with the other two men in flat pursuit . . .' (58).

form, comments on techniques of narration and description, style, language, orthography: '. . . maybe "crowds" is not a noun but a verb and the subject will be in the next line . . .' (102).

meaning, implications and interpretations of specific words or specific lines in the poem: 'Nondescript implies to me unimportant implying that this express is no more important than any other express train' (43).

reader, introspective comments on the reader's associations, likes, dislikes, and what the reader is doing: '. . . what I expect to follow will probably not interest me greatly the title in another language already shuts down my red-neck curiosity . . .' (98).

poet, comments on the poet's name, personality, background, intention: 'I keep thinking this is Pound . . .' (131).

other themes, for instance comments on overall themes: 'I expect it's going to talk about a train station maybe the hustle and bustle of it' (10), '. . . could be about the station itself. Maybe it's haunted' (27).

In terms of these categories, the scripts were analysed by one single analyst (G.L.), who classified the responses as presented in Table 10.1. These rough statistics suggest a few general observations. Chunks 1, 6, and 7 provoked the largest total numbers of observations, chunks 5 and 8 the fewest (chunk 8 being final and thus not a source of further expectations). Of the observations, the overwhelming majority were on character; in descending order, anticipatory comments were then made on action, meaning of lines or words, reader, setting, form, mood, and poet.

One of the interesting features is the number of comments on character after chunks 1, 2, 3, and 6. Obviously chunks 4, 5 and 7, as well as 8, provoke comments on character; that chunks 1, 2, 3, and 6, ostensibly on setting, should call for character interpretations was more unexpected. Similarly, there was a group of anticipations of action after chunk 1 (the title). In general terms such figures suggest that, under these experimental conditions, a large proportion of readers (more than one third) regarded the text as a stimulus towards highly individual fantasies.

As to the comments themselves, one interesting question is to what extent passages on setting, such as the title ('Gare du Midi') and on impersonal action ('A nondescript express in from the South'), provoked comments on matters *other than* setting and action. On the basis of the title alone, in fact as many as 50 of the total 131 informants volunteered comments on character, and after the second passage the number was 44. In the following there are a few examples of this, which were apparently triggered off by these lines:

Table 10.1

	setting		mood		character		action		other themes		poetic form		meaning of words & phrases		POET		READER		TOTALS		
					CONTENT						FORM								exp	dis	total
	exp	dis	exp	dis	exp	dis	exp	dis	exp	dis	exp	dis	exp	dis	exp	dis	exp	dis			
1. Gare du Midi	65	–	16	–	50	–	46	–	78	–	48	4	6	–	7	–	25	4	341	8	349
2. A nondescript express in from the South	11	1	16	2	44	–	34	2	32	2	19	14	30	4	6	–	23	7	215	32	247
3. Crowds round the ticket barrier	17	–	6	2	41	11	58	12	11	–	26	9	14	–	4	1	19	3	196	38	234
4. A face to welcome which the mayor has not contrived bugles or braid	4	–	11	3	105	15	26	5	5	2	9	7	27	–	4	–	10	–	201	32	233
5. Something about the mouth distracts the stray look with alarm and pity.	3	–	5	10	105	11	16	1	2	–	12	8	14	–	3	–	26	3	186	33	219
6. Snow is falling.	74	12	26	6	39	–	19	11	7	9	12	13	31	3	3	1	33	6	244	61	305
7. Clutching a little case, he walks out briskly to infect a city.	3	1	14	6	98	12	16	6	10	–	11	7	53	2	7	1	24	5	236	40	276
8. Whose terrible future may have just arrived.	–	–	14	9	78	8	15	–	6	–	9	6	33	1	4	2	25	7	184	33	217
	177	14	108	38	560	57	230	37	151	13	146	68	208	10	38	5	185	35	1803	277	2080
	191		146		617		267		164		214		218		43		220				

Note
exp. = expectations
dis. = disappointments

199

1   *Gare du Midi*

> 'I would imagine it will tell us about
> the different kinds of people who frequent
> the station either for travel or for
> occupation.' (116)

> 'A train station makes me think of a couple
> standing in front of the train that is
> boarding. They are saying their good-byes
> because the man is going off to war.' (4)

> 'A robber will kidnap a passenger and
> hold her hostage on the train. Other
> passengers are on the train.' (2)

2   *A nondescript express in from the South*

> 'A train full of people – too many to be
> distinct – a usual occurrence. Possibly
> carrying workers, commuters.' (129)

> 'The express . . . is plain – nondescript,
> which invites the reader to continue. For
> someone on the express must be exotic or
> definitely have excitement surrounding
> him/her.' (106)

> '. . . must be a person or persons of note
> on the express arriving at the South
> station. Prisoners or Royalty?' (112)

In general terms, this seems to suggest that there was what one might call a 'character-biased' category of readers, who started by assuming that poems must deal with people, and who used lines describing setting or impersonalized action as triggers for speculations about character.

Similarly passage 6 ('Snow is falling.'), elicited many comments on character, mood and appearance:

6   *Snow is falling*

> 'This is not a physical quality, rather it
> has a reflection of the subject's soul . . .' (120)

> 'Tells how cold and lonely the person is.
> How sad he is.' (13)

'The snow may represent purity and innocence.
the face may be a child.' (20)

'He may be a derlick [*sic!*] riding trains or living
in the station to keep warm.' (53)

'Maybe the traveller is wearing bermuda shorts . . .' (105)

As to the disappointments registered in the protocols, most of
them seemed to concern matters of form:

1   *Gare du Midi*

'I did not expect a French title.' (78)

2   *A nondescript express in from the South*

'Thought the second sentence would be more descriptive.'
(2)

'I thought that the poem would start off with a much
bolder statement; since the poem only has 8 lines I
thought it would have to get to the point fairly quickly.'
(5)

3   *Crowds round the ticket barrier*

'The 'round' bothers me – it is not 'around', it could
be maybe 'crowds' is not a noun but a verb, and the subject
will be in the next line.' (102)

'Why is it a "Barrier" and not a "Booth"?' (74)

4   *a face*
    To welcome which the mayor has not contrived
    Bugles or braid

'I am disappointed that more detail wasn't given
in this line.' (37)

'I am confused by the syntax – I am not sure what the line
means. Is the face the crowd/scene or someone on the
train?' (130)

5   *something about the mouth*
    distracts the stray look with alarm and pity

'I don't know at all where the poem is leading.
It seems like the lines do not follow one another

but are separate and their meanings stand alone
from the other lines.' (28)

6 *Snow is falling*

'Did not expect an all together change. I expected
the next line to flow and answer why or what.' (85)

'Did not expect this abrupt shift to the weather.
Also did not expect such a short, objective description.
The style shift is unusual.' (123)

7 *Clutching a little case,*
He walks out briskly to infect a city

'I never expected to see the word 'infect'.' (124)

8 *Whose terrible future may have just arrived*

'The poem is so different from the title.' (28)

'The poem leaves so much unsettled – unfinished.' (129)

Disappointments recorded after passages 3, 4, 5 and 7 also had to do with character:

3 'Expected this line to talk about people from the train,
rather than people waiting for it.' (123)

'I thought it would be more depth in people: that is involving
a certain group and their relationships.' (5)

4 'Now we are back to an arrival. And only one person and an
important one officially. That I didn't expect.' (124)

'Did not describe people in the crowd.' (26)

5 'I expected to hear about the people/and or passengers'
feelings about what's going on.' (24)

7 'How can someone piteous infect the city?' (124)

'Ooh. I suppose now that the person is not a hero or even an
admired person – that is if he's walking out to infect a city.'
(121)

Passage 5 also brought many disappointments having to do with mood:

'The tone has taken a turn downward. What I
thought was a somewhat happy arrival has
turned into sadness.' (9)

Passage 6 disappointed some readers:

> 'Snow? That makes no sense at all.' (124)

> '. . . makes the reader get off the track . . .' (18)

The physical setting of the poem was also mentioned as a disappointment at this point:

> 'Well so much for the warmth and sunshine.
> I had expected a warm place, a sunny place,
> but this is not what it is.' (103)

After line 8, the whole poem was available for comment. Less than half of the informant group commented on the total meaning. Of these, the majority – 15 per cent of the entire group – regarded the man in the poem as a political figure involved in the overthrow of a regime, a dictator, king or new mayor. Some 10 per cent thought he was a criminal, a gangster or drug dealer or hired gun. Some 8 per cent associated the man with a spread of disease, as a mad doctor; some 6 per cent thought of chemical warfare or a nuclear holocaust or a military spy; and two readers associated the line with religion, Armageddon, and the second coming of Christ.

To illustrate the different problem-solving strategies that came to the fore in the protocols, here are a few quotations. Typical instances revealing a breadth-first strategy include

> 'poem about people or actions involving a train station may be about several people or just a few or all the people in general. I really don't expect a lot from this so far because there are a wide variety of things that could be involved. Happiness as in a reunion, sadness in a departure, new love, old romances – just too many things could happen.'

> 'still not really sure as to what direction this poem will take . . .' (5)

Depth-first strategies seem to underlie

1. 'To be about a woman wanting for her lover to get off the train . . .

2. The train was coming from somewhere in Italy . . . with the man aboard . . .

3. The woman is a part of the crowd waiting for her lover to appear.

4. He's unknown to the crowd, but he is noticed by his lover.

5. The man's mouth has been badly cut and bruised.

6. The couple will soon be able to take a romantic sleigh ride home and cuddle up in front of the fireplace.

7. He is a terrorist who has a bomb in the case. Disappointments: He isn't the woman's lover. It isn't a love poem . . .' (6)

A query of the poet's attitude to a character may also be attributed to a preconceived depth-first view:

'I want to know why the author has the particularly bad attitude about the man in the poem.' (31)

The kind of means-end argument which tries to fit the emerging text to a preconceived conclusion is illustrated in the following:

1. 'I think it will be a poem about slaves in the south trying to get North to be free.

2. Express: you think of train, I think this is the train of people all making their way from the south to the north. Next line will tell about some of the hardships they encountered upon their way north.

3. By this line this is not about slave coming north, for they wouldn't be able to just buy tickets. I expect this is a poem about travlers going from South to North on either business or pleasure.

4. Some sort of business meeting. A short meeting not staying long. Expect some sort of gathering.

5. Well I was all wrong on my second ideal. I think this may be about a person like the elephant man where the people can see the rest of his face. Next I expect it will tell about the person's reactions.

6. Snow is falling – it's most likely winter and the travler has no place to stay and will walk around with no place to go, no one to befriend him.

7. This line says he has a goal to infect a city of what I don't know may be has some sort of disease he is contagous and going to infect other, or may just infect them, the city by his looks.

8. He must be caring a terrible disease of some sort and the city future has just begain to some terrible fate.
Shouldn't a person get to ride the intire poem then, analize it line by line. For each line by itself can mean so many

different things. I thought it being a train from the south it would end up being a happy story about how the slaves reached freedom. This makes a sad poem not knowing what's going to happen to this city. I like happy and funny poems.' (83)

Ever since I. A. Richards's classic experiments, teachers of literature have commented on what they see as oddities in their students' comprehension of literary text. What most impressed us as experimenters was the unexpected liberty several informants took with the text. Some were apt to interpret even the lines describing place and setting, not in terms of things but rather in terms of persons and character. Many of our subjects obviously thought that a poem ought to be about people; if none were mentioned at once, they had to be imagined. In fact some commentators volunteered statements emphasizing their imaginative activities:

'This poem shows that we 'read' images into literature and try to make it meaningful to our life.' (40)

'By doing this I realize how many thoughts and feelings pop into my mind as I read a poem. I am surprised at how many are false . . . This poem is a good choice for this process because by the poem being so vague the reader must use his imagination.' (23)

Several of the subjects were also frustrated by the experiment and voiced their frustrations:

'I am not overly fond of this poem maybe because I wasn't allowed to experience it but was asked to "think" about it. Odd how the two are incompatible in my mind.' (79)

'An exercise of this nature is very frustrating because the true meaning gets lost in all the various possibilities but it does allow you to use your imagination to create your own world of the poem.' (3)

'I didn't like the idea of having to assume. I wanted to see the writing in whole and then go back and pick through it to figure it out – find the meaning. My mind was – is filled with questions, and I felt strange writing down singular meanings without knowing what the future lines contained.' (70)

'Use your imagination to create your own world of a poem' – not a bad description of the process involved in poetry comprehension: use stimuli in the text to activate your knowledge, project your knowledge into a constrained text world, use it to anticipate what comes next and to project what is known or imagined into further imaginations, then check these anticipations and imaginings against the emerging text. This is precisely what is involved in understanding – that is, building a text world around – a literary text.

Notes

We are grateful to Professors Ulla Connor and Richard D. Turner of the Department of English at Indiana University, Indianapolis, for their help in arranging the texts that provided data for the present essay, and to Faber and Faber Ltd, London, and Random House, Inc., New York, for permission to reproduce the first stanza of 'Gare du Midi', from *Collected Poems* by W. H. Auden.

1 It is not our purpose here, to go into semantic theory. But we define 'units of meaning' as units chosen to contrast with other potential units or with zero

References

Tom Bryder, Innehållsanalys som ide och metod (= Publications of the Research Institute of the Åbo Akademi Foundation, 106), Åbo Akademi, 1985

K. A. Ericsson and H. A. Simon, *Protocol Analysis: Verbal Reports as Data* (Cambridge, Mass.: MIT Press), 1984

Irene R. Fairley, 'Experimental Approaches to Language in Literature: Reader Responses to Poems,' *Style*, 13, 4, 1979

Irene R. Fairley, 'On Reading Poems: Visual and Verbal Icons in William Carlos Williams' "Landscape with the Fall of Icarus",' *Studies in Twentieth Century Literature*, 6, 1981–2

Stanley Fish, *Is There a Text in This Class?* (Cambridge, Mass.: Harvard University Press), 1980

Carl H. Frederiksen and Joseph F. Dominic (eds), *Writing: The Nature, Development, and Teaching of Written Communication. Vol. 2 Writing: Process, Development and Communication*, (L. Erlbaum Assocs), 1981

Eberhard Frey, 'Franz Kafka's Style: Impressionistic and Statistical Methods of Analysis,' *Language and Style* XIV, 1, 1981, 53–64

Josue V. Harari (ed.) *Textual Strategies: Perspectives in Post-structuralist Criticism* (New York: Cornell University Press), 1979

Robert C. Holub, *Reception Theory. A Critical Introduction* (London: Methuen), 1984

Wolfgang Iser, 'The Reading Process: A Phenomenological Approach,' in Jane P. Tompkins (ed.), *Reader-Response Criticism from Formalism to Post-Structuralism*, 1980, pp. 50–70

Benjamin Kleinmuntz, (ed.) *Formal Representation of Human Judgment.* (New York: John Wiley & Sons, Inc.), 1968

Allen Newell, 'On the Analysis of Human Problem Solving Protocols,' in P. N. Johnson-Laird and P. C. Wason (eds), *Thinking. Readings in*

Cognitive Science (Cambridge: Cambridge University Press), 1977, pp. 46–61

Gary M. Olson, Susan A. Duffy, and Robert L. Mack, 'Thinking-Out-Loud as a Method of Studying Real-Time Comprehension Processes,' in David E. Kieras and Marcel A. Just (eds), *New Methods in Reading Comprehension Research* (L. Erlbaum Assocs.), 1984, pp. 253–6

I. A. Richards, *Practical Criticism* (New York: Harcourt, Brace and Company), 1929

Louise M. Rosenblatt, *The Reader, the Text, the Poem* (Carbondale: Southern Illinois University), 1978

Marlene Scardamalia and Carl Bereiter, 'Development of Strategies in Text Processing,' in Heinz Mandl, Nancy L. Stein and Tom Trabasso (eds), *Learning and Comprehension of Text* (L. Erlbaum Assocs.) 1984

Sharon Silkey and Alan C. Purves, 'What Happens When we Read a Poem,' *The Journal of Aesthetic Education* 7, 1973, 63–72

Dan Sperber and Deirdre Wilson, *Relevance* (Oxford: Basil Blackwell), 1986

James C. Stalker 'Reader Expectations and the Poetic Line', *Language and Style* XV, 4, 1982, 241–52

Heidi Swarts, Linda S. Flower, and John R. Hayes, 'Designing Protocol Studies of the Writing Process: An Introduction,' in Richard Beach and Lillial S. Bridwell (eds), *New Directions in Composition Research*, (Guildford Press), 1984, pp. 53–71

Deborah Tannen, *That's Not What I Meant!* (New York: William Morrow and Company, Inc.), 1986

Jane P. Tompkins, 'An Introduction to Reader-Response Criticism,' in Jane P. Tompkins (ed.), *Reader-Response Criticism from Formalism to Post-Structuralism*, 1980, pp. 1–7

Amos Tversky, Paul Slovic, and Daniel Kahneman, 'Judgment under Uncertainty: Heuristics and Biases,' in Amos Tversky and Daniel Kahneman (eds), *Judgment under Uncertainty: Heuristics and Biases* (Cambridge: Cambridge University Press), 1982, pp. 3–23

Willie van Peer, *Stylistics and Psychology. Investigations of Foregrounding* (London: Croom Helm), 1986

Marcia Farr Whiteman (ed.), *Writing: The Nature, Development, and Teaching of Written Communication*. Vol. I *Variation in Writing: Functional and Linguistic-Cultural Differences* (L. Erlbaum Assocs.), 1981